THE **BIG** BOOK OF
WORLD
TAPAS

JULIA HARTLEY

THE **BIG** BOOK OF
WORLD
TAPAS

365 DELICIOUS LIGHT BITES
FOR ALL OCCASIONS

DUNCAN BAIRD PUBLISHERS

LONDON

For Richard – the best cook I know.

The Big Book of World Tapas
Julia Hartley

First published in the United Kingdom and Ireland in 2009 by
Duncan Baird Publishers Ltd
Sixth Floor, Castle House
75–76 Wells Street
London W1T 3QH

Conceived, created and designed by Duncan Baird Publishers

Copyright © Duncan Baird Publishers 2009
Text copyright © Julia Hartley 2009
Photography copyright © Duncan Baird Publishers 2009

Managing Editor: Grace Cheetham
Editor: Nicole Bator
Managing Designer: Suzanne Tuhrim
Commissioned photography: William Lingwood
Food Stylist: Mari Mererid Williams
Prop Stylist: Helen Trent

British Library Cataloguing-in-Publication Data:
A CIP record for this book is available from the British Library

ISBN: 978-1-84483-679-6

10 9 8 7 6 5 4 3 2 1

Typeset in Myriad Pro
Colour reproduction by Scanhouse, Malaysia
Printed in China by Imago

Publisher's Note: While every care has been taken in compiling the recipes for this book,
Duncan Baird Publishers, or any other persons who have been involved in working on this
publication, cannot accept responsibility for any errors or omissions, inadvertent or not, that may
be found in the recipes or text, nor for any problems that may arise as a result of preparing one
of these recipes. If you are pregnant or breastfeeding or have any special dietary requirements or
medical conditions, it is advisable to consult a medical professional before following any of the
recipes contained in this book. Ill or elderly people, babies, young children and women who are
pregnant or breastfeeding should avoid the recipes containing uncooked eggs or raw meat or fish.

Notes on the recipes
Unless otherwise stated:
• Use medium eggs, fruit and vegetables
• Use fresh ingredients, including herbs and chillies
• Do not mix metric and imperial measurements
• 1 tsp = 5ml
  1 tbsp = 15ml
  1 cup = 250ml

Author's acknowledgments: My warmest thanks to the whole team at Duncan Baird who helped
bring this book together, in particular, Grace Cheetham for commissioning me and being so
supportive and my amazing editor Nicole Bator for being so patient, encouraging and thorough.
Thank you also to Suzanne Tuhrim for the wonderful design and to William Lingwood and
Mari Williams for bringing the food to life with so many fantastic photographs. I would also like to
thank my children, Francesca and Rocco; Carol Hammick and my father Adam; Hannah Strickland,
Emma and Dani Sanchez, and Simon, Peter and Charlotte Tindall for all their testing, tasting, help
and encouragement. Lastly, my husband Richard, without whom there would have been no book.

CONTENTS

INTRODUCTION

Everybody loves a good party, and one of the best ways to make yours a success is by serving up sensational food. World Tapas are light bites inspired by flavours from around the world. From the tapas bars of Barcelona to the dim sum houses of Shanghai and all points in between, the culture of finger food has never been more popular – or easier to recreate in your own kitchen. The recipes in this book showcase a splendid array of international classics and innovative dishes that are guaranteed to make your party a hit.

Entertaining with world tapas makes it easy to create a menu for every occasion. Whether you're throwing a cocktail party for 50, having the extended family around for Christmas dinner, celebrating a twenty-first birthday or hosting a wedding for 200, everything you need to pull off a stunning event with flair and originality is right here. The little mouthfuls featured in this book can be eaten in one or, at most, two bites. In some cases, the food itself can replace tableware, whether it's a chunk of bread instead of a knife, or a pitta or chapatti as a natural plate. A few recipes may require minimal plates and cutlery, but these have been kept to a minimum to make set-up and clean-up easier on the day of your party.

If you find the prospect of catering for a larger than usual number of people to be daunting, don't worry: on the following pages, you'll find detailed advice on all aspects of effective party planning, as well as a detailed work plan that illustrates how you can break down a menu into manageable steps in the lead-up to your party so that everything runs smoothly.

PLANNING

Once you've made the decision to throw a party and have worked out the basics, such as setting a date and determining how many guests to invite, you need to start planning. This means considering everything from the menu you want to offer, the quantities you'll need and which dishes can be prepared in advance to equipment, timing, presentation and recruiting or hiring people to help. You'll also need to factor in time to plan and go shopping, and don't forget that setting up for a party and getting ready yourself also take time.

MENU

The key to successful catering lies in choosing the right menu, as this is where the majority of your planning will stem from. Choose recipes that feature a variety of ingredients to ensure your menu isn't top-heavy on any one item, such as cheese, cream, bread or chicken. Balance your meat, fish and dessert ratio and remember to include vegetarian options. Also keep in mind which recipes need oven or fridge space or have to be deep-fried or cooked just before serving.

Cost is another important factor. Recipes relying on ingredients such as lobster, foie gras, oysters, beef fillet and salmon will give your menu a sophisticated touch, but they are expensive. To stretch your budget, select a few dishes that feature more economical ingredients, such as crostini and filo pastry. Tailor your menu to the seasons, too. A menu that draws on seasonally available produce usually costs less, and tastes better. Look, for example, for asparagus, broad beans and new potatoes in the spring, or apples, pears and squash in autumn.

QUANTITIES

There's nothing worse than running out of food at a party – but you don't want to face a mountain of leftovers when it's all over, either. With a little planning, these disasters are easily avoided.

One way to judge the quantities you'll need is to visualize all the nibbles you plan to offer per person, arranged on one dinner plate as a main course. If the plate is full, then your quantities are accurate. Although it's natural to question whether a single plateful of small bites will be enough to fill your guests up, it will be. And if you're still not totally convinced – or you're not sure how long your guests will stay – keep a small reserve of olives, nuts, poppodams, tortillas, wontons and other snacks in your store cupboard as back up.

As a general rule, offer three to four light items in place of a starter or before a two-course dinner or lunch. For a three- or four-hour cocktail party or other event where only tapas are going to be served, plan for 10–12 bites per person, and offer a selection of eight to ten dishes. For smaller, more intimate events, create a menu of six to eight dishes and serve them with some form of bread. See the chart below for further advice on calculating quantities for your party.

To determine drink quantities, allow half to three quarters of a bottle of wine or champagne per person. On the whole it is easier to over cater for drink, as it is usually sold sale or return. Do not forget to offer soft drinks, such as water, elderflower cordial or home-made lemonade.

Adapting the Recipes

Each chapter of this book features a selection of recipes most suited to a particular style and size of event, from brunches for 10–12 people, to late-night drinks for six to eight guests, to large celebrations meant to cater to 24–36 or more. You can, however, easily mix and match recipes across chapters to create your ideal menu. The Bruschetta ai Funghi, Mini Quiche Lorraines and Potato Croquettes in the brunches chapter, for example, work brilliantly for big parties; the spring roll, tempura and crostini recipes throughout the book are great for pre-dinner drinks; and many of the cocktail party recipes possess a flair of elegance that makes them perfect for the wedding of your dreams.

Many of the recipes that make large quantities can easily be adapted to make smaller amounts, while low-yield recipes can be scaled up for large parties. For recipes such as skewers, spring rolls and crostini, for example, simply multiply all the ingredients by two or three to get the same great results for a big event, or halve the quantities for a small late-night get-together.

It's important to note that recipes containing flour and eggs, such as pastry, cakes, crème pâtissière and anything battered and deep-fried, can be problematic when scaled. Instead of multiplying the ingredients in such dishes, prepare these recipes as instructed and then make as many individual batches of that recipe as are needed to make the quantity you need.

Also keep in mind that ingredients such as salt, spices and other seasonings should not be scaled proportionally. If you are doubling a recipe, use only about 1½ times the original quantity called for; if halving a recipe, use a little less than half. Taste as you go along, if possible, to make sure the seasonings are right and adjust them as needed.

Other factors may also determine whether a recipe should be doubled or simply made more than once. The size of your pan, baking dish, mixing bowl or oven, for example, may restrict how many times you can make or scale a recipe. Putting too much meat in a dish, for example, will slow down the cooking time and affect the end result. Recipes that require time-consuming last-minute assembly may not be ideal for large numbers, either – although this can be overcome if you organize extra help in the kitchen.

Determining Quantities for Your Party

EVENT	LENGTH OF PARTY	NUMBER OF GUESTS	NUMBER OF BITES PER GUEST	SUGGESTED NUMBER OF RECIPES
BRUNCHES	3 hours	10–12	3–4	3–4
PRE-DINNER DRINKS	1 hour	10–12	2–4	2–4
COCKTAIL PARTIES	3–4 hours	24–36	10–12	8–10
LATE-NIGHT DRINKS	2–3 hours	6–8	6–8	4–6
PARTIES & CELEBRATIONS	4–5 hours	24–36	10–12	6–8
WEDDINGS	3–4 hours	24–36	10–12*	8–10

*This assumes a late-afternoon wedding reception from around 3:00 p.m. to 6:30 p.m. with no lunch or dinner. If the wedding is followed by lunch or dinner, then 6–8 bites per guest will be enough.

SHOPPING

Once you've chosen a menu, it helps to deconstruct it to create a comprehensive shopping list with quantities and a work plan. Go through each recipe in your menu and write down how much of each ingredient is needed.

It is worth noting how long shopping for a party takes, not least because the nature of perishable food means multiple trips will have to be made. Make two lists: one of all the common, non-perishable store cupboard items you'll need, such as oils, vinegars, flour, baking powder, sugar, salt and peppercorns, and buy them well in advance to minimize your last minute shopping.

Create a second list of fresh and perishable foods, such as fruit, vegetables, dairy produce, meat and fish, and plan to shop for these things a few days before your party. Highly perishable items like sushi-grade fish, oysters and delicate fruits such as raspberries should be purchased as close to your event as possible, ideally the morning of your party, or the day before. Many specialist suppliers, such as cheese- and fishmongers, will often deliver to your door for no extra cost, and they can supply larger quantities than you can reasonably buy in the supermarket, which can save you valuable time.

PREPARING AHEAD

Many of the recipes in this book can be prepared partially or completely in advance. See the individual recipes throughout this book for tips on how far ahead you can make each recipe, as well as how to store pre-prepared items.

Before you start preparing the food for your party, make sure your kitchen is neat, clean and organized. You'll need plenty of food storage containers, an organized fridge and clear work surfaces before you begin. This way, nothing will be forgotten or spoiled, and cooking and preparing recipes will be much easier. It's also essential to observe basic food hygiene guidelines when catering so you don't have to throw away contaminated food or risk food poisoning your guests.

When catering, remember to keep work surfaces and hands clean to prevent bacteria spreading; cook and re-heat food (particularly meat) all the way through to kill bacteria; don't let raw food drip onto cooked food as it will contaminate it; and keep food refrigerated at 5°C/41°F to prevent bacteria growing. Do not leave food at room temperature for more than 2 hours (particularly if it is a very hot day) and don't re-heat anything more than once. Store raw food in sealed containers at the bottom of the fridge, make sure cooked food is completely cooled before refrigerating and frozen food is thoroughly defrosted before cooking.

EQUIPMENT

Even if you have a well-equipped kitchen, hiring some additional equipment can help ease the whole catering process. For a large party, a commercial oven or gas hob, refrigerated trailer, and tables and chairs may be useful. Check the internet or your local directory for services that provide equipment delivery and collection.

A selection of basic saucepans, baking tins, roasting trays; good sharp knives, heavy chopping boards that don't wobble, stainless steel mixing bowls, rubber-ended heatproof spatulas, jugs and plastic storage boxes that fit comfortably in the fridge are all essential, and can be rented if you don't have enough. Make sure roasting trays will fit in your oven, though, as some commercial equipment is too large for an average domestic cooker. If you decide to buy a few pans or trays, it's worth spending a little more for high-quality items that will not buckle when hot and throw food all over the oven.

A large plastic tub, metal bath or clean black dustbin all make good ice buckets. If you're chilling wine or champagne that is at room temperature, you'll need to put the ice in the bucket, fill it with water and add the bottles three hours before the party begins. If you're simply keeping cold drinks cool, transfer them to the ice buckets one hour before the party. Make sure the bar is equipped with more than one bottle opener and corkscrew, as these inevitably stray, and provide bar staff with enough serviettes or tea towels to keep the bar area dry.

You'll probably need to hire glasses. A word of advice: hire fifty per cent more than you think you need. Guests inevitably put one glass down and take another – and no one wants to wash up glasses in the middle of a party. Set glasses out well before the party begins, especially for large events.

When hiring glasses, plates or cutlery, ensure that the hire company you are using will take everything back dirty to save you time at the end of the party.

TIMING

Many component parts of a world tapas dish can be made in advance, but assembling too early may affect the end result. When assembling the light bites in this book, it's worth organizing a production line for each recipe in order to speed up the process. If you're delegating the final preparations to someone else, list the recipes in the order in which they need to be made and clearly show the person assembling each one what the finished item should look like.

It isn't necessary for all the food to be ready at the same time. In fact, it's preferable to stagger the food. For a three and a half hour cocktail party with approximately 12 bites allocated per head, have two dishes on offer at the outset and then plan on a new platter of food emerging from the kitchen every 15 minutes or so.

When working out the preparation timings for your party, remember that a brunch or lunchtime event only gives you a morning of late preparation compared to an evening party, which gives you the whole day.

PRESENTATION

Whether concocting small and elaborate creations for a wedding, or simple large platters of fresh and delicious dishes for a family gathering, it's as easy to achieve a relaxed and casual atmosphere as it is something more formal.

One of the charms of catering at home is that you can stamp your own style on your party. It may be that you want to use matching plates, which can be hired at a relatively small cost. Another lovely option is to use your own crockery, particularly non-matching plates that do not usually get much use. Trays and flat baskets lined with white linen serviettes make effective serving platters and have the added advantage of not being too heavy to pass around.

Keep decorations simple, with the emphasis on the ingredients themselves. Use fresh herbs to give platters of crostini or spring rolls a fresh and inviting look. Flowers such as nasturtiums, daffodils, apple blossom and honeysuckle make lovely accents – make sure you choose non-poisonous varieties. Small flowers wilt quickly, so keep them in water or pick them less than an hour before you need them. Other effective decorations include lime leaves, lemon or lime zest, even freshly ground black pepper, sprinklings of paprika or coarsely grated chocolate.

PEOPLE TO HELP

Having help with any size party can be a tremendous support and greatly add to your own enjoyment. Make sure, however, that each person, whether a paid member of staff or a family friend, has a specific role.

Generally, in a formal situation, you should allow one server for every 25 guests and one cook in the kitchen for every 40 guests, depending on the menu. If your event is casual, you may be happy to ask your guests to hand food and drinks around, but even if this is the case, it can be very helpful to have someone in the kitchen assembling the last minute items you've prepared, for example, stuffing new potatoes, frying spring rolls, slicing sushi rolls, assembling the crostini and so on. It is also useful to have someone re-filling empty platters.

If you feel completely in control in the kitchen and do not want any waiting staff, you may consider one or two barmen since opening and handing drinks around is surprisingly time-consuming. A designated bar area, whether it's one or two trestle tables covered with a cloth, a side board or a section of the kitchen, makes life easier by providing smooth access to drinks.

TIME TO PARTY

No matter what kind of party you're throwing, these simple guidelines, your own imagination and the delectable selection of world tapas recipes that follows are guaranteed to make your event a success.

Work Plan

The following work plan illustrates how to break a menu down into manageable steps in the days leading up to your party. Start out by making a list of all the recipes you'll be making. See how much you can prepare ahead of time, keeping in mind your available fridge and freezer space for storing things. Draw up a shopping list and make sure you've got everything you need before you start. The work plan here is tailored for a two-person team to cook and assemble the dishes. Don't forget to make arrangements ahead of time for help on the day of the event – and confirm these arrangements at least two days beforehand. You'll also need to factor in time for setting up the party space – and for getting ready yourself.

THE MENU: Saturday Evening Cocktail Party for 40 Guests
Onion Tartlets *(see page 73)*
Olives with Cumin & Citrus Zest *(see page 72)*
Stilton & Apple Filo Parcels *(see page 75)*
Rare Roast Beef, Tomato & Pesto Crostini *(see page 101)*
Trout Tartare on Artichoke Leaves *(see page 78)*
Duck & Ginger Wontons *(see page 97)*
Green Tandoori Chicken with Poppadoms *(see page 92)*
Panzanella Gem Boats *(see page 76)*
Hazelnut Clusters *(see page 112)*

DAY	TIME	TASK
MONDAY	8:00–8:10 pm	Make and freeze the pastry for the tartlets
	8:10–8:40 pm	Make the Hazelnut Clusters
THURSDAY	6:30–7:30 pm	Shop for remaining ingredients
	7:30 pm	Defrost the tartlet pastry
	8:10–8:30 pm	Make the crostini bases
	8:30–9:15 pm	Make and blind bake the tartlet cases
FRIDAY	7:00–9:10 pm	Make the Crispy Duck for the wontons
	7:10–7:20 pm	Make the Pesto for the Rare Beef, Tomato & Pesto Crostini
	7:20–7:35 pm	Make the green tandoori mix and marinate the chicken
	7:35–8:00 pm	Make the Stilton & Apple Filo Parcels (do not cook)
	8:00–8:25 pm	Make the panzanella for the Panzanella Gem Boats
SATURDAY	10:00	Take the beef for the crostini out of the fridge
	10:05–10:10 am	Make the Olives with Cumin & Lemon Zest
	10:10–10:30 am	Roast the beef for the crostini
	10:30–10:40 am	Prepare the trout tartar mixture
	10:40–11:25 am	Make the filling for the Onion Tartlets
	11:25–11:45 am	Cook the chicken, leave to cool, then slice and store in an airtight container in the fridge
	3:00–3:35 pm	Cook the artichoke for the trout tartar
	3:05–3:35 pm	Prepare the Duck & Ginger Wontons (do not cook)
	5:00–5:20 pm	Assemble and bake the Onion Tartlets
	5:20–5:30 pm	Assemble Panzanella Gem Boats
	5:30–5:50 pm	Slice the beef and assemble the Rare Beef, Tomato & Pesto Crostini
	6:15–6:40 pm	Fry the filo parcels
	6:50–7:00 pm	Assemble the trout tartar and arrange on a plate
ONCE THE PARTY STARTS	7:00–7:15 pm	Cook the Duck & Ginger Wontons
	7:30–7:35 pm	Assemble the Green Tandoori Chicken with Poppadums

BASIC RECIPES

Mint & Yogurt Dip

MAKES: 250ml/9fl oz/1 cup   **PREPARATION TIME:** 5 minutes

250ml/9fl oz/1 cup natural yogurt
leaves from 3 mint sprigs

1 garlic clove
1 small handful coriander leaves

1   Put all the ingredients in a food processor or blender and process for 1 minute
    until smooth.
2   Serve immediately.

PREPARING AHEAD: This can be made up to 1 day in advance and stored in an airtight container
in the fridge.

Salsa Verde

MAKES: 250ml/9fl oz/1 cup   **PREPARATION TIME:** 15 minutes

50g/1³⁄₄oz gherkins, finely chopped
3 tbsp capers
1 small bunch chives, finely chopped
1 large handful parsley, finely
   chopped

4 tbsp olive oil
juice and finely grated zest of 1 lemon
50g/1³⁄₄oz tinned anchovies in oil,
   drained and finely chopped
1 green chilli, finely chopped

1   Put all the ingredients in a bowl and mix well.
2   Serve immediately.

PREPARING AHEAD: This can be made up to 2 days in advance and stored in an airtight container
in the fridge, then served at room temperature.

Pesto

MAKES: 200ml/7fl oz/scant 1 cup   **PREPARATION TIME:** 10 minutes, plus 1 hour resting

1 large handful basil leaves, chopped
125ml/4fl oz/¹⁄₂ cup olive oil, plus
   extra as needed
30g/1oz/¹⁄₄ cup pine nuts

2 tbsp grated Parmesan cheese
1 garlic clove, chopped
salt and freshly ground black pepper

1   Put the basil, oil, pine nuts, Parmesan and garlic in a food processor or blender
    and process for 2 minutes until the mixture forms a paste. If too thick, add more oil,
    taking care not to add too much. Season with salt and pepper.
2   Transfer to an airtight container and leave to stand for at least 1 hour before using.

PREPARING AHEAD: This can be made up to 5 days in advance and stored in an airtight container
in the fridge; it can be frozen for up to 2 weeks. Serve at room temperature.

Sweet Chilli Dip

MAKES: 125ml/4fl oz/½ cup   **PREPARATION TIME:** 5 minutes, plus 1 hour resting

3 tbsp clear honey
1 tbsp rice vinegar
2 tbsp tomato ketchup

1 tsp soy sauce
1 red chilli, deseeded and
   finely chopped

1   Put the honey and vinegar in a bowl and mix well. Stir in the remaining ingredients.
2   Cover and leave to stand for 1 hour, then serve.

PREPARING AHEAD: This can be made up to 2 days in advance and stored in an airtight container in the fridge. Serve at room temperature.

Mayonnaise

MAKES: 250ml/9fl oz/1 cup   **PREPARATION TIME:** 10 minutes

2 very fresh egg yolks, at room
   temperature
1 tsp Dijon mustard

250ml/9fl oz/1 cup olive oil
juice of ½ lemon
salt

1   Put the egg yolks and mustard in a mixing bowl and beat with a wooden spoon for 1 minute until thick and creamy. Very slowly add one third of the oil, 1 tbsp at a time, and beat continuously for 4 minutes until the mixture begins to thicken.
2   Add the remaining oil in a thin, steady stream until stiff and glossy. If the mixture separates, beat another egg yolk in a clean mixing bowl, then slowly whisk in the split mixture in a steady stream. The mayonnaise will re-form. Mix in the lemon juice and season with salt.
3   Transfer to a bowl and serve immediately at room temperature.

PREPARING AHEAD: This can be made up to 2 days in advance and stored in an airtight container in the fridge.

Boiled Chicken

MAKES: 600g/1lb 5oz meat   **PREPARATION TIME:** 15 minutes, plus 30 minutes resting
COOKING TIME: 35 minutes

1 whole chicken, about 1.5kg/3lb 5oz,
   giblets removed
1 carrot, halved

1 onion, halved
1 tsp black peppercorns

1   Put all the ingredients in a large saucepan, cover with cold water and bring to the boil. Reduce the heat to medium-low and simmer for 30 minutes or until cooked through and the juices run clear when the fattest part of a drumstick is pricked with a sharp knife. Carefully remove the chicken from the water and leave to stand for 30 minutes or until cool enough to handle.
2   Remove and discard the skin, then, using your hands, remove all the meat from the bone and tear it into strips. Use immediately or transfer to an airtight container and store in the fridge until ready to use.

PREPARING AHEAD: This can be made up to 1 day in advance and stored in the fridge. You can reserve the cooking liquid and use it in recipes that call for chicken stock.

Crispy Duck

MAKES: 500g/1lb 2oz meat **PREPARATION TIME:** 10 minutes
COOKING TIME: 2 hours 15 minutes

1 whole duck, about 2.25kg/5lb
3 tbsp soft dark brown sugar
1 tsp salt

1 Preheat the oven to 210°C/415°F/Gas 7. Wash the duck inside and out under cold
   running water. Pat dry with a clean tea towel, then pierce 10–12 holes through the
   skin, using a skewer or sharp knife, .
2 Put the sugar, salt and 3 tbsp warm water in a bowl and mix well, then rub the
   mixture all over the duck.
3 Put the duck on a rack over a roasting tin and bake for 20 minutes until pale brown.
   Cover with foil, reduce the oven temperature to 130°C/250°F/Gas 1 and bake for
   a further 1½ hours. Remove the foil and bake for a further 10–15 minutes until the
   skin is dark brown and crispy.

PREPARING AHEAD: This can be made up to 1 day in advance, covered and stored in the fridge.

Savoury Shortcrust Pastry

MAKES: 48 x 5cm/2in tartlet cases **PREPARATION TIME:** 10 minutes, plus 1 hour chilling

250g/9oz/2 cups plain flour
½ tsp salt
140g/5oz cold butter, diced

1 egg
1 egg yolk

1 Put the flour, salt and butter in a food processor and pulse for 1 minute until the
   mixture resembles fine breadcrumbs. Add the egg and egg yolk and process for
   1 minute until the mixture forms a rough dough. Alternatively, put the flour and
   salt in a bowl and rub the butter in, using your fingertips, then add the egg
   and egg yolk and mix well.
2 Shape the dough into a ball, wrap in cling film and chill for 1 hour before using.

PREPARING AHEAD: This can be stored in the fridge for up to 2 days or frozen for up to 2 weeks.

Sweet Shortcrust Pastry

MAKES: 48 x 5cm/2in tartlet cases **PREPARATION TIME:** 10 minutes, plus 1 hour chilling

250g/9oz/2 cups plain flour
140g/5oz cold butter, cubed
115g/4oz/scant 1 cup icing sugar,
   sifted

1 egg
1 egg yolk

1 Put the flour and butter in a food processor and pulse for 1 minute until the
   mixture resembles fine breadcrumbs. Add the icing sugar, egg and egg yolk and
   process for a further 1 minute until the dough comes away from the sides of the
   bowl. Alternatively, put the flour and sugar in a bowl and rub the butter in, using
   your fingertips, then add the egg and egg yolk and mix well.
2 Shape the dough into a ball, wrap in cling film and chill in the fridge for
   1 hour before using.

PREPARING AHEAD: This can be stored in the fridge for up to 2 days or frozen for up to 2 weeks.

Tartlet Cases

MAKES: 48   **PREPARATION TIME:** 30 minutes, plus making the pastry
COOKING TIME: 8–10 minutes for blind-baked cases; 13–17 minutes for baked cases
EQUIPMENT: 5.5cm/2¼in plain or fluted round pastry cutter, 2 x 12-hole mini muffin tins, baking beans

1 recipe quantity Sweet or Savoury
 Shortcrust Pastry, depending on
 the recipe (see page 13)
plain flour, for rolling the pastry

1 Preheat the oven to 180°C/350°F/Gas 4. Take the pastry out of the fridge about
   20 minutes before you need it. On a lightly floured surface, roll the pastry out to
   about 2mm/¹/₁₆in thick. Cut out as many circles as possible, using the pastry cutter.
2 Gather the trimmings, re-roll and repeat until all the pastry has been cut into
   circles. Press 1 circle into each hole of the muffin tins. Line each tartlet case with
   a small square of foil and weigh down with baking beans. Bake for 8–10 minutes
   until pale brown, then remove the baking beans and foil.
3 For recipes calling for blind-baked cases, add the filling to the cases and bake
   according to the recipe.
4 For recipes calling for baked cases, return the tartlets to the oven after removing
   the foil and baking beans and bake for a further 5–7 minutes until golden brown.
   Leave to cool, then add the filling according to the recipe .
5 Repeat with the remaining unbaked pastry circles.

PREPARING AHEAD: Blind-baked tartlet cases can be stored in an airtight container at room
temperature for up to 1 day, then filled and baked according to the recipe. Baked tartlet cases
can be stored in an airtight container at room temperature for up to 1 week.

Croustades

MAKES: 24   **PREPARATION TIME:** 15 minutes   **COOKING TIME:** 4 minutes
EQUIPMENT: 6cm/2½in plain round pastry cutter, 2 x deep 12-hole mini muffin tins

4 sheets filo pastry
15g/½oz butter, melted

1 Preheat the oven to 180°C/350°F/Gas 4. Cut 48 circles out of the pastry, using
   the pastry cutter. Brush 24 of them with the butter and top each one with
   1 of the remaining circles.
2 Gently push 1 circle into each hole of the mini-muffin tins and bake for 4 minutes
   until golden.

PREPARING AHEAD: These can be made up to 1 day in advance and stored in an airtight container
at room temperature.

Pizza Dough

MAKES: 48 x 5cm/2in pizzarettes   **PREPARATION TIME:** 30 minutes, plus 1 hour resting

650g/1lb 7oz/5¼ cups plain flour,
   plus extra for rolling the dough
   and sprinkling
1 tsp salt

1 tsp caster sugar
2 tsp dried active yeast
1 tsp olive oil

1   Sift the flour and salt into a bowl. Add the sugar, yeast, oil and 350ml/12fl oz/
    scant 1½ cups lukewarm water. Mix together for 2–3 minutes until the dough
    comes away from the sides of the bowl. Turn out onto a lightly floured surface
    and knead for 10 minutes until smooth and elastic. Put in a clean bowl, cover
    with a clean, damp tea towel and leave to stand in a warm place for 1 hour until
    doubled in size.
2   Lightly sprinkle a baking sheet with flour. Punch down the dough, turn it onto
    a lightly floured surface and knead for 5 minutes until it forms a smooth ball.
    To make the pizzarette bases, divide the dough into 48 x 30g/1oz balls. Roll each
    ball out to 2mm/¹⁄₁₆in thick, transfer to the baking sheet and follow the recipe
    as required.

Crostini

MAKES: 48 crostini   **PREPARATION TIME:** 5 minutes   **COOKING TIME:** 15 minutes

1 x 50cm/20in baguette, cut into
   48 x 1cm/½in slices
80ml/3fl oz/⅓ cup olive oil

1   Preheat the oven to 170°C/325°F/Gas 3. Put the baguette slices on two baking
    sheets and brush with the oil. Bake for 12–15 minutes, or until lightly toasted.
2   Transfer to a wire rack and leave to cool.

PREPARING AHEAD: These can be stored in an airtight container at room temperature for up
to 1 week.

Crème Pâtissière

MAKES: 250ml/9fl oz/1 cup   **PREPARATION TIME:** 5 minutes   **COOKING TIME:** 15 minutes

185ml/6fl oz/¾ cup milk
4 tbsp caster sugar
2 x 5cm/2in-long strips lemon zest

1 tbsp plain flour
2 egg yolks
½ tsp vanilla extract

1   Put the milk, sugar and lemon zest in a saucepan. Bring to the boil over a medium
    heat, stirring continuously, until the sugar has dissolved. Remove from the heat
    and discard the lemon zest.
2   In a heatproof mixing bowl, whisk together the flour and egg yolks. Slowly add
    the hot milk, whisking well. Strain the mixture back into the saucepan and cook
    over a low heat for 8–10 minutes, stirring continuously, until thick. Do not overheat
    or the eggs will scramble. To test if it is ready, coat a wooden spoon in the mixture
    and run your finger down the back; if the mark remains, the custard is ready.
    Remove from the heat, stir in the vanilla and leave to cool.

PREPARING AHEAD: This can be made up to 1 day in advance and stored in an airtight container
in the fridge.

CHAPTER 1

BRUNCHES

There's something a little decadent about brunch – it's a substantial breakfast that collides so easily with lunch. A meal where the sweet and the savoury can appear in equal measures, and where coffee effortlessly gives way to a Bloody Mary or a glass of champagne.

Whether it's a lazy Sunday morning, a wedding breakfast or a baby shower, brunch is a real treat – and world tapas provide the perfect way to make your get-together stand out. The recipes in this chapter are suitable for 10–12 people, but if you're entertaining a larger group, they can easily be doubled or made in multiple quantities (see page 7).

Your brunch may begin with mouthwatering Blueberry Crêpes and Fruit Kebabs with Yogurt & Honey Dip followed by Quail Eggs Benedict with Caviar and Halloumi & Mint Puffs. Serve up succulent Whisky-Glazed Ham, Potted Prawns and Piedmontese Peppers alongside classic muffins, waffles and Crêpes Suzette, and your guests are guaranteed to savour every bite.

SMOKED SALMON, CREAM CHEESE & CAPER EGG BAGELS (SEE PAGE 27)

001 Cucumber & Apple Sandwiches

MAKES: 24   PREPARATION TIME: 15 minutes

85g/3oz/⅓ cup cream cheese
leaves from 4 mint sprigs
leaves from 4 parsley sprigs
juice and grated zest of ½ lemon

10 slices of white bread
½ cucumber, peeled and finely sliced
2 tart apples, such as Granny Smith,
   peeled, cored and sliced

1   Put the cream cheese, mint, parsley, lemon juice and zest in a food processor
    and pulse until well combined.
2   Spread 5 slices of the bread with the cheese mixture, top with a generous layer
    of the cucumber and a layer of the apple. Cover with the remaining bread.
    Remove the crusts, cut each sandwich into quarters and serve immediately.

PREPARING AHEAD: The herby cream cheese can be made up to 12 hours in advance and stored
in an airtight container in the fridge.

002 Fruit Kebabs with Yogurt & Honey Dip

MAKES: 12   PREPARATION TIME: 20 minutes   EQUIPMENT: 12 x 10cm/4in skewers

½ pineapple, peeled, cored and
   chopped into 2.5cm/1in chunks
1 banana, peeled and sliced
12 strawberries, hulled

125ml/4fl oz/½ cup natural yogurt
2 tsp clear honey
115g/4oz/¾ cup granola or muesli

1   Put 1 piece of the pineapple and banana and 1 strawberry on each skewer.
2   Put the yogurt in a bowl and drizzle the honey over. Sprinkle with the granola
    and serve with the kebabs.

003 Blueberry Crêpes

MAKES: 12   PREPARATION TIME: 10 minutes, plus 30 minutes resting   COOKING TIME: 1 hour

250ml/9fl oz/1 cup milk
15g/½oz butter
150g/5½oz/scant 1¼ cups plain flour
a pinch salt
2 eggs, beaten

225g/8oz/1½ cups blueberries
4 tbsp caster sugar
4 tsp sunflower oil, plus extra
   as needed
140g/5oz/scant ¾ cup crème fraîche

1   Put the milk and butter in a saucepan and heat over a low heat, stirring
    occasionally, for 2–3 minutes until the butter has melted.
2   Sift the flour and salt into a bowl and make a well in the centre. Add the eggs and
    1 tbsp of the milk mixture and whisk until well combined. Add the remaining milk
    mixture and whisk until smooth. Cover the bowl with a clean tea towel and leave
    to stand at room temperature for 30 minutes.
3   Put the blueberries and sugar in a saucepan and cook over a low heat, stirring
    occasionally, for 10 minutes until thickened and the sugar has dissolved. Set aside.
4   Heat 1 tsp of the oil in a 15cm/6in frying pan over a low heat. Remove the pan
    from the heat, add 1 tbsp of the batter and tilt the pan from side to side until the
    base is evenly covered. Return to the heat and cook for 1–2 minutes on each side
    until the crêpe begins to brown. Transfer to a plate and repeat with the remaining
    batter, adding more oil to the pan as needed.
5   Put 1 tsp of the crème fraîche and 1 tsp of the blueberry jam slightly off centre on
    1 crêpe. Fold the crêpe in half twice to form a small triangle, secure with a cocktail
    stick and put on a serving plate. Repeat with the remaining crêpes and serve.

PREPARING AHEAD: The crêpes can be made up to 4 hours in advance and stored in an airtight
container at room temperature. Reheat at 180°C/350°F for 1 minute, then fill, fold and serve.

004 Scotch Pancakes with Honey

MAKES: 20   **PREPARATION TIME:** 10 minutes, plus 10 minutes resting
COOKING TIME: 15 minutes

185ml/6fl oz/³⁄₄ cup milk
15g/¹⁄₂oz unsalted butter
150g/5¹⁄₂oz/scant 1¹⁄₄ cups plain flour
1¹⁄₂ tsp baking powder

2 tbsp caster sugar
1 egg, beaten
2 tbsp sunflower oil
165g/5¾oz/scant ¹⁄₂ cup clear honey

1   Put the milk and butter in a saucepan and heat over a low heat, stirring occasionally, for 2–3 minutes until the butter has melted.
2   Sift the flour and baking powder into a bowl and stir in the sugar. Make a well in the centre, add the egg and slowly pour in the milk mixture. Add the flour and whisk until smooth. Leave to stand at room temperature for 10 minutes.
3   Lightly brush a frying pan with the oil and heat over a medium heat for 1 minute. Drop 5 tbsp of batter into the pan, spacing well apart, and cook for 1–2 minutes until bubbles appear. Turn over and cook for a further 1 minute. Repeat with the remaining batter, adding more oil as needed. It may be necessary to reduce the heat a little so the pancakes do not burn. Serve immediately with the honey.

005 Waffles with Maple Syrup

MAKES: 12   **PREPARATION TIME:** 10 minutes, plus 30 minutes resting
COOKING TIME: 20 minutes   **EQUIPMENT:** electric waffle iron

150g/5¹⁄₂oz/scant 1¹⁄₄ cups plain flour
1 tsp baking powder
¹⁄₂ tsp cinnamon
90g/3¹⁄₄oz/scant ¹⁄₂ cup caster sugar
¹⁄₂ tsp salt

3 eggs, beaten
70g/2¹⁄₂oz unsalted butter, melted
2 tbsp milk
6 tbsp maple syrup

1   Sift the flour, baking powder and cinnamon into a mixing bowl. Add the sugar and salt, then mix in the eggs, melted butter and milk until smooth. Cover with a clean tea towel and leave to stand for 30 minutes.
2   Heat the waffle iron according to the manufacturer's instructions. When it has come to temperature, evenly spoon 2–3 tbsp of the batter into the waffle iron. Be careful not to overfill or the excess batter will spill out when you close the iron. Cook for 3 minutes, or until brown and cooked through. Remove the waffle, using a rubber spatula, and transfer to a serving plate. Repeat with the remaining batter. Cut the waffles in half and serve immediately with the maple syrup.

006 Savoury Waffles

MAKES: 12   **PREPARATION TIME:** 10 minutes, plus 30 minutes resting
COOKING TIME: 20 minutes   **EQUIPMENT:** electric waffle iron

150g/5¹⁄₂oz/scant 1¹⁄₄ cups plain flour
1 tsp baking powder
1 tbsp caster sugar
¹⁄₂ tsp salt
3 eggs, beaten

70g/2¹⁄₂oz butter, melted
4 tbsp milk
90g/3oz Cheddar, Red Leicester or
          Double Gloucester cheese, grated
3 tomatoes, thinly sliced, to serve

1   Sift the flour and baking powder into a bowl, then stir in the sugar and salt. Add the eggs, butter, milk and grated cheese and stir until smooth. Cover with a clean tea towel and leave to stand at room temperature for 30 minutes.
2   Heat the waffle iron according to the manufacturer's instructions. When it has come to temperature, evenly spoon 2–3 tbsp of the batter into the waffle iron. Be careful not to overfill or the excess batter will spill out when you close the iron. Cook for 3 minutes, or until brown and cooked through. Remove the waffle, using a rubber spatula, and transfer to a serving plate. Repeat with the remaining batter. Cut the waffles in half and serve immediately with the tomatoes.

007   Banana, Honey & Granola Yogurt Pots

MAKES: 10   **PREPARATION TIME:** 10 minutes   **EQUIPMENT:** 10 x espresso cups or small ramekins

2 bananas, peeled and sliced
4 tbsp clear honey

300ml/10½fl oz/1¼ cups
  natural yogurt
100g/3½oz/1 heaped cup granola

1   Put 3 banana slices in each of ten espresso cups or small ramekins. Drizzle the honey over and top with 2 tbsp of the yogurt.
2   Sprinkle with the granola and serve.

008 # Brioche Buns

MAKES: 24   **PREPARATION TIME:** 40 minutes, plus 2½ hours rising   **COOKING TIME:** 8 minutes
EQUIPMENT: 24 x 6cm/2½in mini-brioche tins (optional)

175g/6oz butter, softened, plus extra
    for greasing and to serve
1 tbsp caster sugar
2 tbsp milk, warmed
3 tsp dried active yeast

275g/9¾oz/scant 2¼ cups plain flour,
    plus extra for kneading
1 tsp salt
3 eggs
1 egg yolk, beaten with 1 tbsp milk

1   Put the butter and sugar in a food processor. Process for 1–2 minutes until smooth.
2   Put the milk and yeast in a bowl and stir until the yeast has dissolved. Put the flour
    and salt in a bowl. Add the eggs and milk mixture and stir until the mixture is well
    combined and forms a crumbly dough.
3   Add 1 tbsp of the butter mixture and mix, using a wooden spoon, until
    incorporated. Repeat until all the butter has been incorporated and the mixture
    appears very sticky and wet. Continue to mix for 20 minutes until the mixture
    forms a shiny, elastic dough that pulls away from the sides of the bowl. With
    lightly floured hands, briefly knead the dough on a lightly floured surface, shape
    into a ball and transfer to a lightly floured bowl. Cover with a clean damp tea towel
    and leave to rise in a warm, draft-free place for 2 hours until doubled in size.
4   Lightly grease the brioche moulds or a baking sheet. Knead the dough on a lightly
    floured surface for 5 minutes until smooth and elastic. Divide the dough into
    24 portions of equal size and roll into small balls. Put them in the brioche moulds
    or on the baking sheet, lightly brush with the egg yolk mixture and leave to rise
    for 30 minutes. Preheat the oven to 210°C/415°F/Gas 7.
5   Put the brioche in the oven and carefully close the door, making sure you do not
    slam it and release all the air. Bake for 8 minutes until golden. Serve with butter.

PREPARING AHEAD: The dough can be made to the end of step 3 the night before, then covered
with cling film and stored in the fridge.

009 # Halloumi & Mint Puffs

MAKES: 12   **PREPARATION TIME:** 15 minutes   **COOKING TIME:** 15 minutes
EQUIPMENT: 7cm/2¾in plain round pastry cutter

sunflower oil, for greasing
90g/3oz halloumi cheese
4 mint leaves, chopped

plain flour, for rolling the pastry
250g/9oz ready-to-roll puff pastry
1 egg yolk, beaten with 1 tbsp milk

1   Preheat the oven to 180°C/350°F/Gas 4 and lightly grease a baking sheet with oil.
    Break the halloumi into a bowl and mix in the mint.
2   On a lightly floured surface, roll the pastry into a 30 x 20cm/12 x 8in rectangle and
    cut out 12 circles, using the pastry cutter.
3   Put a spoonful of the halloumi mixture on each circle and fold in half, pinching the
    edges together with your fingers to seal. Put the parcels on the baking sheet.
4   Brush with the egg yolk mixture and bake for 15 minutes until golden, then serve.

PREPARING AHEAD: These can be made to the end of step 3 the night before, then covered with
cling film and stored in the fridge until ready to bake.

010 Hash Browns

SERVES: 12   **PREPARATION TIME:** 15 minutes   **COOKING TIME:** 35 minutes

700g/1lb 9oz potatoes, peeled and
  halved lengthways
2 tbsp olive oil

15g/¹/₂oz butter
salt

1   Put the potatoes in a large saucepan, cover with water and bring to the boil.
Boil for 10 minutes until they are soft but still offer some resistance when pierced
with a knife. Drain and leave to cool for a few minutes.
2   Coarsely grate the potatoes onto a plate and season with salt. Shape the potatoes
into 12 patties of equal size, about 4cm/1¹/₂in across and 1.5cm/¾in thick.
3   Put the oil and butter in a frying pan and heat over a medium heat until the butter
has melted. Add the hash browns and fry for 5 minutes on each side until brown,
working in batches to avoid overcrowding the pan. Serve immediately.

PREPARING AHEAD: These can be made to the end of step 2 the night before, then covered with
cling film and stored in the fridge until ready to cook.

011 Potato Croquettes

MAKES: 24   **PREPARATION TIME:** 25 minutes   **COOKING TIME:** 35 minutes

900g/2lb potatoes, peeled
  and chopped
3 eggs
110g/3³/₄oz grated Cheddar cheese

150g/5¹/₂oz/scant 1¹/₄ cups plain flour
100g/3¹/₂oz/1 cup breadcrumbs
80ml/2¹/₂fl oz/¹/₃ cup olive oil

1   Put the potatoes in a large saucepan, cover with water and bring to the boil.
Boil for 10 minutes until soft, then drain. Transfer to a mixing bowl and mash.
2   Beat 1 of the eggs and add it with the cheese to the potatoes and mix well.
Using your hands, shape teaspoonfuls of the potato mixture into 24 x 5cm/
2in-long croquettes.
3   Put the remaining 2 eggs in a bowl and beat. Roll 1 croquette in the flour, dip
it into the beaten eggs and then roll it in the breadcrumbs. Put the croquette
on a plate and repeat with the remaining potato mixture.
4   Heat half of the oil in a frying pan over a medium-high heat. Add the croquettes
and fry for 2 minutes on each side until brown, then drain on kitchen paper.
Work in batches to avoid overcrowding the pan and add the remaining oil
as needed. Serve immediately.

012 Mushroom Beignets

MAKES: 20–24   **PREPARATION TIME:** 5 minutes, plus 30 minutes resting
COOKING TIME: 10 minutes

30g/1oz/¹/₄ cup plain flour
1 egg
4 tbsp milk

1l/35fl oz/4 cups sunflower oil
125g/4¹/₂oz button mushrooms

1   Put the flour, egg, milk and 1 tbsp of the oil in a bowl and mix well. Leave
to stand for 30 minutes.
2   Put the remaining oil in a deep frying pan or wok and heat over a medium-high
heat to 180°C/350°F/Gas 4. Working in small batches, dip the mushrooms in the
batter and carefully drop them into the oil. Fry for 2 minutes until brown and
crispy. Drain on kitchen paper and serve immediately.

013 Bruschetta ai Funghi

MAKES: 12   PREPARATION TIME: 15 minutes   COOKING TIME: 15 minutes

4 tbsp olive oil
250g/9oz mixed mushrooms,
    such as portabello, field and
    shiitake, finely sliced
150g/5oz ciabatta bread, cut into
    12 x 1cm/$^1/_2$in slices

1 garlic clove
juice of 1 lemon
2 tbsp chopped parsley
50g/1$^3/_4$oz Parmesan cheese, grated

1   Heat 2 tbsp of the oil in a frying pan over a medium-high heat. Add the
    mushrooms and fry, stirring occasionally, for 7 minutes until soft.
2   Rub the ciabatta slices with the garlic clove. Heat a ridged griddle pan over a high
    heat for 5 minutes, or until smoking hot, then cook the bread for 2–3 minutes on
    each side until toasted and marked.
3   Drizzle the grilled ciabatta with the remaining oil and top with the mushrooms.
    Squeeze the lemon juice over the bruschetta, sprinkle with the parsley and
    Parmesan and serve immediately.

014 Herby Tapenade-Stuffed Eggs

MAKES: 24   **PREPARATION TIME:** 30 minutes   **COOKING TIME:** 15 minutes

12 eggs, at room temperature
1/2 tsp white wine vinegar
2 tbsp capers
90g/3oz/3/4 cup pitted black olives
8 tinned anchovy fillets in oil, drained

1 tbsp olive oil
juice of 1/2 lemon
20g/3/4oz butter, plus extra as needed
60g/21/4oz/scant 2/3 cup breadcrumbs
1 handful parsley sprigs

1   Bring a saucepan of water to the boil. Add the eggs and vinegar and boil for
    6 minutes, then drain and leave to stand until cool enough to handle.
2   Put the capers, olives, anchovies, oil and lemon juice in a food processor and
    process for 1–2 minutes until the mixture forms a thick paste. Alternatively, grind
    all the ingredients together with a pestle and mortar.
3   Melt the butter in a frying pan over a low heat. Add the breadcrumbs and fry,
    stirring occasionally, for 5 minutes until golden brown. If they seem a little dry
    while frying, add a little more butter.
4   To assemble, peel the eggs and halve them lengthways. Remove the yolks and mix
    them into the olive tapenade, then spoon the tapenade into each egg white half.
    Top with the breadcrumbs and a sprig of parsley and serve.

PREPARING AHEAD: The eggs can be boiled and peeled up to 1 day in advance and stored,
covered, in cold water in the fridge. Do not cut the eggs until ready to use or they will discolour.

015 Smoked Salmon & Scrambled Eggs on Toast

MAKES: 12   **PREPARATION TIME:** 15 minutes   **COOKING TIME:** 4 minutes

40g/11/2oz butter, plus extra
    for buttering the toast
2 eggs, beaten
4 slices of brown bread

125g/41/2oz smoked salmon
    or smoked trout
freshly ground black pepper

1   Heat the butter in a saucepan over a medium-low heat until melted. Add the eggs
    and cook, stirring continuously, for 1 minute until just beginning to set. Remove
    from the heat and continue stirring until the mixture comes together.
2   Toast the bread, then butter it while hot. Put 1 slice of the smoked salmon on each
    piece of toast, quarter and top each piece with 1 spoonful of the scrambled eggs.
    Season with pepper and serve immediately.

016 Kippers on Granary Toast with Lemon

MAKES: 20   **PREPARATION TIME:** 20 minutes   **COOKING TIME:** 18 minutes

5 eggs
1/2 tsp white wine vinegar
200g/7oz kipper fillets

5 slices of Granary bread
30g/1oz butter
juice of 1 lemon

1   Preheat the oven to 180°C/350°F/Gas 4. Bring a saucepan of water to the boil.
    Add the eggs and vinegar and boil for 6 minutes, then drain and leave to stand
    until cool enough to handle.
2   Put the kippers in a baking dish and cover with 250ml/9fl oz/1 cup water.
    Bake for 12 minutes until cooked through. When cool enough to handle, peel
    off the skin and discard.
3   Peel the eggs and slice each one into 4 discs. Toast the bread and butter it while
    still warm, then cut into quarters.
4   Put 1 slice of egg on each piece of toast, divide the kippers evenly on top and
    sprinkle with the lemon juice. Serve immediately.

PREPARING AHEAD: The eggs can be boiled and peeled up to 1 day in advance and stored,
covered, in cold water in the fridge. Do not cut the eggs until ready to use or they will discolour.

017 Quail Egg Spit-in-the-Eye

MAKES: 12   PREPARATION TIME: 10 minutes   COOKING TIME: 5 minutes
EQUIPMENT: 3cm/1¼in and 5cm/2in plain round pastry cutters

6 slices of white bread
1 tbsp olive oil
12 quail eggs

1 tbsp lumpfish caviar
freshly ground black pepper

1 Cut out 2 circles from each slice of bread, using the larger pastry cutter, then
   cut a hole in the centre of each circle, using the smaller pastry cutter.
2 Heat the oil in a frying pan over a medium heat. Add 6 of the large bread circles
   and fry for 1 minute. Turn over and carefully break 1 egg into the hole in each
   circle. Cook for 1 minute, turn the toasts over again and cook for a further
   30 seconds until the yolk sets. Transfer to a serving plate and repeat with the
   remaining bread circles and eggs.
3 Season with pepper, top with ¼ tsp of the caviar and serve.

018 Crumpets with Anchovy Paste

MAKES: 36   PREPARATION TIME: 5 minutes, plus 1 hour resting   COOKING TIME: 20 minutes

50g/1¾oz tinned anchovy fillets in oil
½ tsp celery salt
½ tsp cayenne pepper
½ tsp thyme leaves
¼ tsp ground nutmeg
50g/1¾oz butter, softened

300g/10½oz/heaped 2⅓ cups
   plain flour
½ tsp salt
1 tsp dried active yeast
500ml/17fl oz/2 cups milk
1½ tsp sunflower oil

1 Put the anchovies, celery salt, cayenne pepper, thyme leaves, nutmeg and butter
   in a food processor and process for 2 minutes until smooth. Transfer the anchovy
   paste to a small bowl and refrigerate until needed.
2 Put the flour, salt, yeast and milk in a mixing bowl and whisk until smooth. Cover
   the bowl with a clean tea towel and leave to stand at room temperature for 1 hour.
3 Heat ¼ tsp of the sunflower oil in a non-stick frying pan over a medium heat.
   Drop 5–6 tablespoonfuls of the batter into the pan, spacing well apart. Cook for
   1½ minutes until large holes appear on the surface. Turn and cook for a further
   1½ minutes until golden. Transfer to a serving plate and repeat with the remaining
   batter, adding another ¼ tsp of oil to the frying pan before each new batch.
4 Spread a little of the anchovy paste over each crumpet and serve.

PREPARING AHEAD: The anchovy spread can be made up to 1 week in advance and stored,
covered, in the fridge.

019 Potted Prawns

SERVES: 10   PREPARATION TIME: 5 minutes, plus 1 hour chilling   COOKING TIME: 3 minutes

250g/9oz butter
250g/9oz peeled, cooked brown
   prawns
½ tsp ground mace

½ tsp cayenne pepper
juice of 1½ lemons
10 slices of toast, halved, to serve

1 Heat the butter in a saucepan over a medium-low heat until melted. Stir in the
   prawns, mace, cayenne pepper and lemon juice, then remove from the heat.
2 Transfer the mixture to a deep serving bowl and leave to cool completely at room
   temperature, then cover and refrigerate for 1 hour, or until set. Serve with the toast.

PREPARING AHEAD: This can be made up to 1 day in advance and stored in an airtight container
in the fridge.

020 Piedmontese Peppers

MAKES: 20   **PREPARATION TIME:** 20 minutes   **COOKING TIME:** 20 minutes

125ml/4fl oz/½ cup olive oil, plus
   extra for greasing and drizzling
5 red peppers, quartered
   and deseeded
150g/5½oz goat's cheese, cut into
   20 small pieces
10 cherry tomatoes, quartered

5 tinned anchovy fillets in oil,
   drained and quartered
10 pitted black olives, halved
   (optional)
20 basil leaves
20 slices of ciabatta, toasted, to serve

1　Preheat the oven to 200°C/400°F/Gas 6 and grease a baking sheet with oil.
Put the peppers, skin-side down, on the baking sheet. Put 1 piece of the goat's
cheese, 2 pieces of cherry tomato, 1 anchovy slice and ½ black olive, if using,
into each pepper. Drizzle with the oil and bake for 20 minutes until tender.

2　Remove from the oven and top each pepper with 1 basil leaf. Serve on a slice
of the ciabatta, drizzled with extra oil.

021 Kedgeree Eggs

MAKES: 24   **PREPARATION TIME:** 20 minutes   **COOKING TIME:** 30 minutes

50g/1¾oz/¼ cup basmati rice
12 eggs, at room temperature
1 tsp white wine vinegar
100g/3½oz smoked haddock
10g/¼oz butter
1½ tsp olive oil
1 onion, finely chopped
½ tsp turmeric
1 tsp cumin seeds

2cm/¾in piece root ginger,
   peeled and finely chopped
1 tsp fennel seeds
125ml/4fl oz/½ cup double cream
60g/2¼oz kipper fillet,
   boned and flaked
1 handful parsley leaves,
   finely chopped

1   Bring 500ml/17fl oz/2 cups water to the boil in a saucepan. Add the rice and boil
    for 10 minutes, or until cooked. Drain, transfer to a large bowl and set aside.
2   Meanwhile, bring a large saucepan of water to the boil. Add the eggs and vinegar
    and boil for 6 minutes, then drain and leave to cool.
3   Put the haddock in a deep frying pan and cover with water. Bring to a simmer over
    a low heat and cook for 5 minutes until white yet still firm. Remove from the heat
    and leave the haddock in the water while you cook the remaining ingredients.
4   Heat the butter and oil in a frying pan over a medium heat. Add the onion and fry,
    stirring occasionally, for 5 minutes until softened. Add the turmeric, cumin, ginger
    and fennel and fry for a further 2 minutes until well combined and aromatic.
5   Add the cream and 125ml/4fl oz/½ cup of the cooking water from the haddock.
    Increase the heat to medium-high and bring to a boil. Boil for 5 minutes, stirring
    occasionally, until thick. Remove from the heat.
6   Put the rice in a bowl. Remove the haddock from the water and peel off the skin.
    Break the flesh into the rice. Mix in the creamy onion mixture, kipper and parsley.
7   When ready to serve, peel the eggs and slice in half lengthways. Scoop out the
    yolks and mix them into the kedgeree, then spoon the mixture into the egg
    halves and serve warm.

PREPARING AHEAD: The kedgeree can be made up to 1 day in advance and re-heated
over a medium heat before filling the eggs. The eggs can be boiled and peeled up to 1 day
in advance and stored, covered, in cold water in the fridge. Do not cut the eggs until ready
to use or they will discolour.

022 Smoked Salmon, Cream Cheese, Caper & Egg Bagels

MAKES: 12   **PREPARATION TIME:** 20 minutes   **COOKING TIME:** 12 minutes

2 eggs, at room temperature
½ tsp white wine vinegar
2 tsp capers

3 bagels, halved horizontally
150g/5½oz/⅔ cup cream cheese
125g/4½oz smoked salmon

1   Preheat the oven to 150°C/300°F/Gas 2. Bring a saucepan of water to the boil.
    Add the eggs and vinegar and boil for 6 minutes, then drain and leave to stand
    until cool enough to handle, then peel.
2   Coarsely grate the eggs into a bowl, then stir in the capers.
3   Toast the bagels for 3–4 minutes until golden. Spread the cream cheese over all
    6 halves and cover with the smoked salmon. Top with the caper and egg mixture,
    then cover the bagels with their top halves, quarter and serve.

PREPARING AHEAD: The eggs can be boiled and peeled up to 1 day in advance and stored,
covered, in cold water in the fridge. Do not cut the eggs until ready to use or they will discolour.

023   Fish Pasties

MAKES: 24   **PREPARATION TIME:** 30 minutes   **COOKING TIME:** 40 minutes
EQUIPMENT: 8cm/3in plain round pastry cutter

250g/9oz smoked haddock
750ml/26fl oz/3 cups milk
30g/1oz butter
1 tbsp plain flour, plus extra for rolling
1 handful parsley, finely chopped

1 tbsp capers
sunflower oil, for greasing
500g/1lb 2oz ready-to-roll puff pastry
1 egg yolk, beaten with 1 tbsp milk
salt and freshly ground black pepper

1 Preheat the oven to 180°C/350°F/Gas 4. Put the haddock and 250ml/9fl oz/1 cup of the milk in a baking dish and bake for 15 minutes until the fish is whiter, slightly firm to the touch and a little shrunken.
2 Meanwhile, melt the butter in a non-stick saucepan over a low heat, then stir in the flour. Slowly add the remaining milk, 1 tbsp at a time, stirring continuously, until combined. Continue cooking over a low heat for 10 minutes, stirring, until thickened and smooth.
3 Remove the fish from the oven, peel off the skin and flake the meat into a bowl. Stir in the white sauce, parsley and capers and season with salt and pepper, then leave to cool completely.
4 When ready to assemble, lightly grease a baking sheet with oil. Cut the pastry block in half and, on a lightly floured surface, roll it out into a 32 x 24cm/ 12¾ x 9½in rectangle. Cut out 12 circles, using the pastry cutter. Brush the edge of half of 1 pastry circle with water and put 1 tbsp of the filling slightly off-centre. Fold the pastry in half, pressing down the edges to seal. Put the pasty on the prepared baking sheet and repeat with the remaining pastry and filling.
5 Brush with the egg yolk mixture, bake for 12–15 minutes until golden and serve.

PREPARING AHEAD: These can be made to the end of step 4 up to 2 hours in advance, then covered with cling film and stored in the fridge until ready to bake.

024   Egg & Caper Mayonnaise Sandwiches

MAKES: 12   **PREPARATION TIME:** 15 minutes, plus making the mayonnaise
COOKING TIME: 12 minutes

2 eggs, at room temperature
½ tsp white wine vinegar
2 tinned anchovy fillets in oil, drained and chopped
12 chives, finely chopped

½ recipe quantity Mayonnaise
  (see page 12)
8 slices of white bread, buttered
salt and freshly ground black pepper

1 Bring a saucepan of water to the boil. Add the eggs and vinegar and boil for 6 minutes, then drain and leave to stand until cool enough to handle, then peel.
2 Grate the eggs into a bowl. Add the anchovies, chives and mayonnaise and mix well, then season with salt and pepper.
3 Cut each slice of bread into 3 strips. Put 1½ tsp of the egg mayonnaise on 12 strips and cover with the remaining 12 strips. Press the ends down to seal so that the sandwiches have a 'hump' in the middle, then serve.

PREPARING AHEAD: The eggs can be boiled and peeled up to 1 day in advance and stored, covered, in cold water in the fridge. Do not cut the eggs until ready to use or they will discolour.

25 Salmon Rillettes

SERVES: 10　**PREPARATION TIME:** 10 minutes　**COOKING TIME:** 15 minutes

300g/10½oz 'hot smoked'
　salmon flakes
3 eggs, beaten
185ml/6fl oz/¾ cup double cream

juice of ½ lemon
6 chives, finely chopped
salt and freshly ground black pepper
10 slices of toast, to serve

1　Preheat the oven to 180°C/350°F/Gas 4. Put the salmon flakes, eggs, cream, lemon juice and chives in a bowl and stir well, then season with salt and pepper.
2　Transfer the mixture to a small baking dish and bake for 15–20 minutes until set and the top is beginning to brown. Serve hot or cold with the toast.

26 Quail Eggs Benedict with Caviar

MAKES: 24　**PREPARATION TIME:** 15 minutes　**COOKING TIME:** 20 minutes
EQUIPMENT: 4cm/1½in plain round pastry cutter

6 slices of white bread, crusts
　removed
olive oil, for brushing
4 roast ham slices
juice of ½ lemon
24 quail eggs
30g/1oz lumpfish caviar
salt and freshly ground black pepper

HOLLANDAISE SAUCE
2 egg yolks
100g/3½oz butter, diced
juice of ½ lemon

1　Preheat the oven to 180°C/350°F/Gas 4. Cut 24 circles from the bread, using the pastry cutter, and put them on a baking sheet. Brush with oil and toast for 10 minutes until golden.
2　Cut 24 circles from the ham, using the pastry cutter, and set aside.
3　To make the hollandaise sauce, put the egg yolks, 30g/1oz of the butter and the lemon juice in a heatproof mixing bowl. Rest the bowl over a saucepan of simmering water, making sure that the bottom of the bowl does not touch the water. Gently whisk until the butter has melted. Add the remaining butter, 15g/½oz at a time and whisk continuously until smooth before adding any more. Once all the butter has been added, the hollandaise sauce will be thick, shiny and smooth. Remove the bowl from the heat and set aside.
4　Fill a deep frying pan with water and bring to the boil, then reduce the heat to low so that the water is barely simmering. Add the lemon juice and then carefully crack in the eggs, holding them near the water to help them keep their shape. Poach for 1–2 minutes, then transfer to a plate, using a slotted spoon. Using the pastry cutter or a sharp knife, trim any jagged white edges away for a tidy finish.
5　Put 1 slice of ham on each toast circle and top with 1 egg, followed by 1 tsp of the hollandaise. Top with the caviar, season with salt and pepper and serve.

027 Foie Gras on Brioche

MAKES: 24 **PREPARATION TIME:** 10 minutes, plus making the brioche

125g/4¹/₂oz bloc de foie gras
1 recipe quantity Brioche Buns
    (see page 21), warm

1   Slice the foie gras into 5mm/¹/₄in pieces.
2   Slice the brioche buns in half and spread with the foie gras. Serve immediately.

028 Coronation Chicken Sandwiches

MAKES: 24 **PREPARATION TIME:** 15 minutes, plus making the chicken and mayonnaise

¹/₃ recipe quantity Boiled Chicken
    (see page 12)
140g/5oz/¹/₂ cup mango chutney
¹/₂ recipe quantity Mayonnaise
    (see page 12)

12 seedless white grapes,
    quartered lengthways
12 slices of white or brown
    sandwich bread
salt and freshly ground black pepper

1   Put the chicken, chutney, mayonnaise and grapes in a bowl and mix well, then
    season with salt and pepper.
2   Spread 6 slices of the bread with the mixture and cover with the remaining 6 slices,
    pressing down gently to seal the edges. Just before serving, cut off the crusts and
    cut each sandwich into 4 triangles, then serve.

PREPARING AHEAD: The chicken mixture in step 1 can be made up to 4 hours in advance and
stored in an airtight container in the fridge.

029 Scotch Woodcock on Toast

MAKES: 12 **PREPARATION TIME:** 10 minutes **COOKING TIME:** 2 minutes

50g/1³/₄oz tinned anchovies in oil
70g/2¹/₂oz butter
2 eggs, beaten
3 slices of bread, toasted

¹/₄ tsp cayenne pepper
5 chives, chopped
freshly ground black pepper

1   Put the anchovies, their oil and 30g/1oz of the butter in a food processor and
    process for 1–2 minutes until smooth.
2   Put the remaining butter in a non-stick saucepan and heat over a low heat.
    Add the eggs and cook, stirring continuously, for 1 minute until just beginning
    to set. Remove from the heat.
3   Spread the anchovy butter on the toast. Cut each slice of toast into quarters, then
    top with 1 tsp of the scrambled eggs. Sprinkle with the cayenne pepper and
    chives, season with pepper and serve immediately.

PREPARING AHEAD: The anchovy butter can be made the night before and stored in an airtight
container in the fridge.

30 Piperade

MAKES: 12 **PREPARATION TIME:** 15 minutes **COOKING TIME:** 40 minutes
EQUIPMENT: 900g/2lb loaf tin

1 tbsp olive oil, plus extra for
  greasing and frying
10g/¼oz butter
1 onion, finely chopped
1 garlic clove, finely chopped
1 yellow pepper, deseeded
  and chopped

2 red peppers, deseeded
  and chopped
100g/3½oz ham, finely chopped
6 eggs, beaten
salt and freshly ground pepper

1 Preheat the oven to 180°C/350°F/Gas 4 and grease the loaf tin with oil. Heat the oil and butter in a frying pan over a medium heat. Add the onion and fry, stirring occasionally, for 5 minutes until soft. Stir in the garlic and peppers and cook, stirring occasionally, for a further 5 minutes until tender, adding an additional 1 tsp of oil, if necessary. Stir in the ham and remove from the heat.
2 Add the pepper mixture to the beaten eggs. Season with salt and pepper and pour into the prepared tin. Bake for 25–30 minutes until the eggs have set. Remove from the oven and leave to cool for 10 minutes, then turn out onto a long plate or cutting board. Cut into 6 slices, then halve each slice and serve warm or cold.

31 Country Terrine

SERVES: 10–12 **PREPARATION TIME:** 25 minutes **COOKING TIME:** 1 hour
EQUIPMENT: 8 x 25cm/3¼ x 10in terrine or loaf tin

500g/1lb 2oz pork mince
1 tsp salt
½ tsp ground nutmeg
½ tsp cinnamon
125ml/4fl oz/½ cup double cream
1 tbsp brandy
200g/7oz pork fillet, trimmed and
  cut into 1cm/½in-thick slices

2 boneless, skinless chicken breasts,
  about 125g/4½oz each
1 handful tarragon, finely chopped
15 unsmoked streaky bacon rashers
freshly ground black pepper
1 loaf of French bread, to serve
Dijon mustard, to serve (optional)
mango chutney, to serve (optional)

1 Preheat the oven to 170°C/325°F/Gas 3. Put the pork mince, salt, nutmeg, cinnamon, cream and brandy in a bowl, mix well and set aside. Season the pork fillet with pepper and set aside, then coat the chicken breasts in the tarragon.
2 Using the back of a table knife, stretch the bacon rashers until they are 50 per cent greater in length. Line the base and sides of the terrine with the bacon, leaving some to hang over the edges. Spread ⅓ of the mince mixture evenly across the base of the terrine, then top with the chicken breasts. Spread another ⅓ of the mince over the chicken, then tightly layer the pork fillet on top.
3 Cover with the remaining mince and fold the excess bacon over. Put the lid on the terrine or, if using a loaf tin, cover with a baking sheet and weigh down with something heavy to keep it in place.
4 Put the terrine in an ovenproof baking dish and fill the dish halfway with water. Bake for 1 hour until the sides have begun to pull away from the edges. Leave to cool completely and set before serving.
5 When ready to serve, turn the terrine out onto a serving plate and slice. Serve with the bread and mustard or chutney, if using.

PREPARING AHEAD: This can be made up to 2 days in advance, covered and stored in the fridge.

Scrambled Egg & Bacon Croissants

MAKES: 10   **PREPARATION TIME:** 5 minutes   **COOKING TIME:** 12 minutes

1 tbsp olive oil
10 unsmoked streaky bacon rashers,
    finely chopped
100g/3½oz butter

5 eggs, beaten
10 small croissants, split lengthways
salt and freshly ground black pepper

1   Heat the oil in a frying pan over a medium-high heat. Add the bacon and fry
    for 8–10 minutes until crisp.
2   Heat the butter in a non-stick saucepan over a low heat. Add the eggs and cook,
    stirring continuously, for 1½–2 minutes until just beginning to set. Remove from
    the heat, stir in the bacon and season with salt and pepper.
3   Fill each croissant with the egg mixture and serve immediately.

033 Sweet Whisky-Glazed Roast Ham

SERVES: 10–12   PREPARATION TIME: 10 minutes, plus 2 hours soaking
COOKING TIME: 1 hour 50 minutes

1.6kg/3lb 8oz unsmoked gammon,
  off the bone
2 carrots
1 onion, halved

1 tbsp black peppercorns
2 tbsp Dijon mustard
3 tbsp soft brown sugar
2 tbsp whisky

1 Put the ham in a large basin, cover with water and leave to soak for 2 hours. Drain, transfer the ham to a large saucepan and cover with cold water. Add the carrots, onion and peppercorns, cover with a lid and bring to a low simmer over a medium-low heat. This will take approximately 15 minutes. Remove the lid and skim the surface, using a slotted spoon, to remove the impurities that have gathered on the surface.
2 Reduce the heat to low and continue cooking at a very low simmer, uncovered, for 1 hour and 15 minutes. One or two bubbles should occasionally rise to the surface, but if the water is any hotter, the meat will dry out. Turn the heat off and leave the ham in the water to cool completely. Once cool, peel off the skin, using a sharp knife, if necessary, but leave the thin layer of fat intact. Transfer the ham to a roasting dish.
3 Preheat the oven to 180°C/350°F/Gas 4. Spread the mustard over the fat side of the ham and pat the sugar over the top. Carefully pour over the whisky, trying not to dislodge too much sugar, and bake for 10 minutes.
4 Remove the ham from the oven and spoon over the juices that have collected in the tin. Return to the oven and bake for a further 10 minutes. Transfer the glazed ham to a serving platter and leave to cool. Serve at room temperature.

PREPARING AHEAD: This can be made up to 3 days in advance, covered and stored in the fridge.

034 Cocktail Toads-in-the-Hole

MAKES: 24   PREPARATION TIME: 10 minutes, plus 30 minutes resting
COOKING TIME: 30 minutes   EQUIPMENT: 2 x deep 12-hole mini-muffin tins

115g/4oz/scant 1 cup plain flour
1/4 tsp salt
2 eggs
150ml/5fl oz/scant 2/3 cup milk
1 tbsp olive oil

24 very small cocktail sausages
4 1/2 tsp sunflower oil
2 tbsp Dijon mustard, to serve
  (optional)

1 Sift the flour and salt into a mixing bowl. Add the eggs and mix well to form a thick paste. Slowly add the milk, beating continuously with a wooden spoon until smooth and thick. Leave to rest for 30 minutes at room temperature.
2 Preheat the oven to 200°C/400°F/Gas 6. Heat the olive oil in a frying pan over a medium-high heat. Add the sausages and fry for 2 minutes on each side until brown. Remove from the heat.
3 Put 1/4 tsp of the sunflower oil in each hole of the muffin tins and heat in the oven for 5 minutes until smoking hot. Remove from the oven and immediately spoon 1 tbsp of the batter into each muffin hole. Drop 1 sausage into each hole and return to the oven. Bake for 15 minutes until the batter has risen and turned golden. Serve with the mustard, if using.

035 Croque Monsieur

MAKES: 12   PREPARATION TIME: 10 minutes   **COOKING TIME:** 5 minutes

85g/3oz butter, softened
12 slices of white bread
2 tbsp Dijon mustard
6 slices of ham

200g/7oz hard cheese, such as
  mature Cheddar or Gruyère, thinly
  sliced, plus extra for grating

1   Spread 10g/¼oz of the butter on 6 slices of the bread, then spread with the mustard. Add 1 slice of ham, followed by 1 slice of cheese. Cover with the remaining 6 slices of bread and put the sandwiches in a baking dish. Use two baking dishes, if necessary.
2   Dot the sandwiches with the remaining butter, grate the extra cheese over and bake for 10 minutes until golden. Remove from the oven, cut each sandwich in half and serve.

036 Mini Quiche Lorraines

MAKES: 24   PREPARATION TIME: 15 minutes, plus making the tartlet cases
COOKING TIME: 20 minutes

1 tbsp olive oil
8 rindless streaky bacon rashers,
  finely chopped
100ml/3½fl oz/scant ½ cup
  double cream

1 egg
½ recipe quantity Savoury Tartlet
  Cases, blind-baked (see page 13)
freshly ground black pepper

1   Preheat the oven to 180°C/350°F/Gas 4. Heat the oil in a frying pan over a medium-high heat. Add the bacon and fry, stirring occasionally, for 8–10 minutes until crisp.
2   Put the cream and egg in a bowl, season with pepper and mix well.
3   With the tartlet cases still in their muffin tins, evenly distribute the bacon into the 24 cases. Spoon a scant 1 tsp of the cream mixture into each tartlet case and bake for 8–10 minutes until set and golden. Serve hot or cold.

037 Baked Mediterranean Lamb Kebabs

MAKES: 12   PREPARATION TIME: 15 minutes   **COOKING TIME:** 10 minutes
EQUIPMENT: 12 x 10cm/4in skewers

250g/9oz lamb mince
1 handful parsley leaves,
  coarsely chopped

juice and zest of 1 lemon
salt and freshly ground black pepper

1   If using wooden skewers, soak them in water for at least 30 minutes before cooking. Preheat the oven to 200°C/400°F/Gas 6. Put the mince, parsley, lemon juice and zest in a food processor and process for 1–2 minutes until the mixture forms a fine mince. Season with salt and pepper.
2   Divide the mince into 12 portions of equal size and shape around the pointed end of the skewers. Put the skewers on a baking sheet.
3   Bake for 10 minutes until brown, then serve hot.

PREPARING AHEAD: The kebabs can be made to the end of step 2 up to 1 day in advance, covered and stored in the fridge. Leave to stand at room temperature for 30 minutes before baking.

038 Banana Bread

SERVES: 12   PREPARATION TIME: 25 minutes   COOKING TIME: 55 minutes
EQUIPMENT: 900g/2lb loaf tin

125g/4¹/₂oz unsalted butter, plus extra for greasing and to serve (optional)
280g/10oz/scant 1¹/₄ cups caster sugar
1 tsp vanilla extract
2 eggs
2 ripe bananas, peeled and mashed
80ml/2¹/₂fl oz/¹/₃ cup natural yogurt
1 tsp baking powder

300g/10¹/₂oz/scant 2¹/₂ cups plain flour

ICING (OPTIONAL)
185g/6¹/₂oz/1¹/₂ cups icing sugar
2 tbsp cream cheese
1 banana, mashed
juice of ¹/₂ lemon

1   Preheat the oven to 180°C/350°F/Gas 4. Lightly grease and flour the loaf tin. Put the butter and sugar in a food processor and process for 2–3 minutes until smooth. Add the vanilla extract, eggs and bananas and process for a further 1 minute until well mixed.
2   Put the yogurt in a mixing bowl and stir in the baking powder. Leave to stand for 2–3 minutes, or until bubbles begin to appear on the surface.
3   Sift the flour into a large mixing bowl and add the banana and yogurt mixtures. Stir until smooth, then pour the mixture into the prepared loaf tin.
4   Bake for 55 minutes, or until a skewer or cocktail stick instered into the centre comes out clean. Remove from the oven and leave to cool in the tin.
5   Meanwhile, make the icing, if using. Put all the icing ingredients in a bowl and mix well. Turn the banana bread out of the tin, spread the icing over the top and serve. If not using the icing, serve plain or with butter.

PREPARING AHEAD: The banana bread can be made the night before, wrapped in foil and stored at room temperature. Ice it immediately before serving, if desired.

039 Orange & Almond Sponge Fingers

MAKES: 24   PREPARATION TIME: 20 minutes   COOKING TIME: 10 minutes

butter, for greasing
4 eggs, separated
90g/3¹/₄oz/heaped ¹/₃ cup caster sugar
100g/3¹/₂oz/heaped ³/₄ cup plain flour, plus extra for dusting

100g/3¹/₂oz/¹/₂ cup cream cheese
100g/3¹/₂oz/¹/₂ cup crème fraîche
100g/3¹/₂oz/scant 1 cup icing sugar
juice of ¹/₂ orange, plus extra to taste
30g/1oz/¹/₃ cup flaked almonds

1   Preheat the oven to 190°C/375°F/Gas 5. Grease and flour two baking sheets or line them with baking parchment. Put the egg yolks and 70g/2¹/₂oz/scant ¹/₃ cup of the caster sugar in a bowl and whisk together for 3 minutes until pale and the mixture forms a ribbonlike pattern when drizzled over the surface of the mixture.
2   Put the egg whites and the remaining sugar in a clean bowl and whisk, using a clean whisk, for 3 minutes until stiff peaks form.
3   Sift the flour into the egg yolk mixture and gently fold together, using a metal spoon, then fold in the egg whites, a third at a time, until well combined.
4   Gently spoon heaped teaspoonfuls of the mixture onto the prepared baking sheets to form 24 x 6cm/2¹/₂in sponge fingers, about 1cm/¹/₂in thick. Bake for 10 minutes, then remove from the oven and transfer immediately to a cooling rack.
5   Put the cream cheese, crème fraîche, icing sugar and orange juice in a bowl and mix well. Top each biscuit with a generous spoonful of this mixture, then sprinkle with the flaked almonds and serve immediately.

040 Blueberry & Goji Berry Muffins

MAKES: 12   **PREPARATION TIME:** 10 minutes   **COOKING TIME:** 15–20 minutes
EQUIPMENT: 12-hole muffin tin

210g/7$\frac{1}{2}$oz/1$\frac{2}{3}$ cups plain flour
2 tsp baking powder
100g/3$\frac{1}{2}$oz/heaped $\frac{1}{2}$ cup soft
   brown sugar
1 egg

200ml/7fl oz/scant 1 cup milk
55g/2oz butter, melted, plus extra
   for greasing
40g/1$\frac{1}{2}$oz/$\frac{1}{3}$ cup goji berries
225g/8oz/1$\frac{1}{2}$ cups blueberries

1   Preheat the oven to 200°C/400°F/Gas 6 and line the muffin tin with muffin papers. Sift the flour and baking powder into a bowl and mix in the sugar. Beat in the egg and milk, mixing until well combined, then add the butter and stir until smooth. Add the berries and gently fold together until well mixed.

2   Spoon the mixture into the muffin tins and bake for 15–20 minutes until risen and a cocktail stick inserted into the centre of one of the muffins comes out clean. Transfer to a cooling rack. Serve warm or at room temperature.

PREPARING AHEAD: The batter can be made to the end of step 1 the night before, then transferred to an airtight container and stored in the fridge until ready to bake.

041 Madeleines

MAKES: 24   PREPARATION TIME: 15 minutes   COOKING TIME: 12 minutes
EQUIPMENT: 8cm/3¼in madeleine tin

100g/3½oz/scant ½ cup caster sugar
2 eggs
100g/3½oz/heaped ¾ cup plain flour
1 tbsp baking powder

100g/3½oz butter, melted,
    plus extra for greasing
2 tsp orange blossom water

1   Preheat the oven to 200°C/400°F/Gas 6. Put the sugar and eggs in a bowl and beat, using a whisk or electric handheld mixer, for 2 minutes until pale. Sift in the flour and baking powder and carefully fold together. Gently stir in the butter and orange blossom water.

2   Lightly grease the madeleine tin, or skip this step if using a silicone mould. Fill the moulds three-quarters full, then bake for 12 minutes. Remove from the oven and leave to cool for only 10 minutes before serving slightly warm.

042 Apple Strudels

MAKES: 12   PREPARATION TIME: 30 minutes, plus 1 hour soaking the raisins
COOKING TIME: 20 minutes

55g/2oz unsalted butter
30g/1oz/scant ⅓ cup breadcrumbs
60g/2oz/½ cup raisins, soaked in
    4 tbsp rum or calvados for 1 hour
1 large cooking apple, such as
    Bramley or Granny Smith, peeled,
    cored and finely chopped

1 tsp ground cinnamon
4 tbsp caster sugar
juice of ½ lemon
8 filo pastry sheets

1   Heat 15g/½ oz of the butter in a frying pan over a low heat. Add the breadcrumbs and fry, stirring occasionally, for 5 minutes until golden. Transfer to a mixing bowl. Drain the raisins and add them to the breadcrumbs, along with the apple, cinnamon, sugar and lemon juice. Stir until well combined.

2   Melt the remaining butter in a small saucepan over a low heat. Put 1 filo pastry sheet on a clean work surface, keeping the rest covered with a clean damp tea towel while you work. Brush the pastry with a little of the melted butter, then cover with a second filo sheet and brush again with butter. Cut the filo lengthways into 3 long strips.

3   Position 1 pastry strip vertically in front of you. Put 1 heaped tbsp of the filling at the bottom end of the pastry, leaving a little space between the edges of the pastry and the filling. Fold the bottom-right corner of the pastry diagonally up over the filling to form a triangle, then fold the bottom-left corner up the left edge, keeping the triangular shape. Continue folding until you reach the end of the pastry and the filling is enclosed. Repeat with the remaining pastry and filling.

4   Put the apple strudels on a baking sheet, brush with the remaining butter and bake for 15 minutes until golden brown. Serve warm.

043 Carrot Cake with Orange-Cream Icing

SERVES: 12 **PREPARATION TIME:** 20 minutes **COOKING TIME:** 1 hour
EQUIPMENT: 900g/2lb loaf tin

butter, for greasing
150g/5¹/₂oz/scant 1¹/₄ cups plain flour,
   plus extra for flouring
1 tsp baking powder
1 tsp ground cinnamon
1 tsp ground nutmeg
1 tsp ground allspice
1 tsp ground coriander
230g/8¹/₄oz carrots, coarsely grated
70g/2¹/₂oz/heaped ¹/₂ cup raisins
3 eggs

100g/3¹/₂oz/heaped ¹/₂ cup soft dark
   brown sugar
4 tbsp sunflower oil
40g/1¹/₂oz/¹/₄ cup pine nuts
juice and zest of 1 orange

ICING
80ml/2¹/₂fl oz/¹/₃ cup whipping cream
80g/2³/₄oz/scant ¹/₃ cup cream cheese
juice and zest of ¹/₂ small orange
80g/2³/₄oz/scant ²/₃ cup icing sugar,
   sifted

1   Preheat the oven to 180°C/350°F/Gas 4. Grease and flour the loaf tin and line the
   base with baking parchment. Sift the flour and baking powder into a bowl, then
   stir in the cinnamon, nutmeg, allspice and coriander.
2   Add the carrots, raisins, eggs, sugar, oil, pine nuts, and orange juice and zest. Mix
   well until smooth. Pour the mixture into the tin and bake for 1 hour. Remove from
   the oven and leave to cool completely before icing.
3   Meanwhile, make the icing. Put the cream in a bowl and beat, using a whisk or
   handheld electric mixer, for 1–2 minutes until stiff. Add the cream cheese, orange
   juice and sugar and mix until smooth. Turn the cake out onto a serving plate and
   spread the icing over the top and sides. Sprinkle with the orange zest and serve.

PREPARING AHEAD: The cake can be made the night before, wrapped in foil and stored at room
temperature. Ice it immediately before serving.

044 Crêpes Suzette

MAKES: 12 **PREPARATION TIME:** 10 minutes, plus 30 minutes resting
COOKING TIME: 50 minutes

250ml/9fl oz/1 cup milk
70g/2¹/₂oz unsalted butter
150g/5¹/₂oz/scant 1¹/₄ cups plain flour
a pinch salt
2 eggs, beaten
4 tsp sunflower oil, plus extra
   as needed

juice of 1 orange
juice of ¹/₂ lemon
70g/2¹/₂oz/heaped ¹/₂ cup icing sugar
1–2 tbsp orange liqueur, such
   as Cointreau or Grand Marnier

1   Heat the milk and 15g/¹/₂oz of the butter in a saucepan over a low heat until the
   butter has melted.
2   Sift the flour and salt into a bowl and make a well in the centre. Add the eggs and
   1 tbsp of the milk mixture and whisk well. Add the rest of the milk and continue to
   whisk until smooth. Cover the bowl with a clean tea towel and leave to stand at
   room temperature for 30 minutes.
3   Heat 1 tsp of the oil in a 15cm/6in frying pan over a low heat. Remove the pan
   from the heat, add 1 tbsp of the batter and tilt the pan from side to side until the
   base is evenly covered. Return to the heat and cook for 1–2 minutes on each side
   until the crêpe begins to brown. Transfer to a plate and repeat with the remaining
   batter, adding more oil to the pan as needed.
4   Cut each crêpe in half and fold each half over and over again to form a small
   triangle. Secure with a cocktail stick and put in a heatproof dish until ready to serve.
5   When ready to serve, preheat the oven to 180°C/350°F/Gas 4. Put the orange
   and lemon juices, sugar, liqueur and the remaining butter in a saucepan and heat
   over a low heat, stirring occasionally, for 2–3 minutes until the butter has melted.
   Pour the sauce over the crêpes and bake for 10 minutes until heated through,
   then serve.

045 Churros & Cinnamon Cream

MAKES: 24 **PREPARATION TIME:** 5 minutes, plus 45 minutes resting
COOKING TIME: 15 minutes **EQUIPMENT:** pastry bag with 1cm/½in nozzle

55g/2oz unsalted butter
2 tbsp caster sugar, plus extra
  for sprinkling
150g/5½oz/scant 1¼ cups plain flour
¼ tsp salt

½ tsp baking powder
125ml/4fl oz/½ cup double cream
½ tsp ground cinnamon
1l/35fl oz/4 cups sunflower oil

1 Put the butter, 1 tbsp of the sugar and 250ml/9fl oz/1 cup water in a saucepan and
   heat over a medium-low heat, stirring occasionally, for 2–3 minutes until the butter
   has melted and the sugar has dissolved. Remove from the heat and stir in the flour,
   salt and baking powder until the mixture forms a smooth, thick, slightly sticky
   dough that pulls away from the sides of the pan. Remove from the heat and
   transfer to a bowl. Leave to stand, covered, for 45 minutes.
2 In a large bowl, whisk the cream for 1 minute until slightly thickened. Whisk in the
   cinnamon and remaining sugar and set aside.
3 Heat the oil in a deep saucepan to 160°C/315°F. Put the churros mixture in the
   pastry bag and pipe a few 10cm/4in rows of the batter into the oil, working in
   batches to avoid overcrowding the pan. Fry for 2–3 minutes until brown, then
   remove from the oil, using a slotted spoon, and drain on kitchen paper. Repeat
   with the remaining batter.
4 Sprinkle the churros with sugar and serve warm with the cinnamon cream.

CHAPTER 2

PRE-DINNER DRINKS

A few light bites with a drink are an important prelude to any meal. They whet the appetite, ensure no one drinks on an empty stomach and can act as an icebreaker. Designed for small gatherings of 10–12 people, this chapter features both simple and more elaborate recipes from around the world with flavours to set just the right mood – and ensure that everyone still has room for dinner.

Plan your menu so that it complements the meal that will follow. Pre-dinner tapas can precede a starter, or replace one entirely. For light bites before a starter, plan only a few simple items per head, such as Naan Breadsticks with Masala Dip, Spiced Nuts or Padrón Peppers. If you're skipping the starter, go for a selection of three or four more extravagant, intensely flavoured dishes, such as Mini Beef Rossinis, Chicken Gyoza, Cauliflower & Paneer Pakoras and Artichoke Hearts Stuffed with Tuna & Capers. Most of the recipes in this chapter can be made partly or completely in advance to ease any pressure in the kitchen – and so you'll be free to entertain your guests and enjoy the party yourself.

SEAFOOD TARTLETS (SEE PAGE 58)

046　Grissini Sticks

MAKES: 48　**PREPARATION TIME:** 20 minutes, plus 1½ hours resting
COOKING TIME: 12 minutes

300g/10½oz/scant 2½ cups strong
　white bread flour, plus extra
　for kneading
1 tsp dried active yeast

½ tsp salt
1 tbsp olive oil, plus extra
　for brushing

1　Put the flour, yeast, salt and oil in a bowl. Add 200ml/7fl oz/scant 1 cup lukewarm water in a slow, steady stream and mix, using a wooden spoon, for 2 minutes until the mixture comes together. Continue mixing the dough for a further 5 minutes until smooth and elastic.

2　Turn the dough out onto a lightly floured surface and knead, using your hands, for 2 minutes, then shape into a ball. Transfer to a clean bowl, cover with a clean damp tea towel and leave to rest for 1½ hours.

3　Preheat the oven to 190°C/375°F/Gas 5. Divide the dough in half. Keep one half under the tea towel while you roll out the other half into a 30 x 20cm/12 x 8in rectangle on a lightly floured surface. Cut the dough in half lengthways, then cut it into 24 x 1cm/½in strips. Roll each one into a cylinder, increasing its length by half.

4　Put the grissini sticks on a baking sheet and lightly brush them with olive oil, then sprinkle with salt. Repeat with the remaining dough, then bake for 10–12 minutes until golden and crispy.

PREPARING AHEAD: These can be made up to 1 day in advance and stored in an airtight container at room temperature.

047　Naan Breadsticks with Masala Dip

MAKES: 24　**PREPARATION TIME:** 10 minutes, plus 2 hours resting　**COOKING TIME:** 5 minutes

335g/11¾oz/2⅔ cups plain flour,
　sifted, plus extra for kneading
1 tsp caster sugar
105ml/3¾fl oz/scant ½ cup
　natural yogurt
1 tsp garam masala

1 handful coriander leaves
4 tbsp olive oil
juice of a lemon
50g/1¾oz butter, melted
salt and freshly ground black pepper

1　Put the flour in a bowl. Make a well in the centre and add the sugar and 1 tbsp of the yogurt. Mix the flour into the centre, then add 250ml/9fl oz/1 cup lukewarm water and continue mixing, using your hands, for 5 minutes until the mixture forms a dough. Turn the dough out onto a lightly floured surface and knead, using your hands, for 3 minutes until smooth and elastic. Transfer to a clean bowl, cover with a clean damp tea towel and leave to rise for 2 hours, or until doubled in size.

2　Meanwhile, make the masala dip. Put the garam masala, coriander leaves, oil, lemon juice and the remaining yogurt in a food processor and process for 1 minute until smooth. Season with salt and pepper, transfer to a serving bowl and set aside.

3　Preheat the grill to high and line a baking sheet with baking parchment. Divide the dough into 12 pieces of equal size and shape each one into a 10cm/4in-long oval. Put them on the baking sheet and brush with half of the butter.

4　Grill for 3 minutes until the surface blisters, then remove from the grill, turn over and brush with the remaining butter. Grill for a further 1–2 minutes until golden and slightly puffed. Cut each naan in half and serve with the dip.

PREPARING AHEAD: The dip can be made up to 1 day in advance and stored in an airtight container in the fridge. Stir well before serving at room temperature.

048 Cheese & Thyme Pastry Sticks

MAKES: 30 **PREPARATION TIME:** 15 minutes **COOKING TIME:** 12 minutes

55g/2oz mature Cheddar cheese,
  grated
2 tbsp Dijon mustard

leaves from 1 thyme sprig
plain flour, for rolling the pastry
250g/9oz ready-to-roll puff pastry

1 Preheat the oven to 180°C/350°F/Gas 4. Put the Cheddar, mustard and thyme
   in a bowl and mix well.
2 On a lightly floured surface, roll the pastry into a 45 x 15cm/18 x 6in rectangle.
   Spread the cheese mixture over it, then roll into a long log and flatten slightly so
   that it measures about 50 x 10cm/20 x 4in, then cut it into 30 x 1cm/½in strips.
3 Transfer to a baking sheet and bake for 12 minutes until golden brown and slightly
   puffed. Leave to cool for 10 minutes, then serve.

049 Dukka with Olive Oil & Pitta Breads

SERVES: 10–12 **PREPARATION TIME:** 5 minutes **COOKING TIME:** 5 minutes

60g/2¼oz/heaped ⅓ cup pine nuts
70g/2½oz/½ cup flaked almonds
70g/2½oz/½ cup pistachio nuts,
  shelled
1 tsp cumin seeds

1 tsp coriander seeds
1 tsp salt
250ml/9fl oz/1 cup olive oil
24 mini pitta breads, cut into
  2½ x 5cm/1 x 2in strips

1 Preheat the oven to 130°C/250°F/Gas 1. Put the nuts, cumin, coriander and salt
   in a food processor and process for 1–2 minutes until the mixture resembles large,
   coarse breadcrumbs. Transfer to a serving bowl. Put the oil in another serving bowl.
2 Put the pitta bread strips on a baking sheet and heat in the oven for 5 minutes
   until warmed through. Transfer to a serving plate and serve with the dukka and oil,
   dipping the bread first in the oil and then the dukka.

050 Wonton Crisps

SERVES: 10 **PREPARATION TIME:** 15 minutes, plus making the dip **COOKING TIME:** 15 minutes

200g/7oz wonton wrappers
1l/35fl oz/4 cups sunflower oil

1 recipe quantity Sweet Chilli Dip
  (see page 12), to serve

1 Cut each wonton wrapper into four squares, using a pair of kitchen scissors. Using
   your thumb and forefinger, pinch the centre of each square to form a flower shape.
2 Heat the oil in a deep saucepan to 180°C/350°F. Carefully drop a few of the wonton
   flowers into the oil and fry for 1 minute until golden. Work in batches to avoid
   overcrowding the pan. Remove the wontons from the oil, using a slotted spoon,
   and drain on kitchen paper. Repeat with the remaining wontons, bringing the oil
   back to temperature before each batch. Serve with the dip.

051 Tortilla Crisps & Tomato Salsa

SERVES: 10–12 **PREPARATION TIME:** 10 minutes **COOKING TIME:** 20 minutes

8 soft corn tortillas, about 18.5cm/
  7¹/₂in across
1l/35fl oz/4 cups sunflower oil
200g/7oz cherry tomatoes, quartered
4 tbsp olive oil

1 green chilli, deseeded and
  finely chopped
1 small garlic clove, finely chopped
1 small handful coriander leaves
salt and freshly ground black pepper

1 Cut each tortilla into 8 triangles. Cover a baking sheet with kitchen paper.
Heat the sunflower oil in a deep saucepan or wok to 180°C/350°F. Carefully drop
a few of the tortillas into the oil, working in batches to avoid overcrowding the pan,
and fry for 1 to 2 minutes until beginning to brown. Remove, using a slotted spoon,
and drain on the kitchen paper. Do not overlap them or they will not crisp.
2 To make the salsa, put all the remaining ingredients in a bowl and mix well. Serve
with the tortilla crisps.

PREPARING AHEAD: The salsa can be made up to 1 day in advance and stored in an airtight
container in the fridge.

052 Hummus with Pitta Bread

SERVES: 10 **PREPARATION TIME:** 8 minutes **COOKING TIME:** 5 minutes

400g/14¹/₂oz tinned chickpeas,
  drained and rinsed
2 tbsp tahini
1 garlic clove, coarsely chopped
juice of 1 lemon
80ml/2¹/₂fl oz/¹/₃ cup olive oil

20 mini pitta breads
1 tsp paprika
1 small handful parsley, chopped,
  to serve
salt and freshly ground black pepper

1 Preheat the oven to 130°C/250°F/Gas 1. Put the chickpeas, tahini, garlic, lemon
juice, 4 tbsp of the oil and 4 tbsp water in a food processor. Process for 2–3 minutes
until smooth. Season with salt and pepper and transfer to a serving bowl.
2 Put the pitta breads on a baking sheet and heat in the oven for 5 minutes until
warmed through. Sprinkle the paprika and parsley over the hummus, drizzle over
the remaining oil and serve with the pitta breads.

PREPARING AHEAD: The hummus can be made up to 1 day in advance and stored in an airtight
container in the fridge.

053 Babaganoush with Pitta Bread

SERVES: 10 **PREPARATION TIME:** 5 minutes **COOKING TIME:** 25 minutes

3 aubergines
1 garlic clove, coarsely chopped
4 tbsp olive oil

10 mini pitta breads
salt and freshly ground black pepper

1 Preheat the oven to 200°C/400°F/Gas 6. Put the whole aubergines on a baking
sheet and bake for 25 minutes until soft and the skin is wrinkled, then set aside
until cool enough to handle. Lower the oven temperature to 130°C/250°F/Gas 1.
2 Peel the skin off the aubergines and then slice them in half. Scoop out as many
seeds as you can and discard. Put the pulp, garlic and oil in a food processor and
process for 1 minute until smooth, then season with salt and pepper.
3 Put the pitta breads on a baking sheet and heat in the oven for 5 minutes until
warmed through. Serve the babaganoush with the pitta breads.

PREPARING AHEAD: The babaganoush can be made up to 1 day in advance and stored
in an airtight container in the fridge. Warm it slightly in a saucepan before serving.

54 Watermelon, Orange, Feta & Lime Skewers

MAKES: 12   **PREPARATION TIME:** 25 minutes   **EQUIPMENT:** 12 skewers

1kg/2lb 2oz watermelon, rind
    removed and fruit cut into 12 cubes
2 oranges, peeled and cut into
    12 cubes

200g/7oz feta cheese, cut into
    12 cubes
12 mint leaves
juice and finely grated zest of 1/2 lime
freshly ground black pepper

1 Put 1 piece of the watermelon and orange on each skewer, then add 1 mint leaf
   and 1 piece of the feta.
2 Squeeze the lime juice over the skewers and sprinkle with the zest. Season with
   pepper and serve.

Deep-Fried Camembert with Sweet Chilli Dip

MAKES: 12 **PREPARATION TIME:** 10 minutes, plus making the dip **COOKING TIME:** 5 minutes

1 x 250g/9oz Camembert circle,
   cut into 12 equal triangles
2 eggs, beaten
100g/3½oz/1 cup breadcrumbs

1l/35fl oz/4 cups sunflower oil
1 recipe quantity Sweet Chilli Dip
   (see page 12), to serve

1 Dip 1 Camembert triangle in the egg, then roll it in the breadcrumbs to coat.
   Transfer to a plate, then repeat with the remaining cheese.
2 Heat the oil in a deep saucepan or wok to 180°C/350°F, or until a few breadcrumbs
   sizzle and float when dropped in. Carefully drop 4 cheese triangles into the oil
   and fry for 1 minute until golden, then remove, using a slotted spoon, and drain
   on kitchen paper. Repeat with the remaining cheese, working in batches to avoid
   overcrowding. Serve with the sweet chilli dip.

056 Cheese & Mustard Bites

MAKES: 24   PREPARATION TIME: 15 minutes   COOKING TIME: 8–10 minutes

55g/2oz mature Cheddar cheese, grated
55g/2oz Red Leicester, Double
  Gloucester or other hard cheese,
  grated

5 tbsp plain flour
50g/1³/₄oz butter
1 egg
2 tbsp Dijon mustard

1 Preheat the oven to 200°C/400°F/Gas 6. Put all the ingredients in a bowl and mix well until the mixture forms a sticky dough.
2 Shape the dough into 24 balls of equal size and flatten slightly into 2cm/1in patties. Put them on a baking sheet and bake for 8–10 minutes until golden brown. Leave to cool for 10 minutes, then serve.

057 Spiced Nuts

SERVES: 10   PREPARATION TIME: 5 minutes   COOKING TIME: 2 minutes

1¹/₂ tsp olive oil
250g/9oz/1²/₃ cups mixed nuts, such
  as pecans, walnuts, Brazil, almonds,
  cashews and hazelnuts

¹/₂ tsp celery salt
¹/₂ tsp cayenne pepper
1 tsp ground coriander
salt

1 Heat the oil in a frying pan over a medium heat. Add the nuts, celery salt, cayenne pepper and coriander and fry for 2 minutes until the nuts are completely coated and warmed through.
2 Season with salt and set aside to cool to room temperature, then serve.

058 Broccoli & Parmesan Fried Bread

SERVES: 12   PREPARATION TIME: 10 minutes   COOKING TIME: 15 minutes

200g/7oz broccoli florets
1 garlic clove, unpeeled
30g/1oz Parmesan cheese, grated
juice of ¹/₂ lemon

4 tbsp olive oil
3 slices of bread, quartered
salt

1 Bring a saucepan of water to the boil. Add the broccoli and garlic and boil for 2 minutes until the broccoli just starts to turn tender. Drain, then peel the garlic clove. Leave to cool for 10 minutes. Set aside 12 small broccoli florets. Pat the remaining broccoli dry between two clean tea towels, removing as much excess water as possible.
2 Put the broccoli, garlic, Parmesan, lemon juice and 2 tbsp of the oil in a food processor and process for 2 minutes until smooth.
3 Heat the remaining oil in a frying pan over a medium-high heat. Add the bread and fry for 1–2 minutes on each side until golden. Drain on kitchen paper.
4 Spoon the broccoli purée onto the fried bread. Top each bread with 1 broccoli floret, season with salt and serve.

059 Mushrooms à la Greque

SERVES: 10   PREPARATION TIME: 10 minutes   COOKING TIME: 10 minutes

350g/12oz button mushrooms
4 tbsp olive oil
2 tsp coriander seeds
leaves from 4 thyme sprigs

zest of 1 lemon, cut into 4 long strips,
   using a vegetable peeler
salt and freshly ground black pepper
bread, to serve

1   Put the mushrooms, oil, coriander, thyme, lemon zest and 250ml/9fl oz/1 cup water
in a saucepan and bring to the boil. Boil for 10 minutes, stirring occasionally, until
the mushrooms are soft and light brown. Leave to cool.
2   Season with salt and pepper, then serve with bread and cocktail sticks.

PREPARING AHEAD: This can be made up to 1 day in advance and stored in an airtight container
in the fridge. Serve at room temperature.

060 Aubergine Tempura

MAKES: 24   PREPARATION TIME: 10 minutes, plus 1 hour resting   COOKING TIME: 8 minutes

1 aubergine, cut into
   24 x 1cm/$\frac{1}{2}$in-thick pieces
1 tbsp salt
100g/3$\frac{1}{2}$oz/heaped $\frac{3}{4}$ cup plain flour
1 egg, beaten

1l/35fl oz/4 cups sunflower oil
salt
125ml/4fl oz/$\frac{1}{2}$ cup soy sauce,
   to serve

1   Put the aubergine in a colander and sprinkle with the salt. Cover with a saucer
and leave to stand for 1 hour, then squeeze to extract as much water as possible.
2   Put the flour, egg and 125ml/4fl oz/$\frac{1}{2}$ cup ice-cold water in a bowl and stir until
the mixture just comes together.
3   Heat the oil in a deep saucepan or wok to 180°C/350°F. Dip the aubergine into
the batter and carefully drop them, a few at a time, into the oil, working in batches
to avoid overcrowding the pan. Fry for 1–2 minutes until brown and crispy, then
remove, using a slotted spoon, and drain on kitchen paper. Repeat with the
remaining aubergine, making sure to bring the oil back to temperature before
each batch. Season with salt and serve immediately with soy sauce.

061 Cauliflower & Paneer Pakoras

MAKES: 48 pakoras   PREPARATION TIME: 5 minutes   COOKING TIME: 30 minutes

250g/9oz/2$\frac{1}{4}$ cups gram flour
2 tsp garam masala
$\frac{1}{2}$ tsp baking powder
$\frac{1}{4}$ tsp salt, plus extra for seasoning
1l/35fl oz/4 cups sunflower oil

$\frac{1}{2}$ cauliflower, cut into 24 bite-sized
   florets
200g/7oz paneer cheese, cut into
   24 x 2cm/$\frac{3}{4}$in cubes
1 lemon, halved

1   Put the flour, garam masala, baking powder and salt in a bowl and mix well.
Add 325ml/11fl oz/scant 1$\frac{1}{3}$ cups cold water and stir until smooth.
2   Heat the oil in a deep saucepan or wok to 180°C/350°F. Dip the cauliflower and
paneer pieces into the batter to coat completely. Carefully drop them into the oil,
working in batches to avoid overcrowding the pan, and fry for 2–3 minutes until
golden and crispy. Remove, using a slotted spoon, and drain on kitchen paper.
Repeat with the remaining cauliflower and paneer, making sure to bring the oil
back to temperature before each batch.
3   Squeeze the lemon halves over the pakoras, sprinkle with salt and serve.

062 Crostini with Fennel & Mayonnaise

MAKES: 24 **PREPARATION TIME:** 30 minutes, plus 1 hour marinating and making the mayonnaise and crostini

1 small fennel bulb, halved, cored
  and finely sliced
1 tbsp olive oil
juice of 1/2 lemon
1/2 recipe quantity Mayonnaise
  (see page 12)

12 anchovy fillets in oil, drained
  and halved (optional)
1/2 recipe quantity Crostini
  (see page 15)
salt and freshly ground black pepper

1 Put the fennel, oil and lemon juice in a bowl and mix well, then season with salt and pepper. Cover and leave to marinate for up to 1 hour.
2 Spread 1 heaped tsp of the mayonnaise onto each of the crostini. Top with 1 tbsp of the fennel and 1 anchovy half, if using. Drizzle with the marinating juices left in the bowl and serve.

063 Fennel Coleslaw

SERVES: 12 **PREPARATION TIME:** 20 minutes

2 small fennel bulbs, halved, cored
  and finely sliced
3 celery sticks, finely sliced
4 carrots, peeled and grated
2 spring onions, cut into
  5mm/1/4in pieces

juice of 1 lemon
125ml/4fl oz/1/2 cup olive oil
1 tsp salt
freshly ground black pepper
12 slices of French bread, or
  6 wholemeal rolls, halved, to serve

1 Put the fennel, celery, carrots and spring onion in a bowl and mix well. Mix in the lemon juice, oil and salt.
2 Season with pepper and serve with the bread.

064 Vegetable Spring Rolls

MAKES: 20 **PREPARATION TIME:** 35 minutes, plus making the dip **COOKING TIME:** 10 minutes

1 large carrot, peeled and grated
1/4 red cabbage, finely chopped
55g/2oz bean sprouts, broken up
4cm/11/2in piece root ginger, peeled
  and finely grated
1 small handful coriander leaves,
  coarsely chopped

1 small red chilli, finely chopped
1 spring onion, finely chopped
20 spring roll wrappers, 11cm/41/4in
  square
1l/35fl oz/4 cups sunflower oil
1 recipe quantity Sweet Chilli Dip
  (see page 12), to serve

1 Put all the ingredients, except the wrappers and oil, in a bowl and mix well.
2 Position a spring roll wrapper as a diamond on a work surface. Put 1 tbsp of the vegetable mixture across the bottom half and fold the bottom corner over the filling. Fold in the sides to encase the filling and roll up to form a parcel. Dab a little water on the end and press to seal. Repeat with the remaining wrappers.
3 Heat the oil in a deep saucepan or wok to 180°C/350°F, or until a small piece of spring roll wrapper sizzles when dropped in. Fry the spring rolls for 2 minutes until golden, working in batches to avoid overcrowding the pan. Remove from the pan, using a slotted spoon, and drain on kitchen paper. Bring the oil back to temperature before each batch. Serve warm with the dip.

PREPARING AHEAD: These can be made to the end of step 2 up to 1 day in advance and stored in an airtight container in the fridge until ready to cook.

065 Onion Bhajis

SERVES: 10   **PREPARATION TIME:** 5 minutes   **COOKING TIME:** 12 minutes

100g/3½oz/scant 1 cup gram flour
140g/5oz/heaped ¾ cup rice flour
1l/35fl oz/4 cups sunflower oil

2 onions, finely sliced
1 tsp cayenne pepper

1   Put the gram and rice flours in a bowl and gradually whisk in 375ml/13fl oz/
    1½ cups water, 125ml/4fl oz/½ cup at a time, until smooth.
2   Heat the oil in a deep saucepan or wok to 180°C/350°F. Dip the onion slices into
    the batter and then carefully drop them in the oil, working in batches to avoid
    overcrowding the pan, and fry for 2–3 minutes until golden brown. Remove, using
    a slotted spoon, and drain on kitchen paper. Repeat with the remaining onion,
    making sure to bring the oil back to temperature before each batch.
3   Sprinkle with the cayenne pepper and serve immediately.

066 Spinach & Paneer Parathas

MAKES: 24   **PREPARATION TIME:** 30 minutes   **COOKING TIME:** 1 hour

2 tbsp olive oil, plus extra for
    brushing
250g/9oz spinach, washed, dried
    and stems discarded
1 tbsp garam masala
1 garlic clove, finely chopped

30g/1oz paneer cheese,
    finely chopped
150g/5½oz/scant 1¼ cups plain flour,
    plus extra for rolling the dough
1 tsp sunflower oil

1   Put 1 tbsp of the olive oil in a large saucepan, add the spinach and cook, covered,
    over a medium heat for 3–4 minutes until wilted. Transfer the spinach to a colander
    and press down with a saucer to squeeze out as much excess water as possible,
    then chop finely.
2   Heat the remaining olive oil in a frying pan over a medium heat. Add the garam
    masala and garlic and cook for 1 minute until aromatic, then stir in the spinach
    and paneer. Remove from the heat and leave to cool.
3   Put the flour, sunflower oil and 80ml/2½fl oz/⅓ cup water in a bowl and mix
    together, using your hands. Add an additional 1–2 tbsp of water if the mixture is
    too dry. Knead the dough for 2 minutes until smooth, then divide it into 12 pieces
    of equal size. Roll each piece into a 3cm/1¼in ball.
4   Press an indentation in the centre of each ball, using your thumb. Put 1 tbsp of the
    spinach mixture into the indentation, then bring the edges of the dough up and
    over the filling and press it together to seal. Flatten the balls slightly in your palms,
    then, on a well floured surface, roll them into 10cm/4in circles. Transfer the rolled-
    out parathas to a plate until ready to cook.
5   Heat a heavy frying pan over a high heat for 3–4 minutes until hot. Put 1 paratha
    in the pan and cook for 1–2 minutes until the surface begins to blister. Lightly
    brush the top with olive oil and season with salt, then turn it over and cook for
    a further 1–2 minutes until brown and blistered. Transfer to a plate and repeat
    with the remaining parathas. Cut each paratha in half and serve immediately.

067 Tabouleh in Little Gem Lettuce Boats

MAKES: 30 **PREPARATION TIME:** 25 minutes, plus at least 8 hours soaking

125g/4½oz/⅔ cup bulgar wheat
135g/4½oz cucumber, halved
  lengthways, deseeded and
  finely diced
1 handful mint leaves, finely chopped
1 handful parsley leaves,
  finely chopped

2 tbsp olive oil
60g/2¼oz/scant ½ cup black pitted
  olives, coarsely chopped
juice and finely grated zest of 1 lemon
30 Little Gem lettuce leaves, about
  2 heads
salt and freshly ground black pepper

1 Put the bulgar wheat in a bowl, add 500ml/17fl oz/2 cups cold water and leave
  to soak for 8 hours or overnight.
2 Drain the bulgar wheat through a clean tea towel, squeezing out as much of the
  water as possible. Put the bulgar wheat in a clean bowl. Mix in the cucumber, then
  add the mint, parsley, oil, olives, lemon juice and zest and mix well. Season with
  salt and pepper.
3 Put 1 tbsp of tabouleh on the end of each lettuce leaf and serve.

PREPARING AHEAD: The tabouleh can be made up to 4 hours in advance, covered and stored
in the fridge. Leave it at room temperature for 20 minutes before assembling and serving.

068 Goat's Cheese & Walnut Crostini

MAKES: 24 PREPARATION TIME: 10 minutes, plus making the crostini

90g/3 oz/³/₄ cup walnuts, finely
  chopped
2 tsp walnut oil
150g/5¹/₂oz soft goat's cheese

¹/₂ recipe quantity Crostini
  (see page 15)
24 rocket leaves
salt

1 Put the walnuts and oil in a small bowl and mix well.
2 Spread 1 tsp of the cheese onto each of the crostini, add 1 rocket leaf and top
   with ¹/₂ tsp of the walnut mixture. Season with salt and serve.

069 Padrón Peppers

SERVES: 10 PREPARATION TIME: 5 minutes COOKING TIME: 5 minutes

1 tbsp olive oil
200g/7oz Padrón peppers
salt

1 Heat the olive oil in a frying pan over a medium-high heat. Add the peppers and
   cook for 3 minutes until brown and blistered on all sides.
2 Season with salt, transfer to a serving bowl and serve.

070 Sage & Anchovy Fritters

MAKES: 24 PREPARATION TIME: 30 minutes COOKING TIME: 20 minutes

150g/5¹/₂oz/scant 1¹/₄ cups plain flour
1 egg
50g/1³/₄oz tinned anchovy fillets
  in oil, drained

48 large sage leaves
1l/35fl oz/4 cups sunflower oil

1 Sift the flour into a bowl. Add the egg and 125ml/4fl oz/¹/₂ cup cold water and stir
   until smooth, then set aside.
2 Put the anchovies in a food processor and pulse until the mixture forms a paste.
   Alternatively, grind them to a paste, using a pestle and mortar. Spread
   24 of the sage leaves with ¹/₂ tsp of the anchovy paste, then cover with the
   remaining 24 leaves.
3 Heat the oil in a deep saucepan or wok to 180°C/350°F. Dip the sage and anchovy
   sandwiches into the batter and carefully drop them into the oil, working in batches
   to avoid overcrowding the pan. Fry for 3 minutes until brown. Remove, using
   a slotted spoon, and drain on kitchen paper, then serve.

071 ## Smoked Salmon Mousse

MAKES: 24   PREPARATION TIME: 10 minutes

125g/4½oz smoked salmon
100g/3½oz/½ cup crème fraîche
4 tbsp soured cream

juice of ½ lemon
freshly ground black pepper
6 slices of toast, quartered, to serve

1   Put 100g/3½oz of the salmon in a food processor. Add the crème fraîche, soured cream and lemon juice and process for 1–2 minutes until smooth.
2   Spread 2 tsp of mousse onto each piece of toast. Top with a sliver of the remaining smoked salmon, sprinkle with pepper and serve.

072 Cherry Tomatoes Stuffed with Anchoïade

MAKES: 20   **PREPARATION TIME:** 20 minutes

20 cherry tomatoes
1 handful parsley leaves,
    stems removed
55g/2oz/scant ½ cup black
    pitted olives

50g/1¾oz tinned anchovy fillets
    in oil, drained
2 tbsp capers
1 garlic clove
1 tbsp olive oil

1   Slice the top off each cherry tomato and carefully scoop out and discard the seeds,
    using a small spoon. Put the tomatoes on a serving plate and cut away a small
    piece from the bottom of any that wobble.
2   To make the anchoïade, put the parsley, olives, anchovies, capers, garlic and oil in a
    food processor and process for 2 minutes until the mixture forms a coarse paste.
    Divide the mixture into the tomatoes and serve.

PREPARING AHEAD: The anchoïade in step 2 can be made up to 1 day in advance and stored
in an airtight container in the fridge.

073 Crab & Guacamole on Rye Bread

MAKES: 12　**PREPARATION TIME:** 15 minutes　**EQUIPMENT:** 4cm/1½in fluted round pastry cutter

1 avocado, halved and stoned
85g/3oz cherry tomatoes, quartered
1 tbsp olive oil
juice of ½ lemon
6 slices of rye bread

6 thin slices of Edam cheese,
　about 6cm/2½in square
150g/5¼oz crab meat, about
　1 dressed crab
freshly ground black pepper

1　Scoop out the avocado flesh and put it in a bowl. Add the tomatoes, oil and lemon juice and mix well.
2　Cut out 2 circles from each slice of bread, using the pastry cutter. Do the same with the Edam.
3　Cover each bread circle with 1 cheese circle. Add 1 rounded tsp of the guacamole and top this with ½ tsp of the crab meat. Sprinkle with pepper and serve.

074 Avocado & Crab Lettuce Leaves

MAKES: 24　**PREPARATION TIME:** 5 minutes, plus making the mayonnaise
COOKING TIME: 10 minutes

1 recipe quantity Mayonnaise
　(see page 12)
1 tsp paprika
juice of ½ lemon
100g/3½oz crab meat

24 Little Gem lettuce leaves
1 avocado, peeled, halved, stoned
　and thinly sliced
salt and freshly ground black pepper

1　Put the mayonnaise, paprika and lemon juice in a bowl and mix well. Season with salt and pepper, then stir in the crab meat.
2　Put 1 tbsp of the crab mixture onto each lettuce leaf. Top with 2 slices of the avocado and serve immediately.

075 Prawn, Chive & Egg Toasts

MAKES: 12　**PREPARATION TIME:** 10 minutes　**COOKING TIME:** 5 minutes

3 slices of bread
40g/1½oz butter
2 eggs, beaten

75g/2⅔oz small peeled prawns
5 chives, chopped
salt and freshly ground black pepper

1　Toast the bread and cut each slice into four pieces.
2　Heat 30g/1oz of the butter in a saucepan over a medium-low heat until melted. Add the eggs and cook, stirring continuously, for 1–1½ minutes until just beginning to set. Remove from the heat and season with salt and pepper.
3　Put the prawns and the remaining butter in a saucepan and heat over a medium heat for 2 minutes until warmed through. Put ½ tsp of the scrambled eggs onto each piece of toast, top with a few of the prawns and sprinkle with the chives. Serve immediately.

Prawn & Herb Mayonnaise Eggs

MAKES: 12   **PREPARATION TIME:** 10 minutes, plus making the mayonnaise
COOKING TIME: 7 minutes

6 eggs, at room temperature
1/2 tsp white wine vinegar
1/2 recipe quantity Mayonnaise
    (see page 12)
5 chives, chopped

80g/3oz peeled, cooked small prawns
1 tsp cayenne pepper
salt and freshly ground black pepper

1   Bring a saucepan of water to the boil. Add the eggs and vinegar and boil for
    6 minutes, then drain and leave to stand until cool enough to handle, then peel.
2   Slice the eggs in half lengthways, remove the yolks and put them in a bowl. Set the
    whites aside. Add the mayonnaise to the yolks and mash together. Stir in the chives
    and season with salt and pepper.
3   Spoon the mayonnaise mixture into the egg whites and top with 3 or 4 of the
    prawns. Sprinkle with the cayenne pepper and serve.

PREPARING AHEAD: The eggs can be boiled and peeled up to 1 day in advance and stored,
covered, in cold water in the fridge. Do not cut the eggs until ready to use or they will discolour.

077   Sesame Prawn Toasts

MAKES: 24   **PREPARATION TIME:** 15 minutes   **COOKING TIME:** 12 minutes

100g/3 1/2 oz peeled, cooked prawns
3cm/1 1/4 in piece root ginger, peeled
    and finely chopped

3 slices of white bread, crusts
    removed
55g/2oz/heaped 1/3 cup sesame seeds
375ml/13fl oz/1 1/2 cups sunflower oil

1   Put the prawns and ginger in a food processor and process for 1–2 minutes until
    the mixture forms a paste.
2   Cut each slice of bread into 8 rectangles and generously spread both sides with
    the prawn paste. Put the sesame seeds on a plate and press the bread into the
    seeds to coat both sides.
3   Heat the oil in a deep saucepan or wok over a medium-high heat until a few
    crumbs or sesame seeds sizzle when dropped in. Working in batches, fry the toasts
    for 1–2 minutes on each side until golden. Remove from the oil and drain on
    kitchen paper. Serve immediately.

078   Smoked Salmon & Dill Pinwheels

MAKES: 20   **PREPARATION TIME:** 15 minutes

100g/3 1/2 oz/1/2 cup cream cheese
a few dill fronds, finely chopped
juice of 1/2 lemon
4 thin slices of brown bread,
    crusts removed

120g/4 1/4 oz smoked salmon,
    thinly sliced
freshly ground black pepper

1   Put the cream cheese, dill and lemon juice in a bowl and mix well.
2   Flatten each slice of bread, using a rolling pin. Spread with equal portions of the
    cream cheese, then top with the smoked salmon and season with pepper.
3   Put 1 slice of the bread on a clean work surface with the long side nearest to you.
    Roll the bread up into a tight log, then slice it into 5 equal-sized pieces. Repeat with
    the remaining slices of bread and serve immediately.

PREPARING AHEAD: These can be made up to 12 hours in advance, wrapped, uncut, in cling film
and stored in the fridge. Serve at room temperature.

079 Vietnamese Crab Rolls

MAKES: 24   PREPARATION TIME: 30 minutes

12 Vietnamese rice paper wrappers
140g/5oz crab meat
juice of $\frac{1}{2}$ lemon
olive oil, for greasing
70g/2$\frac{1}{2}$oz alfalfa sprouts

125g/4$\frac{1}{2}$oz cucumber, peeled
 and cut into thin strips
1 handful coriander leaves
1 handful mint leaves
4 tbsp soy sauce, to serve

1 Soak each spring roll wrapper in warm water for 20 seconds, or until soft. Gently shake off the excess water, put the wrappers on a plate and cover with a clean damp tea towel or cling film. Put the crab meat and lemon juice in a bowl and mix.
2 Grease a large plate with oil and put 1 of the wrappers on it. Put 2 tsp crab meat, a few alfalfa sprouts, a few cucumber strips, 2 coriander leaves and 2 mint leaves in the centre of the wrapper. Fold the bottom of the wrapper over the filling, then fold in the sides and roll upwards to form a roll. Transfer the roll to a clean plate and cover with cling film. Repeat with the remaining wrappers and filling.
3 Cut each crab roll in half at a slight angle and serve with the soy sauce.

080 Seafood Tartlets

MAKES: 24 **PREPARATION TIME:** 45 minutes, plus making the tartlet cases
COOKING TIME: 12 minutes

675g/1lb 8oz mussels
125ml/4fl oz/½ cup double cream
1 egg, beaten

½ recipe quantity savoury Tartlet
  Cases, blind-baked (see page 14)
60g/2¼oz peeled, cooked prawns
salt and freshly ground black pepper

1   Discard any mussels with broken shells or that do not close when tapped. Pull
    out the beards and put the mussels in a basin of cold water. Soak for 10 minutes,
    then change the water. Soak for a further 10 minutes, then drain and rinse.
2   Put 250ml/9fl oz/1 cup water in a large saucepan and bring to the boil. Add the
    mussels and cook for 2 minutes, covered, or until all the mussels are open. Discard
    any that have not opened.
3   Transfer the mussels to a colander and leave to cool for 10 minutes, then remove
    them from their shells and chop coarsely. Preheat the oven to 180°C/350°F/Gas 6.
4   Put the cream and egg in a bowl and mix well, then season lightly with salt and
    pepper. With the tartlet cases still in their muffin tins, fill each one with 2 prawns
    and 1 tsp of the chopped mussels. Add 1 tbsp of the egg and cream mixture and
    bake for 10 minutes until just set and beginning to brown. Serve immediately.

081 Prawn Beignets

MAKES: 24 **PREPARATION TIME:** 5 minutes **COOKING TIME:** 5 minutes

100g/3½oz/scant 1 cup gram flour
1 tsp baking powder
2 tsp vegetable oil

1l/35fl oz/4 cups sunflower oil
24 large peeled, cooked king prawns

1   Put the flour, baking powder, vegetable oil and 100ml/3½fl oz/scant ½ cup water
    in a bowl and mix until smooth.
2   Heat the sunflower oil in a deep saucepan or wok to 180°C/350°F. Dip the prawns
    in the batter and, working in batches to avoid overcrowding the pan, fry for
    1 minute until golden and crispy. Remove, using a slotted spoon, and drain
    on kitchen paper, then serve.

082 Artichoke Hearts Stuffed with Tuna & Capers

MAKES: 12 **PREPARATION TIME:** 20 minutes

1 very fresh egg yolk
4 tbsp olive oil
90g/3oz tinned yellow fin tuna,
  crumbled

1 tbsp capers, plus 12 to serve
400g/14oz bottled artichoke hearts,
  about 6 hearts, halved horizontally
freshly ground black pepper

1   Put the egg yolk in a bowl and whisk in the oil 1 tbsp at a time until the mixture
    starts to thicken into a mayonnaise, then stir in the tuna and capers.
2   Spoon the tuna mayonnaise onto the artichoke halves, top each one with 1 caper
    and season with pepper. Serve immediately or keep in the fridge, covered, for
    up to 2 hours before serving.

PREPARING AHEAD: The tuna mayonnaise in step 1 can be made up to 1 day in advance and
stored in an airtight container in the fridge.

083 Salmon Sushi Rolls

MAKES: 24   **PREPARATION TIME:** 20 minutes, plus 20 minutes resting
COOKING TIME: 20 minutes   **EQUIPMENT:** sushi mat

210g/7½oz/1 cup sushi rice
1 tsp caster sugar
1 tbsp rice vinegar
2 tsp mirin
2 tsp sake
¼ tsp salt

360g/12¾oz smoked salmon
125ml/4fl oz/½ cup rice wine
    vinegar mixed with 125ml/4fl oz/
    ½ cup water
100g/3½oz/scant ½ cup
    salmon caviar

1   Cook the sushi rice according to the packet instructions. Set aside to rest
    for 20 minutes.
2   Put the sugar, rice vinegar, mirin, sake and salt in a bowl and mix well. Stir this
    mixture into the rice.
3   Put the sushi mat in a landscape position in front of you and cover with a piece
    of cling film. Put one quarter of the salmon evenly across the mat, leaving
    a 2.5cm/1in gap along the top. Dip your hands into the vinegar and water
    mixture to make handling the rice easier, then spread some of the sushi rice
    over the salmon in a thin layer.
4   Starting at the bottom edge and working upwards, roll the mat tightly around
    the salmon and rice, pulling the cling film away as you roll to prevent it being
    rolled into the sushi roll. Slowly peel back the mat and wrap the sushi roll in the
    cling film, then transfer to the fridge while you make 3 more sushi rolls.
5   When ready to serve, slice each sushi roll into 6 pieces of equal size, using a very
    sharp knife. Top each piece with scant ½ tsp of the caviar and serve.

PREPARING AHEAD: The sushi rolls can be made up to 4 hours in advance, wrapped, uncut,
in cling film and stored in the fridge. Slice and serve at room temperature.

084 Smoked Mackerel, Manchego & Spinach

MAKES: 12   **PREPARATION TIME:** 15 minutes   **COOKING TIME:** 5 minutes

1 tbsp olive oil
250g/9oz spinach, washed, dried
    and stems discarded
12 slices of baguette, 5mm/¼in-thick

70g/2½oz smoked mackerel, broken
    into 12 or 24 flakes
50g/1¾oz Manchego cheese, grated
freshly ground black pepper

1   Heat the oil in a large saucepan over a medium heat. Add the spinach and
    cook, covered, for 3–4 minutes until wilted. Transfer the spinach to a colander
    and press down with a saucer to squeeze out as much excess water as possible,
    then chop coarsely.
2   Put 1 tbsp of the spinach on each slice of bread. Top with 1–2 mackerel flakes
    and sprinkle with the Manchego. Season with pepper and serve.

085 Chicken Gyoza

MAKES: 24 **PREPARATION TIME:** 30 minutes **COOKING TIME:** 15 minutes

2 boneless, skinless chicken breasts,
  about 150g/5½oz each, chopped
3 spring onions, coarsely chopped
3 chillies, chopped, plus extra, sliced,
  for the soy sauce
1 small bunch chives, chopped

½ tsp salt
24 gyoza wrappers
225g/8oz tinned bamboo shoots,
  drained and chopped
1 tbsp olive oil
125ml/4fl oz/½ cup soy sauce

1 Put the chicken, spring onions, chillies, chives and salt in a food processor and
   process for 2–3 minutes until the mixture forms a fine mince.
2 Hold a gyoza wrapper in the palm of one hand and dab a little water around the
   edge, using your finger. Spoon 1 tsp of the mince into the centre, add a few of the
   bamboo shoots and fold the wrapper into a semi-circle, pressing the edges
   together to enclose the filling. Pinch 3 pleats along the sealed edge and set aside.
   Repeat with the remaining wrappers and filling.
3 Heat the oil in a frying pan over a medium heat. Working in batches, fry the gyoza
   for 2 minutes on each side until brown, then remove from the pan.
4 Put the soy sauce and sliced chillies in a dipping bowl.
5 Bring a large pan of water to the boil. Add the gyoza, working in batches to avoid
   overcrowding the pan, and cook for 1 minute until they float to the surface.
   Remove, using a slotted spoon. Bring the water back to the boil before each new
   batch. Serve immediately with the soy sauce.

PREPARING AHEAD: These can be made to the end of step 2 up to
8 hours in advance, covered and stored in the fridge.

086 Seared Duck Breast & Blackcurrant Toasts

MAKES: 24   PREPARATION TIME: 25 minutes   COOKING TIME: 20 minutes
EQUIPMENT: 4cm/1½in plain round pastry cutter

8 slices of white bread
1 tsp oil, plus extra for brushing
165g/5¾oz duck breast

¼ tsp salt, plus extra to season
100g/3½oz/½ cup cream cheese
3 tbsp blackcurrant jam

1 Preheat the oven to 160°C/315°F/Gas 2–3. Cut 3 circles from each slice of bread, using the pastry cutter. Brush each circle with a little oil, put them on a baking sheet and bake for 8–10 minutes until just golden.
2 Put the duck breast in a colander and pour boiling water over the top. Pat dry with a clean tea towel, then rub all over with the salt.
3 Heat the oil in a frying pan over a high heat. Add the duck and cook, skin-side down, for 5 minutes until brown and crispy. Turn and cook for a further 2–3 minutes, or until brown on the outside but still pink in the centre. Remove and leave to rest for 5 minutes, then cut into 24 thin slices.
4 Put the cream cheese in a bowl and mix until smooth. Spread each toast circle with 1 tsp of the cream cheese, cover with 1 slice of the duck and top with scant ½ tsp of the jam. Serve immediately.

087 Smoked Chicken & Mango California Rolls

MAKES: 24   PREPARATION TIME: 30 minutes, plus 20 minutes resting
COOKING TIME: 20 minutes   EQUIPMENT: sushi mat

210g/7½oz/1 cup sushi rice
1 tsp caster sugar
1 tbsp rice vinegar
2 tsp mirin
2 tsp sake
¼ tsp salt
4 nori sheets
125ml/4fl oz/½ cup rice wine
   vinegar mixed with 125ml/4fl oz/
   ½ cup water

2 tbsp wasabi powder mixed with
   2 tbsp water
25g/1oz smoked chicken, sliced
½ mango, peeled, stoned and sliced
   into thin strips
30g/1oz pickled ginger, to serve
4 tbsp soy sauce, to serve

1 Cook the sushi rice according to the packet instructions. Set aside to rest for 20 minutes.
2 Put the sugar, rice vinegar, mirin, sake and salt in a bowl and mix well. Stir this mixture into the rice.
3 Put the sushi mat in a landscape position in front of you and cover with a sheet of nori, shiny-side down. Dip your hands into the vinegar and water mixture to make handling the rice easier, then spread some of the sushi rice across the nori in a thin layer, leaving a 2.5cm/1in gap along the top.
4 Spread a thin layer of wasabi paste across the top third of the rice. Add a line of the chicken and then a line of mango slices. Starting at the bottom edge and working upwards, roll the mat around the nori and filling to form a log. Slowly peel back the mat and seal the edge of the nori with a dab of water. Repeat with the remaining nori sheets.
5 When ready to serve, slice each sushi roll into 6 pieces of equal size, using a very sharp knife. Serve with the pickled ginger and soy sauce.

PREPARING AHEAD: The uncut sushi rolls can be wrapped in cling film and stored in the fridge for up to 4 hours before slicing, but should be served at room temperature.

088　Coarse Pork Pâté

SERVES: 10　PREPARATION TIME: 10 minutes　COOKING TIME: 30 minutes

450g/1lb pork mince
160ml/5¼fl oz/scant ⅔ cup
　double cream
1 tbsp brandy

90g/3¼oz cornichons
　(small gherkins), finely chopped
55g/2oz/scant ⅓ cup capers, drained
1 baguette, cut into 20 slices
salt and freshly ground black pepper

1　Preheat the oven to 170°C/325°F/Gas 3. Put the pork, cream, brandy, gherkins and capers in a large bowl. Season with salt and pepper and mix well, using a wooden spoon. Transfer the mixture to a shallow 20cm/8in square baking dish and press down firmly to level the surface, then cover with foil.

2　Bake for 30 minutes until the pâté is firm to the touch. Serve warm or allow to cool completely and serve at room temperature with the baguette.

089　Pork & Gorgonzola Gyoza

MAKES: 36　PREPARATION TIME: 30 minutes　COOKING TIME: 30 minutes

500g/1lb 2oz pork mince
3½ tsp hot horseradish, freshly grated
160ml/5¼fl oz/scant ⅔ cup
　double cream
1 handful coriander leaves,
　finely chopped

½ tsp salt
55g/2oz Gorgonzola cheese
36 gyoza wrappers
1 tbsp olive oil
125ml/4fl oz/½ cup soy sauce,
　to serve

1　Put the pork, horseradish, cream, coriander, salt and Gorgonzola in a bowl and mix well.

2　Hold a gyoza wrapper in the palm of one hand and dab a little water around the edge, using your finger. Spoon 1 tsp of the mince into the centre and fold the wrapper into a semi-circle, pressing the edges together to enclose the filling. Pinch 3 pleats along the sealed edge and set aside. Repeat with the remaining wrappers and filling.

3　Heat the oil in a frying pan over a medium heat. Working in batches, fry the gyoza for 2 minutes on each side until brown, then remove from the pan.

4　Bring a large pan of water to the boil. Add the gyoza, working in batches to avoid overcrowding the pan, and cook for 1 minute until they float to the surface. Remove, using a slotted spoon, and serve immediately with the soy sauce.

PREPARING AHEAD: These can be made to the end of step 2 up to 8 hours in advance, covered and stored in the fridge.

090　Mini Beef Rossinis

MAKES: 12　PREPARATION TIME: 20 minutes, plus making the pâté　COOKING: 5 minutes
EQUIPMENT: 4cm/1½in and 5cm/2in plain round pastry cutters

200g/7oz beef fillet, about
　2.5cm/1in thick
6 slices of white bread
1 tbsp olive oil, plus extra for drizzling

½ recipe quantity Chicken Liver Pâté
　(see page 132)
3 tsp Dijon mustard
6 chives, finely chopped

1　Preheat the oven to 170°C/325°F/Gas 3. Cut 12 circles from the beef, using the small pastry cutter, and set aside. Cut 2 circles from each slice of bread, using the large pastry cutter. Put the bread circles on a baking sheet, drizzle with a little oil and bake for 5 minutes until toasted.

2　Heat the oil in a frying pan over a high heat. Add the beef circles and cook for 30 seconds on each side until brown, working in batches if necessary.

3　Spread each toast circle with 1 tsp of the pâté and cover with 1 beef circle. Top with ¼ tsp of the mustard, sprinkle with the chives and serve.

091 **Lamb & Rosemary Bread Brochettes**

MAKES: 12   **PREPARATION TIME:** 15 minutes, plus 1–2 hours marinating
COOKING TIME: 15 minutes   **EQUIPMENT:** 12 x 10cm/4in skewers

250g/9oz lamb fillet, cut into
   4cm/1½in cubes
leaves from 2 rosemary sprigs,
   chopped, plus extra sprigs to serve

2 garlic cloves
2 tbsp olive oil
125g/4½oz ciabatta bread, cut
   into 12 x 4cm/1½in cubes

1   Put all the ingredients in a bowl, mix well and leave to marinate in the fridge,
covered, for 1–2 hours.
2   If using wooden skewers, soak them in water for at least 30 minutes before
cooking. Put 1 cube of bread and 1 cube of lamb on each skewer. Heat a griddle
pan over a medium-high heat until hot.
3   Cook the brochettes for 4–6 minutes, turning halfway through, until the bread
is brown and the lamb is seared on the outside and still slightly pink in the centre.
Serve immediately on a bed of rosemary sprigs.

092　Pissaladière

SERVES: 12　**PREPARATION TIME:** 15 minutes　**COOKING TIME:** 25 minutes

4 tbsp olive oil, plus extra for drizzling
6 onions, thinly sliced
500g/1lb 2oz ready-to-roll puff pastry

12 tinned anchovy fillets, in oil, drained
120g/4¹/₄oz/1 cup pitted black olives,
　halved

1　Preheat the oven to 180°C/350°F/Gas 4. Heat the oil in a frying pan over
　a medium-low heat. Add the onions and cook for 10 minutes, stirring occasionally,
　until soft and beginning to caramelize.
2　Cut the puff pastry in half and roll each half out into a 30 x 25cm/12 x 10in
　rectangle. Put the pastry rectangles on two baking sheets and divide the
　onions between them. Arrange the anchovy fillets in a diagonal pattern across
　the onions and sprinkle with the olives. Drizzle with a little oil and bake for
　15 minutes until the pastry is puffed and light golden brown around the edges.
3　Cut each pissaladière into 6 pieces and serve warm.

093 Pork Empanadas

MAKES: 12 **PREPARATION TIME:** 30 minutes **COOKING TIME:** 15 minutes
EQUIPMENT: 9cm/3½in plain round pastry cutter

250g/9oz pork mince
1 garlic clove, finely chopped
½ tsp salt
½ tsp cayenne pepper
a large pinch saffron
1 tsp white wine vinegar

seeds from 3 cardamom pods
plain flour, for rolling the pastry
500g/1lb 2oz ready-to-roll puff pastry
1 egg yolk, beaten with 1 tbsp milk
salt

1 Preheat the oven to 180°/350°/Gas 4. Put the pork, garlic, salt, cayenne pepper, saffron, vinegar and cardamom seeds in a bowl and mix well. On a lightly floured surface, roll half the pastry out into a 20 x 30cm/8 x 12in rectangle.
2 Cut out 6 circles, using the pastry cutter. Put 1 tbsp of the pork mixture slightly off centre on each circle, then fold over to form a semi-circle. Press the edges together to seal and transfer to a baking sheet. Repeat with the remaining pastry.
3 Brush the empanadas with the egg yolk mixture and sprinkle with salt. Bake for 12–15 minutes until puffed and golden. Serve immediately.

PREPARING AHEAD: These can be made to the end of step 2 up to 6 hours in advance, covered with cling film and stored in the fridge before being brushed with the egg yolk mixture and baked.

094 Pork Rillettes

SERVES: 10 **PREPARATION TIME:** 10 minutes, plus 3½ hours resting and cooling
COOKING TIME: 2 hours

500g/1lb 2oz pork belly, deboned
1 tsp salt
500ml/17fl oz/2 cups white wine

3 bay leaves
½ tsp coriander seeds
12 slices of toast, quartered, to serve

1 Remove the rind, but not the fat, from the pork belly and discard. Rub the pork all over with the salt. Leave to stand at room temperature for 1 hour.
2 Cut the meat into three big chunks and put them in a frying pan with a lid. Add the remaining ingredients. Cook, covered, over a very low heat for 2 hours until very tender, making sure that the liquid barely simmers.
3 Remove from the heat and leave to cool in the pan for 30 minutes.
4 Transfer the pork to a clean work surface and set the cooking liquid aside. Using two forks, scrape off the fat and pull the pork into thin strands, then transfer to a small serving dish with a lid. Add 125ml/4fl oz/½ cup of the cooking liquid, cover and leave the pork to set for 2 hours. Serve at room temperature with the toast.

095 Beef Stuffed with Olives

MAKES: 24 **PREPARATION TIME:** 20 minutes **COOKING TIME:** 20 minutes

300g/10½oz top rump beef
165g/5¾oz/1⅓ cups pitted
   black olives

50g/1¾oz tinned anchovies in oil,
   drained
1 tbsp grated horseradish

1 Preheat the oven to 180°C/350°F/Gas 4. Slice the beef as thinly as possible, then flatten each slice, using a rolling pin, and cut into 3cm/1¼in-wide strips.
2 Put the olives, anchovies and horseradish in a food processor and process for 1–2 minutes until the mixture forms a paste. Spread the beef strips with the olive paste and roll up tightly. Secure the ends with cocktail sticks and put the parcels in a baking dish.
3 Bake for 20 minutes until brown. Serve immediately.

PREPARING AHEAD: These can be made to the end of step 2 up to 6 hours in advance, covered with cling film and stored in the fridge. Leave at room temperature for 20 minutes before baking.

CHAPTER 3

COCKTAIL PARTIES

Cocktail parties are a great way to entertain lots of guests at once.

They also have a certain transience that you need to prepare for:

guests may make only a brief appearance; they may arrive late or

not at all; or they may bring along a friend or two. The recipes in

this chapter take all of that into consideration. With a little planning

(see page 6) and the right combination of hot and cold, and sweet

and savoury items, there's no need to worry that your party will

be anything but a massive success.

   All of the dazzling dishes here are designed for 24–36 guests,

and they can be eaten in one mouthful while mingling over

cocktails. Serve up classic tapas such as Paprika-Chicken Pinchos

and Spinach, Raisin & Pine Nut Puff-Pastry Parcels. Then give your

selection an international flair with delicious dishes that highlight

exciting flavours from every corner of the Mediterranean to the

Far East and beyond. Add a touch of the exotic with stunning dishes

like Salmon Teriyaki or Coconut Thai Chicken Skewers. Mix in a few

favourite cocktail bites, such as Peppercorn Beef with Béarnaise

Sauce, Asparagus Tartlets and Chocolate Fondue, and your party

will be an evening to remember.

COD & GREMOLATA SPOONS *(SEE PAGE 77)*

096   Asparagus Tartlets

MAKES: 24   **PREPARATION TIME:** 15 minutes   **COOKING TIME:** 15 minutes
EQUIPMENT: 2 x 12-hole mini muffin tins, 5.5cm/2¼in plain round pastry cutter

butter, for greasing
plain flour, for rolling the pastry
   and flouring
250g/9oz ready-to-roll puff pastry
24 asparagus spears, 10cm/4in long

1 egg
125ml/4fl oz/½ cup double cream
1 tbsp grated Parmesan cheese
salt and freshly ground black pepper

1 Preheat the oven to 180°C/350°F/Gas 4 and lightly grease and flour the muffin tins.
   On a lightly floured surface, roll the pastry into a 25 x 34cm/10 x 13½in rectangle.
   Cut out 24 circles, using the pastry cutter, and gently press each one into a hole
   of the muffin tin. Working from the tip downwards, cut each asparagus spear into
   4cm/1¾in pieces and discard the remaining woody ends.
2 Bring a saucepan of water to the boil. Add the asparagus and cook for 1 minute,
   then drain immediately. Put 1 asparagus tip and 1 stem in each pastry case. It does
   not matter if they stick out a bit.
3 Put the egg, cream and Parmesan in a bowl and mix well. Season with salt and
   pepper and spoon 1–2 tsp of the mixture into each pastry case. Bake for 12–14
   minutes until puffed and brown. Serve immediately.

097   Avocado, Blue Cheese & Caramelized Onion Wraps

MAKES: 24   **PREPARATION TIME:** 20 minutes   **COOKING TIME:** 20 minutes

30g/1oz butter
5 tbsp olive oil
2 onions, finely sliced
2 avocados, halved and stoned
4 tortilla wraps, 25cm/10in round

110g/3¾oz blue cheese, broken
   into small pieces
2 handfuls rocket leaves
juice of ½ lemon
salt and freshly ground black pepper

1 Put the butter and 3 tbsp of the oil in a frying pan and heat over a low heat until
   the butter has melted. Stir in the onion. Increase the heat to medium-low and
   cook, stirring occasionally, for 20 minutes until soft and golden brown.
2 Scoop the avocado pulp into a bowl and mash it, using a fork, until smooth. Spread
   half of the avocado over each tortilla wrap, then divide the caramelized onion over
   the avocado. Sprinkle with the cheese and rocket leaves and season with salt and
   pepper. Drizzle the wraps with the remaining 2 tbsp of the oil and the lemon juice.
3 Roll each tortilla wrap fairly tightly, folding the sides over the filling as you go. Just
   before serving, slice each wrap into 6 pieces and secure with a cocktail stick.

PREPARING AHEAD: These can be made up to 4 hours in advance, wrapped, uncut, in cling film
and stored in the fridge. Slice just before serving.

098 Brie & Cranberry Croutes

MAKES: 24   **PREPARATION TIME:** 15 minutes   **COOKING TIME:** 20 minutes

150g/5¹/₂oz cranberries
70g/2¹/₂oz/scant ¹/₃ cup caster sugar
6 slices of white bread, cut into
   quarters

olive oil, for brushing the bread
250g/9oz Brie cheese, cut into
   24 pieces

1 Preheat the oven to 170°C/325°F/Gas 3. Put the cranberries, sugar and 4 tbsp water in a large saucepan over a medium-low heat and cook, stirring occasionally, for 10 minutes until the cranberries have popped. Transfer to a clean, heatproof bowl and set aside.
2 Brush the bread with oil and put on a baking sheet. Bake for 5 minutes until lightly golden. Remove from the oven and top each toast with 1 piece of the Brie. Return to the oven and bake for a further 5 minutes, or until the cheese has melted.
3 Top each toast with 1 tsp of the cranberry sauce and serve immediately.

PREPARING AHEAD: The cranberry sauce can be made up to 1 week in advance, covered and stored in the fridge.

099 Mixed Mushrooms & Thyme Cream Vol-au-Vents

MAKES: 36   **PREPARATION TIME:** 40 minutes   **COOKING TIME:** 30 minutes
EQUIPMENT: 3cm/1¼in and 4cm/1½in plain round pastry cutters

3 tbsp olive oil, plus extra for greasing
500g/1lb 2oz ready-to-roll puff pastry
plain flour, for rolling the pastry
1 egg, beaten
500g/1lb 2oz mixed mushrooms,
   finely diced

leaves from 4 thyme sprigs
160ml/5¹/₄fl oz/scant ²/₃ cup double
   cream
salt and freshly ground black pepper

1 Preheat the oven to 190°C/375°F/Gas 5 and lightly grease a baking sheet. Cut the pastry in half and, on a lightly floured surface, roll one half of it into a 25 x 30cm/ 10 x 12in rectangle. Cut out 36 pastry circles, using the large pastry cutter. Put 18 of the circles on the baking sheet, brush with the beaten egg and cover with the remaining pastry circles. Repeat with the remaining half of the pastry.
2 Using the small pastry cutter, carefully press an incision through the centre of the top layer of each pastry circle. Brush the edges of the top circle with the remaining egg and bake for 8 minutes until golden.
3 Remove from the oven, transfer to a cooling rack and leave to cool for 5 minutes. Remove the inner circle from the centre of each vol-au-vent case, using a small, sharp knife and your fingertips, and set them aside to use as lids, if desired.
4 Heat the oil in a frying pan over a medium heat. Add the mushrooms and fry, stirring, for 12 minutes until soft and brown. Add the thyme leaves, season with salt and pepper and cook for a further 3 minutes until well mixed and aromatic. Add the cream and cook, stirring occasionally, for a further 5 minutes until beginning to brown and thicken. Spoon the filling into each vol-au-vent case, cover the openings with the pastry lids, if desired, and serve warm.

100　Nutty Tofu

MAKES: 24　PREPARATION TIME: 15 minutes, plus 30 minutes–1 hour marinating
COOKING TIME: 5 minutes

5 tsp pine nuts
5 tsp shelled pistachio nuts
5 tsp sesame seeds
5 tsp finely chopped coriander leaves
juice and finely grated zest of 1 lemon
1½ tsp Tabasco sauce

3 tbsp olive oil
½ tsp salt
375g/13oz firm tofu, cut into
　24 x 2.5cm/1in squares
freshly ground black pepper

1　Put the pine nuts, pistachio nuts and sesame seeds in a dry frying pan and heat over a medium heat, stirring continuously, for 5 minutes until golden. Transfer to a food processor, add the coriander leaves and pulse for 30 seconds until the mixture resembles coarse breadcrumbs.

2　Put the lemon juice, Tabasco sauce, oil and salt in a bowl. Season with pepper and whisk well. Put the tofu in a serving bowl and pour the dressing over. Gently stir in the nut mixture. Leave to stand at room temperature for 30 minutes to 1 hour, then serve.

101　Patty-Pan Squash Stuffed with Ratatouille

MAKES: 24　PREPARATION TIME: 15 minutes　COOKING TIME: 10 minutes

3 tbsp vegetable oil
1 courgette, finely chopped
1 small aubergine, finely chopped
1 garlic clove, finely chopped
125g/4½oz cherry tomatoes,
　finely chopped

1 small handful basil leaves,
　finely chopped
24 small patty-pan squash,
　about 4cm/1½in in diameter
salt and freshly ground black pepper

1　Heat the oil in a frying pan over a medium heat. Add the courgette and aubergine and cook, stirring occasionally, for 5 minutes until soft and beginning to brown. Add the garlic and tomatoes and cook for a further 3 minutes until the tomatoes have broken down and are incorporated. Remove the pan from the heat, stir in the basil and season with salt and pepper, then set the ratatouille aside.

2　Using a small, sharp knife, cut away the top stem and surrounding flesh from each squash to make a natural saucer.

3　Bring a large saucepan of lightly salted water to the boil. Add the squash and cook for 2 minutes until just soft, but still firm enough to hold the filling. Drain, then transfer the squash to a bowl of cold water.

4　When ready to serve, remove the squash from the water and pat dry with a clean tea towel. Top each squash with 1 tsp of the ratatouille and serve.

PREPARING AHEAD: The ratatouille in step 1 can be made up to 1 day in advance and stored in an airtight container in the fridge.

02 Mini Poppadoms with Raita

MAKES: 48   **PREPARATION TIME:** 20 minutes

2 tomatoes, finely chopped
½ cucumber, deseeded and
   finely diced
¼ red onion finely sliced
1 tsp cumin seeds
1 small garlic clove, finely chopped

juice of ½ lime
1 small handful coriander leaves,
   finely chopped
250ml/9fl oz/1 cup natural yogurt
48 mini poppadoms
salt and freshly ground black pepper

1 Put the tomatoes, cucumber, onion, cumin and garlic in a bowl. Add the lime
   juice, coriander leaves and yogurt and mix well. Season with salt and pepper.
2 Spoon the raita onto the poppadoms and serve immediately.

103 Spinach, Raisin & Pine Nut Puff-Pastry Parcels

MAKES: 16 **PREPARATION TIME:** 20 minutes, plus 30 minutes soaking
COOKING TIME: 20 minutes **EQUIPMENT:** 2 x 12-hole non-stick muffin tins

65g/2¼oz/½ cup raisins
30g/1oz/scant ¼ cup pine nuts
1 tbsp olive oil
250g/9oz spinach, washed, dried
    and stems discarded

plain flour, for rolling the pastry
250g/9oz ready-to-roll puff pastry
30g/1oz Gorgonzola cheese, chopped
1 egg yolk, beaten with 1 tbsp milk

1 Put the raisins in a heatproof bowl, cover with boiling water and leave to stand for 30 minutes. Put the pine nuts in a dry frying pan and heat over a medium heat, stirring continuously, for 2 minutes until golden. Transfer to a bowl and set aside.
2 Preheat the oven to 180°C/350°F/Gas 4. Heat the oil in a large pan over a medium heat. Add the spinach and cook for 3–5 minutes until wilted. Transfer to a colander and squeeze out as much excess water as possible, then chop. Drain the raisins.
3 On a lightly floured surface, roll the pastry into a 24cm/9½in square. Cut out 16 x 6cm/2½in squares, using a knife, and gently press them into the tins. Divide the spinach, Gorgonzola and raisins into them and brush with the egg yolk mixture.
4 Bake for 12–15 minutes until golden. Sprinkle with the pine nuts and serve.

104 Olives with Cumin & Citrus Zest

SERVES: 24 **PREPARATION TIME:** 5 minutes, plus 1–2 hours marinating (optional)

450g/1lb mixed olives
1 tsp cumin seeds
juice and grated zest of 1 lemon

finely grated zest of 1 orange
2 tbsp olive oil

1 Put all the ingredients in a bowl and mix well.
2 Serve immediately or leave to marinate at room temperature for 1–2 hours and then serve.

105 Beetroot Crisps

SERVES: 24 **PREPARATION TIME:** 20 minutes **COOKING TIME:** 30 minutes

2kg/4lb 8oz large beetroot, washed
1l/35fl oz/4 cups sunflower oil
salt

1 Finely slice the beetroot by passing them through the slicing blade of a food processor or mandoline, or cut by hand, using a sharp knife.
2 Heat the oil in a deep saucepan or wok to 180°C/350°F, or until a piece of beetroot sizzles and floats when dropped into the oil.
3 Carefully drop a few beetroot slices into the oil and fry for 5 minutes until crisp, working in batches to avoid overcrowding the pan. Remove from the oil, using a slotted spoon, and drain on kitchen paper, then transfer to a cooling rack. Repeat with the remaining beetroot. Season with salt and leave the crisps to cool and dry completely before serving.

106 Mushroom Tartlets

MAKES: 24 **PREPARATION TIME:** 10 minutes, plus making the tartlet cases
COOKING TIME: 10 minutes

3 tbsp olive oil
250g/9oz button mushrooms,
   cut into quarters
leaves from 3 thyme sprigs

2 garlic cloves, finely chopped
250ml/9fl oz/1 cup double cream
½ recipe quantity savoury Tartlet
   Cases, baked (see page 14)

1 Heat the oil in a frying pan over a medium heat. Add the mushrooms and thyme
leaves and fry, stirring occasionally, for 5–6 minutes until beginning to soften and
brown. Add the garlic, reduce the heat a little and cook, stirring occasionally, for
a further 2 minutes until the garlic has softened but has not begun to brown.
2 Stir in the cream and cook over a medium heat for 2 minutes until slightly reduced.
3 Spoon the mixture into the tartlet cases and serve immediately.

PREPARING AHEAD: The mushrooms in step 1 can be made up to 12 hours in advance and stored
in an airtight container in the fridge.

107 Onion Tartlets

MAKES: 24 **PREPARATION TIME:** 20 minutes, plus making the tartlet cases
COOKING TIME: 30 minutes

2 tbsp raisins
15g/½oz butter
1 tbsp olive oil
1 large onion, finely sliced
4 tbsp white wine
1 large egg, beaten

125ml/4fl oz/½ cup double cream
a generous pinch salt
½ recipe quantity savoury Tartlet
   Cases, blind-baked (see page 14)
freshly ground black pepper

1 Put the raisins in a heatproof bowl and cover with 125ml/4fl oz/½ cup boiling
water. Leave to stand for 30 minutes, then drain. Meanwhile, preheat the oven
to 170°C/325°F/Gas 3. Heat the butter and oil in a frying pan over a medium
heat until the butter has melted. Add the onion and fry, stirring occasionally,
for 10 minutes until soft and just beginning to brown.
2 Add the wine and drained raisins and turn up the heat to medium-high. Cook for
5 minutes until the liquid has evaporated, stirring occasionally to ensure that the
bottom does not burn, then remove from the heat.
3 Put the egg, cream and salt in a large bowl, season with pepper and beat lightly.
Add the onion mixture and mix well. Put 1–2 tsp of the mixture into each tartlet
case and bake for 12–15 minutes until set and slightly brown. Serve warm or cold.

PREPARING AHEAD: The onions in step 1 can be made up to 12 hours in advance and stored
in an airtight container in the fridge.

108   Polenta Bruschetta

MAKES: 24   **PREPARATION TIME:** 25 minutes   **COOKING TIME:** 25 minutes

190g/6¾oz/heaped 1¼ cups polenta
2 tbsp olive oil
1 garlic clove

24 cherry tomatoes,
   quartered lengthways
15g/½oz Parmesan cheese
salt and freshly ground black pepper

1   Bring 750ml/26fl oz/3 cups water to the boil in a large saucepan. Stir in the polenta and remove from the heat. Leave to stand, covered, for 5 minutes until all the water has been absorbed.

2   Line a baking sheet with greaseproof paper and spread the polenta evenly across the sheet so that it is 1.5cm/⅝in thick. Turn onto a board, peel off the paper and cut the polenta into 24 x 2cm/¾in squares.

3   Heat a ridged griddle pan over a high heat for 3–4 minutes until hot. Brush the polenta squares with the oil, then rub with the garlic clove. Working in batches, put them on the pan and cook for 5 minutes on each side until clearly marked.

4   Top each polenta square with 4 pieces of the tomato and season with salt and pepper. Grate the Parmesan, if using, over the top and serve.

PREPARING AHEAD: The polenta can be made to the end of step 2 up to 8 hours in advance and stored in an airtight container in the fridge.

109   Potato Samosas

MAKES: 24   **PREPARATION TIME:** 40 minutes, plus making the dip   **COOKING TIME:** 35 minutes

300g/10½oz potatoes, peeled and
   coarsely chopped
1 tbsp olive oil
1 large onion, finely chopped
1 large tomato, finely chopped
3 chillies, finely chopped
1 x 2cm/¾in piece root ginger,
   peeled and finely chopped
1½ tsp coriander seeds

1½ tsp mustard seeds
1½ tsp cumin seeds
8 filo pastry sheets
55g/2oz butter, melted
375ml/13fl oz/1½ cups sunflower oil,
   plus extra as needed
salt and freshly ground black pepper
1 recipe quantity Mint & Yogurt Dip
   (see page 11), to serve

1   Put the potatoes in a saucepan, cover with water and bring to the boil. Boil for 10 minutes, or until tender, then drain.

2   Meanwhile, heat the olive oil in a frying pan over a medium heat. Add the onion and fry, stirring occasionally, for 5 minutes until soft and translucent. Add the tomato, chillies, ginger and coriander, mustard and cumin seeds and cook for a further 2 minutes until well combined and aromatic. Add the potatoes and stir until well coated in the onion mixture. Remove from the heat and leave to cool.

3   Put 1 filo pastry sheet on a clean work surface, keeping the rest covered with a clean damp tea towel while you work. Brush the pastry with a little of the melted butter, then cover with a second filo sheet and brush again with butter. Cut the filo lengthways into 6 long strips.

4   Position 1 pastry strip vertically in front of you. Put 1 tbsp of the filling at the bottom end of the pastry, leaving a little space between the edges of the pastry and the filling. Fold the bottom-right corner of the pastry diagonally up over the filling to form a triangle, then fold the bottom-left corner up the left edge, keeping the triangular shape. Continue folding until you reach the end of the pastry and the filling is enclosed. Repeat with the remaining pastry and filling.

5   Heat the oil in a deep saucepan or wok until a small piece of pastry sizzles when dropped in. Fry the samosas for 1–2 minutes on each side until golden brown, working in batches to avoid overcrowding the pan. Remove from the pan, using a slotted spoon, and drain on kitchen paper. Repeat with the remaining samosas, adding more oil to the pan if necessary. Serve hot, warm or cool with the dip.

PREPARING AHEAD: These can be made to the end of step 4 up to 1 day in advance, covered and stored in the fridge.

10 Stilton & Apple Filo Parcels

MAKES: 24   **PREPARATION TIME:** 40 minutes   **COOKING TIME:** 25 minutes

85g/3oz Stilton cheese
1 apple, peeled, cored and
    finely chopped
juice of ½ lemon

8 filo pastry sheets
55g/2oz butter, melted
375ml/13fl oz/1½ cups sunflower oil,
    plus extra as needed

1   Crumble the Stilton into a bowl. Add the apple and lemon juice and mix well.
2   Put 1 filo pastry sheet on a clean work surface, keeping the rest covered with a
    clean damp tea towel while you work. Brush the pastry with a little of the melted
    butter, then cover with a second filo sheet and brush again with butter. Cut the
    filo lengthways into 6 long strips.
3   Position 1 pastry strip vertically in front of you. Put 1 tbsp of the filling at the
    bottom end of the pastry, leaving a little space between the edges of the pastry
    and the filling. Fold the bottom-right corner of the pastry diagonally up over the
    filling to form a triangle, then fold the bottom-left corner up the left edge, keeping
    the triangular shape. Continue folding until you reach the end of the pastry and
    the filling is enclosed. Repeat with the remaining pastry and filling.
4   Heat the oil in a deep saucepan or wok until a small piece of pastry sizzles when
    dropped in. Fry the parcels for 1–2 minutes on each side until golden brown,
    working in batches to avoid overcrowding the pan. Remove from the pan, using
    a slotted spoon, and drain on kitchen paper. Repeat with the remaining parcels,
    adding more oil to the pan if necessary. Serve warm.

PREPARING AHEAD: These can be made to the end of step 3 up to 4 hours in advance, covered
and stored in the fridge.

111 Feta-Filled Sweet Peppers

MAKES: 24   **PREPARATION TIME:** 10 minutes

100g/3¹/₂oz feta cheese
24 bottled sweet peppers, about
    175g/6oz drained weight

juice of ¹/₂ lemon
freshly ground black pepper

1 Crumble the feta into a bowl, then spoon 1 tsp of it into each pepper.
2 Sprinkle the peppers with the lemon juice, season with pepper and serve.

PREPARING AHEAD: These can be made up to 12 hours in advance and stored in an airtight container in the fridge.

112 Panzanella Gem Boats

MAKES: 24   **PREPARATION TIME:** 15 minutes, plus 1–12 hours chilling
COOKING TIME: 20 minutes

1 red pepper
6 yellow cherry tomatoes,
    finely chopped
6 red cherry tomatoes,
    finely chopped
3 tinned anchovy fillets in oil,
    drained and chopped

6 basil leaves, torn
150g/5¹/₂oz ciabatta, broken into
    small pieces and toasted
1 tsp balsamic vinegar
4 tbsp olive oil
2 Little Gem lettuce hearts
salt and freshly ground black pepper

1 Preheat the oven to 180°C/350°F/Gas 4. Put the whole pepper in a baking dish and bake for 20 minutes until the skin is wrinkled and the pepper soft. Set aside until cool enough to handle, then remove the skin, stalk and seeds and chop coarsely.
2 Put the pepper, tomatoes, anchovies, basil, ciabatta, vinegar and oil in a bowl. Season with salt and pepper, mix well, cover, and chill in the fridge for 1–12 hours.
3 When ready to serve, put 1 tbsp of the panzanella on the end of each gem lettuce leaf and serve.

113 New Potatoes Stuffed with Crème Fraîche & Caviar

MAKES: 24   **PREPARATION TIME:** 15 minutes   **COOKING TIME:** 45 minutes

24 new potatoes
200g/7oz/heaped ³/₄ cup
    crème fraîche
50g/1³/₄oz lumpfish roe

1 Preheat the oven to 190°C/375°F/Gas 5. Put the potatoes on a baking sheet and bake for 30–45 minutes until tender, then remove from the oven and leave to cool.
2 Slice the top off each potato and carefully scoop out most of the flesh, using a teaspoon. The centre can be used in a recipe that calls for mashed potato.
3 Fill each potato with 1 tsp of the crème fraîche, top with ¹/₂ tsp of the roe and serve.

14 Sun-Dried Tomato, Tapenade & Fontina Crostini

MAKES: 24   PREPARATION TIME: 15 minutes   COOKING TIME: 5 minutes

2 tbsp capers
30 pitted black olives
8 tinned anchovy fillets in oil, drained
1 tbsp olive oil
juice of ½ lemon
24 thin slices of baguette

24 sun-dried tomatoes,
  about 100g/3½oz
100g/3½oz fontina cheese,
  thinly sliced
freshly ground black pepper

1 Put the capers, olives, anchovies, oil and lemon juice in a food processor
   and blend for 1 minute until the mixture forms a thick paste. Alternatively,
   grind all the ingredients together, using a pestle and mortar.
2 Preheat the grill to high. Spread 1 heaped tsp of the tapenade onto each
   slice of bread, cover with 1 slice each of sun-dried tomato and fontina. Put the
   breads on a grill pan and grill for 3–5 minutes or until the cheese has melted
   and is bubbling. Season with pepper and serve.

15 Cod & Gremolata Spoons

MAKES: 24   PREPARATION TIME: 15 minutes   COOKING TIME: 15 minutes
EQUIPMENT: 24 Chinese soup spoons (available in Chinese supermarkets)

1 garlic clove
4½ tsp olive oil
1 small handful parsley,
  coarsely chopped
juice and zest of 1 lemon
200g/7oz/2 cups breadcrumbs

1 skinless cod fillet,
  about 480g/1lb 1oz
70g/2½oz/heaped ½ cup plain flour
1 egg, beaten
salt and freshly ground black pepper

1 Preheat the oven to 200°C/400°F/Gas 6. Put the garlic, oil, parsley, lemon juice and
   zest and ½ cup of the breadcrumbs in a food processor and pulse for 30 seconds
   until well mixed and the garlic is chopped. Set the gremolata aside.
2 Season the cod well with salt and pepper. Dip the cod in the flour, then in the egg,
   followed by the remaining breadcrumbs to coat. Put the fish in a baking dish and
   bake for 15 minutes until golden.
3 Break the cod into 3cm/1¼in nuggets. Put the Chinese spoons on a serving platter
   and divide the fish evenly among them. Top with 1 tsp of the gremolata and serve.

116 Trout Tartare on Artichoke Leaves

MAKES: 24 **PREPARATION TIME:** 20 minutes, plus 2 hours marinating
COOKING TIME: 30 minutes

150g/5½oz sea trout, skinned and
   finely chopped
1 spring onion, finely chopped
1 large handful parsley, chopped

2 tbsp capers, finely chopped
1 globe artichoke
freshly ground black pepper
1 lime, cut into small wedges, to serve

1   Put the trout, spring onion, parsley and capers in a bowl and mix well. Season with pepper and leave to marinate, covered, in the fridge for 2 hours.
2   Bring a large saucepan of water to the boil. Add the artichoke and boil for 25–30 minutes, or until you can easily pull a leaf off the artichoke. Drain, transfer to a bowl of cold water for 5 minutes, then drain again.
3   Remove 24 large, regular-shaped leaves from the artichoke. Put 1 heaped tsp of the trout tartar on the end of each artichoke leaf and serve with the lime wedges.

PREPARING AHEAD: The trout tartar in step 1 can be made up to 1 day in advance and stored in an airtight container in the fridge.

117 Breaded Haddock Croquettes

MAKES: 24 **PREPARATION TIME:** 20 minutes, plus making the dip **COOKING TIME:** 35 minutes

450g/1lb potatoes, peeled and cubed
250g/9oz skinless, boneless haddock
90g/3¼oz/scant 1 cup breadcrumbs
6 dill sprigs, finely chopped
150g/5½oz/scant 1¼ cups plain flour

2 tbsp sunflower oil, plus extra
  as needed
salt and freshly ground black pepper
1 recipe quantity Sweet Chilli Dip
  (see page 12), to serve

1 Put the potatoes in a pan, cover with water and bring to the boil. Boil for
  15 minutes until tender, then drain.
2 Put the haddock in a large frying pan and cover with water, bring to a simmer over
  a low heat and poach for 5 minutes until white and cooked through but still firm.
  Remove the fish, using a slotted spoon, and break it up into a mixing bowl. Add the
  breadcrumbs, dill and potatoes and mash together. Season the mixture with salt
  and pepper and shape into 24 log-shaped croquettes of equal size.
3 Roll the croquettes in the flour to coat lightly.
4 Heat 1 tbsp of the oil in a frying pan over a medium-high heat. Working in batches,
  fry the croquettes for 2–3 minutes on each side until golden. Remove from the
  pan, using a slotted spoon, and drain on kitchen paper. Serve hot with the sweet
  chilli dip.

PREPARING AHEAD: These can be made to the end of step 2 up to 6 hours in advance, covered
with cling film and stored in the fridge.

118 Cherry Tomatoes Stuffed with Seared Tuna

MAKES: 24 **PREPARATION TIME:** 20 minutes **COOKING TIME:** 2 minutes

24 cherry tomatoes
125g/4½oz tuna fillet
2 tsp soy sauce

2 tsp olive oil
½ cucumber, finely diced

1 Slice the top off each cherry tomato and carefully scoop out and discard the seeds,
  using a small spoon. Put the tomatoes on a serving plate and cut away a small
  piece from the bottom of any that wobble.
2 Heat a frying pan for 2 minutes over a high heat until hot, then add the tuna and
  sear for 45 seconds on each side until brown. The centre will still be raw. Remove
  from the pan and cut into pieces small enough to fit inside the cherry tomatoes.
3 Mix the soy sauce and oil together in a bowl. Fill each tomato with 1 tsp of the
  tuna, followed by ¼ tsp of the dressing. Sprinkle 3–4 pieces of the cucumber over
  the top and serve.

119 Salmon & Dill Croquettes

MAKES: 24 **PREPARATION TIME:** 30 minutes **COOKING TIME:** 40 minutes

300g/10¹/₂oz small potatoes, peeled
300g/10¹/₂oz salmon fillets
1 large handful dill, finely chopped
2 tbsp capers, drained and chopped
2 tbsp double cream

150g/5¹/₂oz/scant 1¹/₄ cups plain flour
1 egg, beaten
100g/3¹/₂oz/1 cup breadcrumbs
2 tbsp olive oil
salt

1 Put the potatoes in a saucepan, cover with water and bring to the boil. Boil for 15 minutes until tender, then drain. Transfer to a bowl and mash coarsely.
2 Put the salmon fillets, skin-side up, in a frying pan and cover with water. Bring to the boil over a medium-low heat, then immediately turn off the heat and leave to stand for 4 minutes until pale pink on the outside and slightly darker in the centre.
3 Remove the fillets from the water and peel off the skin. Break the fish up into the bowl of potatoes. Add the dill, capers and cream, mix well and season with salt. Shape the mixture into 24 logs of equal size, using your hands.
4 Roll each croquette in the flour to coat, dip it in the egg and then roll it in the breadcrumbs to coat.
5 Heat the oil in a frying pan over a medium-high heat . Working in batches, fry the croquettes for 2–3 minutes on each side until brown and crisp. Serve immediately.

PREPARING AHEAD: These can be made to the end of step 3 up to 6 hours in advance, covered with cling film and stored in the fridge.

120 Seafood Brochettes

MAKES: 24 **PREPARATION TIME:** 20 minutes **COOKING TIME:** 10 minutes
EQUIPMENT: 24 x 10cm/4in skewers

24 large peeled king prawns
1 monkfish fillet, about 185g/6¹/₂oz,
   cut into 48 x 2.5cm/1in chunks
24 scallops

120g/4¹/₂oz/scant 1¹/₄ cups
   breadcrumbs
olive oil, to drizzle
juice of ¹/₄ lemon
salt

1 If using wooden skewers, soak them in cold water at least 30 minutes before grilling. Put 1 prawn on a skewer, followed by 1 piece of the monkfish, 1 scallop and another piece of monkfish. Repeat with the remaining skewers.
2 Heat the grill to high. Turn each brochette in the breadcrumbs to coat and drizzle with the oil. Put the brochettes directly on the grill rack over a baking sheet and grill for 5 minutes on each side until the scallops and monkfish are white and the prawns are pink.
3 Transfer the brochettes to a serving platter and season with salt. Drizzle the lemon juice over them and serve immediately.

121 Tuna, Carrot & Onion Open Sandwiches

MAKES: 24   PREPARATION TIME: 25 minutes   COOKING TIME: 15 minutes

2 tbsp olive oil
2 onions, thinly sliced
4 carrots, peeled and finely grated
2 tbsp red wine vinegar
1 tsp Dijon mustard

24 slices of baguette
250g/9oz tinned yellow fin tuna,
    broken into teaspoon-sized flakes
freshly ground black pepper

1   Heat the oil in a frying pan over a medium-low heat. Add the onions and cook,
    stirring occasionally, for 15 minutes until very soft and just beginning to brown.
2   Put the carrots in a bowl. Mix together the vinegar and mustard and stir the
    mixture into the carrots.
3   Put 1 tbsp of the onion on each slice of bread, add 1 tsp of the tuna and top with
    some of the carrot mixture. Season with pepper and serve.

122 Beetroot, Herring & Crème Fraîche Toasts

MAKES: 24   PREPARATION TIME: 20 minutes   COOKING TIME: 50 minutes

1 beetroot
6 slices of white bread, crusts removed
150g/5¹/₂oz/scant ²/₃ cup crème
    fraîche

1 small handful rocket
120g/4¹/₄oz herring, cut into
    24 x 2.5cm/1in squares
freshly ground black pepper

1   Put the beetroot in a saucepan, cover with water and bring to the boil. Boil for
    40–45 minutes until a knife easily goes through to the centre. Drain and leave
    to stand until cool enough to handle, then peel and finely chop.
2   Preheat the oven to 160°C/315°F/Gas 2–3. Cut each slice of bread into 4 squares
    and put them on a baking sheet. Bake for 5 minutes until lightly toasted.
3   Spread each toast square with 1 heaped tsp of the crème fraîche, top with 1 rocket
    leaf, 1 piece of the herring and a few pieces of the beetroot. Season with pepper
    and serve.

PREPARING AHEAD: The beetroot in step 1 can be cooked up to 1 day in advance and stored,
unchopped, in an airtight container in the fridge.

123 Coconut Prawns

MAKES: 24   PREPARATION TIME: 10 minutes   COOKING TIME: 5 minutes

1 lemongrass stalk, finely chopped
250ml/9fl oz/1 cup coconut milk
¹/₂ large red chilli
1 tbsp peeled and grated root ginger

200g/7oz peeled, cooked
    king prawns
grated zest of 1 lime

1   Put the lemongrass, coconut milk, chilli and ginger in a saucepan and bring
    to the boil, then remove from the heat and leave to cool to room temperature.
2   Put the prawns in a serving bowl and sprinkle with the lime zest. Pour the coconut
    sauce over the prawns, mixing so they are completely covered, and serve with
    cocktail sticks.

124 Herb Crêpes with Smoked Salmon & Crème Fraîche

MAKES: 35 **PREPARATION TIME:** 25 minutes, plus 30 minutes resting
COOKING TIME: 30 minutes

250ml/9fl oz/1 cup milk
15g/¹/₂oz butter
150g/5¹/₂oz/scant 1¹/₄ cups
   plain flour
¹/₂ tsp salt
2 eggs
a few dill sprigs, chopped

2 tsp olive oil, plus extra as needed
140g/5oz/scant ³/₄ cup
   crème fraîche
350g/12oz smoked salmon,
   thinly sliced
freshly ground black pepper

1 Put the milk and butter in a saucepan and heat over a low heat until the butter has melted.
2 Sift the flour and salt into a large bowl and make a well in the centre. Add the eggs and 1 tbsp of the milk mixture and beat, using a balloon whisk, until well combined. Add the remaining milk mixture and continue to whisk for 1–2 minutes until smooth. Cover the bowl with a clean tea towel and leave to rest at room temperature for 30 minutes.
3 Stir the dill into the batter. Heat the oil in a 20cm/8in frying pan over a medium heat. Remove the pan from the heat, add 2 tbsp of the batter and tilt the pan from side to side until the base is evenly covered. Return to the heat and cook for 1–2 minutes on each side until the crêpe begins to brown. Transfer to a plate and repeat with the remaining batter, adding more oil to the pan as needed.
4 Spread 2 tbsp of the crème fraîche over each crêpe and top with a few slices of the salmon. Roll the crêpes into tight rolls, then cut each one into 7 x 2.5cm/1in pieces and serve immediately.

125 Salmon, Eel & Prawn Nigiri

MAKES: 24 **PREPARATION TIME:** 20 minutes, plus 20 minutes resting
COOKING TIME: 20 minutes

105g/3³/₄oz/¹/₂ cup sushi rice
¹/₂ tsp caster sugar
1¹/₂ tsp rice vinegar
1 tsp mirin
1 tsp sake
a pinch salt
8 large peeled, cooked prawns,
   peeled

100g/3¹/₂oz smoked eel
4 tbsp rice wine vinegar mixed with
   4 tbsp water
1 tbsp wasabi paste
100g/3¹/₂oz salmon fillet, thinly sliced
   and cut into 8 strips
125ml/4fl oz/¹/₂ cup soy sauce,
   to serve

1 Cook the sushi rice according to the packet instructions. Set aside to rest for 20 minutes.
2 Put the sugar, rice vinegar, mirin, sake and salt in a bowl and mix well. Stir this mixture into the rice.
3 Using a sharp knife, make a deep incision along the back of each prawn, so it can open up into a butterfly shape. Repeat with the eel.
4 Dip your hands into the vinegar and water mixture and shape the rice into 24 slightly rounded 2.5cm/1in-high rectangles.
5 Dab a little wasabi onto each rice rectangle. Cover 8 of the rice rectangles with 1 piece of the eel, 8 with the salmon and 8 with 1 prawn each. Serve immediately with the soy sauce.

126 Tuna & Japanese Mayo Sushi

MAKES: 24   **PREPARATION TIME:** 30 minutes, plus 20 minutes resting and making the mayonnaise
COOKING TIME: 20 minutes   **EQUIPMENT:** sushi mat

210g/7$\frac{1}{2}$oz/1 cup sushi rice
1 recipe quantity Mayonnaise
  (see page 12)
1 tsp wasabi paste
1 tsp caster sugar
1 tbsp rice vinegar
2 tsp mirin
2 tsp sake
$\frac{1}{4}$ tsp salt

125ml/4fl oz/$\frac{1}{2}$ cup rice wine
  vinegar, mixed with 125ml/4fl oz/
  $\frac{1}{2}$ cup water
4 nori sheets
185g/6$\frac{1}{2}$oz tuna fillet, cut into
  1cm/$\frac{1}{2}$in-square strips
15g/$\frac{1}{2}$oz pickled ginger, to serve
125ml/4fl oz/$\frac{1}{2}$ cup soy sauce,
  to serve

1 Cook the sushi rice according to the packet instructions. Set aside to rest for
   20 minutes. Put the mayonnaise and wasabi paste in a bowl, mix well and set aside.
2 Put the sugar, rice vinegar, mirin, sake and salt in a bowl and mix well. Stir this
   mixture into the rice.
3 Put the sushi mat in a landscape position in front of you and lay a sheet of nori
   on top, shiny-side down. Dip your hands into the vinegar and water mixture and
   spread a thin layer of the rice over the nori, leaving a 4cm/1$\frac{1}{2}$in gap along the top.
4 Spread 2 tbsp of the wasabi mayonnaise across the top half of the rice. Put $\frac{1}{4}$ of
   the tuna over this in a line. Tightly roll the mat upwards to create a log, then peel
   back the mat and seal the edge of the nori with a dab of water. Repeat with the
   remaining nori. Slice each of the sushi rolls into 6 x 2.5cm/1in pieces, using a very
   sharp knife. Serve with the ginger and soy sauce.

PREPARING AHEAD: The uncut sushi rolls can be wrapped in cling film and stored in the fridge
for up to 4 hours before slicing, but should be served at room temperature.

127   Scallops Wrapped in Pancetta

MAKES: 24   PREPARATION TIME: 15 minutes   COOKING TIME: 15 minutes

24 Queen or small scallops,
  white flesh only
12 slices of pancetta, cut in half

1 lemon, cut into wedges, to serve
1 small handful rocket leaves, to serve

1   Preheat the oven to 180°C/350°F/Gas 4. Roll each scallop tightly in 1 strip
    of the pancetta and put on a baking sheet.
2   Bake for 15 minutes until the scallops are white and the pancetta is cooked
    through, then serve immediately with the lemon wedges and rocket.

PREPARING AHEAD: These can be made to the end of step 1 up to 8 hours in advance,
covered with cling film and stored in the fridge.

128 Salmon Teriyaki

MAKES: 24 **PREPARATION TIME:** 10 minutes, plus 1 hour marinating **COOKING TIME:** 4 minutes

6 tbsp dry sherry
4 tbsp clear honey
4 tbsp light soy sauce

2 tsp white wine vinegar
500g/1lb 2oz salmon fillet, skin on
2 tbsp olive oil

1 Put the sherry, honey, soy sauce and vinegar in a bowl and mix well. Add the salmon and turn it around in the marinade a few times to coat. Leave to stand at room temperature for 1 hour.
2 Heat the oil in a frying pan over a medium-high heat. Add the salmon, skin-side down and fry for 2 minutes, adding half the marinade after 1 minute. Turn the salmon over and add the rest of the marinade. Cook for a further 2 minutes until the salmon is completely coated in the teriyaki sauce but still raw in the centre.
3 Cut the salmon in half lengthways, then cut widthways into 24 slices and serve.

PREPARING AHEAD: This can be made to the end of step 1 up to 8 hours in advance, covered with cling film and stored in the fridge.

129 Salmon Tikka Skewers

MAKES: 12 double or 24 single skewers **PREPARATION TIME:** 30 minutes, plus 2 hours marinating **COOKING TIME:** 6 minutes **EQUIPMENT:** 12 or 24 x 10cm/4in skewers

1 tbsp olive oil
4^1/$_2$ tsp finely chopped root ginger
1^1/$_2$ tsp ground coriander
1^1/$_2$ tsp paprika

1^1/$_2$ tsp cumin seeds
50g/1^3/$_4$oz butter, softened
450g/1lb skinless salmon fillet,
    cut into 24 x 3cm/1^1/$_2$ in cubes

1 Heat the oil in a frying pan over a low heat. Add the ginger, coriander, paprika and cumin and fry for 2 minutes, stirring continuously, until well mixed and aromatic. Remove from the heat and leave to cool.
2 Put the spices and butter in a food processor and process for 1 minute until soft and well combined. Put the salmon in a non-metallic bowl and rub the spicy butter onto the salmon cubes, then leave to marinate, covered, in the fridge for 1 hour.
3 If using wooden skewers, soak them in cold water for at least 30 minutes before grilling. Preheat the grill to high and line a baking sheet with baking parchment. Put 1–2 salmon cubes on each skewer and put the skewers on the baking sheet. Grill for 3–4 minutes until pale pink and coated in melted butter, then serve.

PREPARING AHEAD: This can be made to the end of step 2 up to 8 hours in advance, covered with cling film and stored in the fridge

130 Seared Tuna & Cucumber Parcels

MAKES: 24 **PREPARATION TIME:** 15 minutes **COOKING TIME:** 2 minutes

2 tsp olive oil
250g/9oz tuna fillet, trimmed
1 cucumber

250ml/9fl oz/1 cup soy sauce,
    to serve

1 Heat the oil in a frying pan over a medium heat. Add the tuna and fry for 40 seconds on each side until brown. The centre of the fillet will still be slightly raw.
2 Slice the tuna into 24 x 1cm/^{1}/$_2$in strips. Slice the cucumber lengthways into 24 thin strips, using a potato peeler.
3 Put 1 strip of tuna on each strip of cucumber, then roll the cucumber around the tuna to form a parcel and secure with a cocktail stick. Serve with the soy sauce.

131 Curried Mussels

MAKES: 24   PREPARATION TIME: 15 minutes, plus 20 minutes soaking
COOKING TIME: 12 minutes

680g/1lb 8oz mussels
1 tbsp sunflower oil
1 onion, finely chopped
1 tsp turmeric
1/2 tsp cumin seeds

1/2 tsp ground coriander
1/2 tsp hot chilli powder
a few coriander leaves
finely chopped cucumber (optional)

1   Discard any mussels with broken shells or that do not close when tapped. Pull
    out the beards and put the mussels in a basin of cold water. Soak for 10 minutes,
    then change the water. Soak for a further 10 minutes, then drain and rinse.
2   Put 250ml/9fl oz/1 cup water in a large saucepan and bring to the boil. Add the
    mussels and cook for 2 minutes, covered, or until all the mussels have opened.
    Discard any that have not opened. Transfer the mussels to a colander and leave
    to cool for 5 minutes, or until cool enough to handle, then remove the empty top
    shells and discard.
3   Heat the oil in a frying pan over a medium heat. Add the onion, turmeric, cumin,
    ground coriander and chilli powder and fry, stirring occasionally, for 5 minutes
    until the onion has begun to soften. Add 125ml/4fl oz/1/2 cup water and simmer
    for a further 5 minutes until the liquid has almost completely evaporated. Remove
    from the heat and leave to cool.
4   Top each mussel with 1 tsp of the onion mixture, 1 coriander leaf and some
    cucumber, if using, then serve.

PREPARING AHEAD: The mussels can be made to the end of step 3 up to 8 hours in advance
and stored in an airtight container in the fridge.

132 Bacon-Stuffed Mussels

MAKES: 24   PREPARATION TIME: 25 minutes, plus 20 minutes soaking
COOKING TIME: 17 minutes

680g/1lb 8oz mussels
8 unsmoked streaky bacon rashers,
   finely chopped

100g/31/2 oz/1 cup breadcrumbs
olive oil

1   Discard any mussels with broken shells or that do not close when tapped. Pull
    out the beards and put the mussels in a basin of cold water. Soak for 10 minutes,
    then change the water. Soak for a further 10 minutes, then drain and rinse.
2   Preheat the oven to 190°C/375°/Gas 5. Put 250ml/9fl oz/1 cup water in a large
    saucepan and bring to the boil. Add the mussels and cook for 2 minutes, covered,
    or until all the mussels have opened. Discard any that have not opened. Transfer
    the mussels to a colander and leave to cool for 5 minutes, or until cool enough
    to handle, then remove the empty top shells and discard.
3   Put the mussels in their half-shells face-up on a baking sheet. Divide the bacon
    pieces into the shells, then cover with the breadcrumbs and push down slightly
    to pack the filling in.
4   Drizzle the mussels with oil and bake for 10–15 minutes until the breadcrumbs
    are golden. Serve immediately.

PREPARING AHEAD: The mussels can be made to the end of step 3 up to 8 hours in advance
and stored in an airtight container in the fridge.

133 Oysters with Beetroot & Horseradish

MAKES: 24   **PREPARATION TIME:** 30 minutes   **EQUIPMENT:** oyster knife and protective glove

80ml/2¹/₂fl oz/¹/₃ cup double cream
3 tsp grated horseradish
juice of ¹/₂ lemon
2 cooked beetroot, peeled and
   finely chopped

24 oysters
6 cornichons (small gherkins),
   finely chopped
4 tbsp vodka
crushed ice

1 Put the cream in a large bowl and whip, using a whisk or handheld electric mixer for 1–2 minutes, or until soft peaks form. Add the horseradish and lemon juice and fold together until well mixed. Stir the beetroot into the cream mixture and set aside until needed.

2 To shuck the oysters, wear a protective glove or use a folded tea towel as a barrier between the hand holding the oyster and the oyster. Hold the oyster, flat-side up, and push the tip of the oyster knife as far as you can into the shell at the narrow end and prize it open. Remove the top shell and the muscle attaching the oyster to its shell. If not serving immediately, pack the shucked oysters, in their bottom shells, in crushed ice and keep in the fridge for up to 2 hours.

3 In a small bowl, mix together the cornichons and vodka. Put 1 tsp of the beetroot cream onto the narrow end of each oyster shell and top with ¹/₂ tsp of the gherkins in vodka. Set the oyster shells on crushed ice and serve immediately.

134 Seafood Tomatoes

MAKES: 24 **PREPARATION TIME:** 20 minutes, plus 20 minutes soaking
COOKING TIME: 5 minutes

350g/12¹/₂oz mussels
24 cherry tomatoes
1 tsp olive oil
12 peeled, cooked prawns,
  coarsely chopped

1 garlic clove, finely chopped
salt and freshly ground black pepper

1   Discard any mussels with broken shells or that do not close as soon as tapped. Pull out the beards and put the mussels in a basin of cold water. Leave to soak for 10 minutes, then change the water, leave for a further 10 minutes and drain again.
2   Meanwhile, slice the top off each cherry tomato and carefully scoop out and discard the seeds, using a small spoon. Put the tomatoes on a serving plate and cut away a small piece from the bottom of any that wobble.
3   Put 125ml/4fl oz/¹/₂ cup water in a saucepan and bring to the boil. Add the mussels and cook for 2 minutes, covered, or until all the mussels have opened. Discard any that have not opened. Transfer the mussels to a colander and leave to cool for 5 minutes, or until cool enough to handle.
4   Remove the mussels from their shells and chop coarsely.
5   Heat the oil in a frying pan over a medium heat. Stir in the mussels, prawns and garlic and cook, stirring occasionally, for 2 minutes until heated through. Divide the seafood mixture into the tomatoes, season with salt and pepper and serve

PREPARING AHEAD: The mussels can be made to the end of step 3 up to 8 hours in advance and stored in an airtight container in the fridge.

135 Prawn & Glass Noodle Spring Rolls

MAKES: 32 **PREPARATION TIME:** 45 minutes, plus making the dip **COOKING TIME:** 15 minutes

100g/3¹/₂oz glass noodles
60g/2¹/₄oz cooked, peeled prawns,
  chopped
1 carrot, grated
1 tbsp peeled and finely grated
  root ginger
70g/2¹/₂oz bean sprouts, broken up
90g/3¹/₄oz pak choi, finely chopped

1 handful coriander leaves,
  finely chopped
juice of ¹/₂ lime
32 x 11cm/4¹/₄in-square spring roll
  wrappers
1l/35fl oz/4 cups sunflower oil
1 recipe quantity Sweet Chilli Dip
  (see page 12), to serve

1   Bring a saucepan of water to the boil. Add the noodles and cook for 2 minutes. Drain and leave to cool, then transfer to a bowl. Add the prawns, carrot, ginger, bean sprouts, pak choi, coriander leaves and lime juice and mix well.
2   Position a spring roll wrapper as a diamond on a work surface. Put 1 tbsp of the vegetable mixture across the bottom half and fold the bottom corner over the filling. Fold in the sides to encase the filling and roll up to form a parcel. Dab a little water on the end and press to seal. Repeat with the remaining wrappers.
3   Heat the oil in a deep saucepan or wok to 180°C/350°F, or until a small piece of spring roll wrapper sizzles when dropped in. Fry the spring rolls for 1 minute until golden, working in batches to avoid overcrowding the pan. Remove from the pan, using a slotted spoon, and drain on kitchen paper. Bring the oil back to temperature before each batch. Serve warm with the dip.

PREPARING AHEAD: These can be made to the end of step 2 up to 8 hours in advance and stored in an airtight container in the fridge.

136 Seared Tuna & Ginger Mayonnaise on Prawn Crackers

MAKES: 24 **PREPARATION TIME:** 15 minutes, plus making the mayonnaise
COOKING TIME: 2 minutes

1 recipe quantity Mayonnaise
  (see page 12)
2.5cm/1in piece root ginger,
  peeled and grated

1 tbsp olive oil
350g/12oz tuna fillet
24 prawn crackers
24 coriander leaves

1   Put the mayonnaise and ginger in a bowl, mix well and set aside.
2   Heat the oil in a frying pan over a medium heat. Add the tuna and fry for 1 minute on each side until brown. The centre of the fillet will still be raw. Remove from the pan and cut the tuna into 24 x 2cm/¾in squares and leave to cool.
3   Put 1 cube of tuna on each prawn cracker, spoon over ½ tsp of the ginger mayonnaise and top with 1 coriander leaf. Serve immediately.

137 Almond Mussels

MAKES: 24 **PREPARATION TIME:** 30 minutes, plus 20 minutes soaking and 1 hour chilling
COOKING TIME: 2 minutes

680g/1lb 8oz mussels
90g/3¼oz/1 cup flaked almonds
1 slice of day-old bread,
  crust removed

1 handful parsley leaves
6 tbsp olive oil
juice of ½ lemon

1   Discard any mussels with broken shells or that do not close when tapped. Pull out the beards and put the mussels in a basin of cold water. Soak for 10 minutes, then change the water. Soak for a further 10 minutes, then drain and rinse.
2   Put 250ml/9fl oz/1 cup water in a large saucepan and bring to the boil. Add the mussels and cook for 2 minutes, covered, or until all the mussels are open. Discard any that have not opened. Transfer the mussels to a colander and leave to cool for 5 minutes, or until cool enough to handle, then remove the empty top shells and discard.
3   Put the almonds, bread, parsley, oil and lemon juice in a food processor and process for 1 minute, or until the mixture resembles coarse crumbs. Top each mussel with 1 tsp of the mixture, then chill, covered, in the fridge for 1 hour before serving.

PREPARING AHEAD: The mussels can be made to the end of step 3 up to 8 hours in advance and stored in an airtight container in the fridge.

138 Prawn Tempura

MAKES: 24   **PREPARATION TIME:** 10 minutes   **COOKING TIME:** 10 minutes

100g/3½oz/heaped ¾ cup plain flour
1 egg, beaten
1l/35fl oz/4 cups sunflower oil

24 peeled, cooked large king prawns
 with tails
2 lemons, cut into wedges

1   Put the flour, egg and 125ml/4fl oz/½ cup ice-cold water in a bowl and stir until
the mixture just comes together.

2   Heat the oil in a deep saucepan or wok to 180°C/350°F, or until a little of the
tempura batter sizzles and floats when dropped in. While the oil is heating, dip the
prawns in the tempura batter to coat. Working in batches to avoid overcrowding
the pan, fry the prawns for 1–2 minutes until golden brown. Remove from the pan,
using a slotted spoon, and drain on kitchen paper. Repeat with the remaining
prawns, bringing the oil back to temperature before each batch.

3   Serve immediately with the lemon wedges.

39 Sweet & Sour Prawns

MAKES: 24 **PREPARATION TIME:** 10 minutes **COOKING TIME:** 10 minutes

125ml/4fl oz/½ cup rice vinegar
95g/3½ oz/½ cup soft brown sugar
1 tsp soy sauce
2 tbsp tomato ketchup
1 tbsp arrowroot, mixed with 1 tsp
   cold water to form a paste

1 tsp olive oil
200g/7oz king prawns,
   peeled and cooked
2 tsp black sesame seeds

1   Put the vinegar, sugar, soy sauce and ketchup in a saucepan and bring to the boil over a medium-low heat, stirring until the sugar has dissolved. Increase the heat to medium and boil for a further 5 minutes until syrupy. Remove from the heat and leave to cool to room temperature, then add the arrowroot paste.

2   Heat the oil in a frying pan over a medium-high heat. Add the prawns and cook, stirring occasionally, for 1–2 minutes until heated through. Reduce the heat to low and stir in the sauce. Remove from the heat, sprinkle with the sesame seeds and serve with cocktail sticks.

40 Whole Prawn & Coriander Spring Rolls

MAKES: 32 **PREPARATION TIME:** 30 minutes, plus making the dip **COOKING TIME:** 15 minutes

32 peeled, cooked large king prawns
   with tails
32 x 11cm/4¼in-square spring
   roll wrappers
60g/2¼oz root ginger, peeled and
   finely sliced into 32 matchsticks

32 coriander leaves
1l/35fl oz/4 cups sunflower oil
1 recipe quantity Sweet Chilli Dip
   (see page 12), to serve

1   Put 1 prawn on the edge of a spring roll wrapper so that the tail extends over the edge of the wrapper. Top the prawn with a strip of ginger and a coriander leaf. Fold the edge of the wrapper over the filling to cover, then roll tightly to form a spring roll. Dab a little warm water on the end and press to seal. Repeat with the remaining prawns.

2   Heat the oil in a deep saucepan or wok to 180°C/350°F, or until a small piece of spring roll wrapper sizzles when dropped in. Fry the spring rolls for 1 minute until golden, working in batches to avoid overcrowding the pan. Remove from the pan, using a slotted spoon, and drain on kitchen paper. Bring the oil back to temperature before each batch. Serve warm with the dip.

PREPARING AHEAD: These can be made to the end of step 1 up to 8 hours in advance and stored in an airtight container in the fridge.

141 Green Tandoori Chicken with Poppadoms

MAKES: 24   **PREPARATION TIME:** 25 minutes, plus 2–4 hours marinating
COOKING TIME: 20 minutes

2 boneless, skinless chicken breasts,
  about 125g/4½oz each
24 mini poppadoms
24 coriander leaves

MARINADE
1 small handful mint leaves
1 small handful coriander leaves
125ml/4fl oz/½ cup natural yogurt
1 garlic clove
1 green chilli, stem removed
1 heaped tsp ground cumin
juice of 1 lemon
1 tsp salt

1   To make the marinade, put all the marinade ingredients in a food processor
    and process for 1–2 minutes until smooth, then transfer to a shallow dish.
2   Add the chicken to the marinade and turn to coat. Cover with cling film and leave
    to marinate in the fridge for 2–4 hours.
3   Preheat the oven to 180°C/350°F/Gas 4. Drain the chicken and transfer it to
    a baking dish. Bake for 15–20 minutes, or until cooked through and the juices run
    clear when the meat is pierced with a sharp knife.
4   Cut the chicken into thin strips and divide equally onto the poppadoms. Top each
    one with 1 coriander leaf and serve immediately.

PREPARING AHEAD: This can be made to the end of step 2 up to 1 day in advance and stored
in the fridge.

142 Chicken & Bacon Tartlets

MAKES: 24   **PREPARATION TIME:** 20 minutes, plus making the tartlet cases and mayonnaise
COOKING TIME: 25 minutes

2 tbsp olive oil
5 rindless streaky bacon rashers,
  finely chopped
1 boneless, skinless chicken breast,
  about 185g/6½oz

½ recipe quantity savoury Tartlet
  Cases, baked (see page 14)
1 recipe quantity Mayonnaise
  (see page 12)
salt and freshly ground black pepper

1   Heat 1 tbsp of the oil in a frying pan over a medium-high heat. Add the bacon and
    fry for 10 minutes until crispy. Remove from the pan and drain on kitchen paper.
2   Add the remaining oil to the frying pan and heat over a medium-high heat. Add
    the chicken and cook for 15 minutes, turning halfway through, until cooked
    through and the juices run clear when the meat is pierced with a sharp knife.
    Season with salt. Transfer to a plate and leave to rest for 5 minutes, then cut the
    chicken into thin strips.
3   When ready to serve, fill each tartlet case with 1 tsp of the mayonnaise. Top
    with 2–3 strips of the chicken and a sprinkling of the bacon. Season with pepper
    and serve.

PREPARING AHEAD: The bacon and chicken in steps 1 and 2 can be made up to 4 hours
in advance and stored in separate airtight containers in the fridge. Leave to stand at room
temperature for 20 minutes before assembling the tartlets.

43 Chinese Chicken Croustades

MAKES: 24 **PREPARATION TIME:** 25 minutes, plus making the chicken and croustades
COOKING TIME: 5 minutes

1 tsp olive oil
1/3 recipe quantity Boiled Chicken, chopped (see page 12)
1/2 large carrot, peeled and finely diced
1 tbsp light soy sauce
1 tbsp black bean sauce

1 recipe quantity Croustades (see page 14)
1/2 cucumber, halved lengthways, deseeded and finely diced
24 coriander leaves
salt and freshly ground black pepper

1   Heat the oil in a frying pan or wok over a medium heat. Add the chicken, carrot and soy and bean sauces and cook for 5 minutes, stirring occasionally, until warmed through. Season with salt and pepper.
2   When ready to serve, put 1 heaped tsp of the chicken mixture in each croustade. Top with some of the cucumber and 1 coriander leaf and serve.

44 Duck Spring Rolls

MAKES: 36 **PREPARATION TIME:** 45 minutes, plus making the duck
COOKING TIME: 10 minutes

1 recipe quantity Crispy Duck, finely chopped (see page 13)
6cm/2½in piece root ginger, peeled and finely chopped
2 carrots, peeled and finely grated
zest of 2 oranges
4 spring onions, trimmed and finely sliced

36 x 11cm/4¼in-square spring roll wrappers
1l/35fl oz/4 cups sunflower oil
250ml/9fl oz/1 cup hoisin sauce, to serve
salt and freshly ground black pepper

1   Put the duck, ginger, carrots, orange zest and spring onions in a bowl. Mix well and season with salt and pepper.
2   Position a spring roll wrapper as a diamond on a work surface. Put 1 tbsp of the duck mixture across the bottom half and fold the bottom corner over the filling. Fold in the sides to encase the filling and roll up to form a parcel. Dab a little water on the end and press to seal. Repeat with the remaining wrappers.
3   Heat the oil in a deep saucepan or wok to 180°C/350°F, or until a small piece of spring roll wrapper sizzles when dropped in. Fry the spring rolls for 1 minute until golden, working in batches to avoid overcrowding the pan. Remove from the pan, using a slotted spoon, and drain on kitchen paper. Bring the oil back to temperature before each batch. Serve warm with the dip.

PREPARING AHEAD: These can be made to the end of step 2 up to 8 hours in advance and stored in an airtight container in the fridge.

145 Coconut Thai Chicken Skewers

MAKES: 24 **PREPARATION TIME:** 15 minutes, plus 1–12 hours marinating
COOKING TIME: 15 minutes **EQUIPMENT:** 24 x 10cm/4in skewers

5 boneless, skinless chicken breasts, about 150g/5½oz each, cut into 48 x 4cm/1½in cubes

MARINADE
1 lemongrass stalk, coarsely chopped
200ml/7fl oz/scant 1 cup coconut cream
125ml/4fl oz/½ cup natural yogurt
1 small red chilli, stem removed
1 small handful coriander leaves
juice of ½ lime

1 Put all the marinade ingredients in a food processor and process for 1–2 minutes until well combined. Transfer to a bowl, add the chicken and stir to coat. Leave to marinate, covered, in the fridge for at least 1 hour and up to 12 hours.
2 If using wooden skewers, soak them in cold water for at least 30 minutes before grilling. Preheat the grill to high. Put 2 cubes of chicken on each skewer and put them on a roasting rack above a baking sheet. Grill for 7–8 minutes on each side until brown. Serve hot.

146 Paprika Chicken Pinchos

MAKES: 36 **PREPARATION TIME:** 35 minutes, plus 1 hour marinating
COOKING TIME: 20 minutes **EQUIPMENT:** 36 x 10cm/4in skewers

6 boneless, skinless chicken thighs, cut into 36 x 3cm/1¼in chunks
2 tbsp olive oil
2 tsp turmeric
2 tsp ground cumin

2 tsp paprika
2 garlic cloves, flattened
½ tsp salt
2 lemons, cut into wedges, to serve

1 Put the chicken in a bowl, add the oil, turmeric, cumin, paprika, garlic and salt and mix well. Cover and leave to marinate at room temperature for 1 hour.
2 If using wooden skewers, soak them in cold water for at least 30 minutes before grilling. Preheat the grill to hot. Put 2 pieces of chicken on each skewer and put them on a baking sheet. Grill for 15–20 minutes, turning half way through, until the chicken is cooked and browning. Squeeze lemon juice, as desired, over the top of the skewers and serve immediately.

PREPARING AHEAD: This can be made to the end of step 1 up to 1 day in advance, covered and stored in the fridge.

147 Sweet Duck & Cucumber Croustades

MAKES: 24 **PREPARATION TIME:** 15 minutes, plus making the duck and croustades

½ recipe quantity Crispy Duck, about 250g/9oz meat, finely chopped (see page 13)
2 tbsp hoisin sauce

135g/4½oz cucumber, finely diced
1 recipe quantity Croustades (see page 14)
24 coriander leaves

1 Put the duck, hoisin sauce and cucumber in a bowl and mix well.
2 Divide the duck mixture into the croustades, top each one with 1 coriander leaf and serve.

PREPARING AHEAD: The duck mixture in step 1 can be made up to 6 hours in advance, covered and stored in the fridge.

148 Chilli Chicken Spring Rolls

MAKES: 24 **PREPARATION TIME:** 40 minutes, plus making the dip **COOKING TIME:** 25 minutes

2 boneless, skinless chicken breasts, about 185g/6½oz each
2 small red chillies, finely chopped
3 sticks of celery, trimmed and finely chopped
3 tbsp light soy sauce

24 x 11cm/4¼in-square spring roll wrappers
1l/35fl oz/4 cups sunflower oil
1 recipe quantity Mint & Yogurt Dip (see page 11), to serve

1 Preheat the oven to 180°C/350°F/Gas 4. Put the chicken in a baking dish and bake for 15 minutes until cooked through and the juices run clear when the meat is pierced with a sharp knife. Remove from the oven, leave to cool, then chop finely.
2 Put the chicken, chillies, celery and soy sauce in a bowl and mix well.
3 Position a spring roll wrapper as a diamond on a work surface. Put 1 tbsp of the chicken mixture across the bottom half and fold the bottom corner over the filling. Fold in the sides to encase the filling and roll up to form a parcel. Dab a little water on the end and press to seal. Repeat with the remaining wrappers.
4 Heat the oil in a deep saucepan or wok to 180°C/350°F, or until a small piece of spring roll wrapper sizzles when dropped in. Fry the spring rolls for 1 minute until golden, working in batches to avoid overcrowding the pan. Remove from the pan, using a slotted spoon, and drain on kitchen paper. Bring the oil back to temperature before each batch. Serve warm with the dip.

PREPARING AHEAD: These can be made to the end of step 3 up to 8 hours in advance and stored in an airtight container in the fridge.

149 Peppercorn Chicken

MAKES: 24 **PREPARATION TIME:** 10 minutes, plus 1 hour marinating
COOKING TIME: 15 minutes

4 tbsp natural yogurt
3cm/1¼in piece root ginger, peeled and finely grated
15 black peppercorns, crushed

juice of 1 lime
2 tbsp olive oil
2 boneless, skinless chicken breasts, about 150g/5½oz each

1 Put the yogurt, ginger, peppercorns, lime juice and 1 tbsp of the oil in a shallow bowl and mix well. Add the chicken and turn well to coat. Leave to marinate, covered, at room temperature for 1 hour.
2 Heat the remaining oil in a frying pan over a medium heat. Add the chicken and marinade and cook for 15 minutes, turning halfway through, until cooked through and the juices run clear when the meat is pierced with a sharp knife.
3 Remove the chicken from the pan and slice into 24 pieces. Serve warm or at room temperature with cocktail sticks.

PREPARING AHEAD: This can be made to the end of step 1 up to 8 hours in advance and stored in the fridge.

150 Chicken & Ham Pies

MAKES: 24 **PREPARATION TIME:** 30 minutes, plus making the chicken
COOKING TIME: 35 minutes **EQUIPMENT:** 7cm/2¾in plain round pastry cutter

½ recipe quantity Boiled Chicken, chopped (see page 12)
2 slices roasted ham, chopped
30g/1oz butter
4½ tsp plain flour, plus extra for rolling the pastry

375ml/17fl oz/1½ cups warm milk
500g/1lb 2oz ready-to-roll puff pastry
1 egg yolk, beaten with 1 tbsp milk
salt and freshly ground black pepper

1 Preheat the oven to 180°C/350°F/Gas 4. Put the chicken and ham in a mixing bowl.
2 Melt the butter in a saucepan over a medium-low heat, then stir in the flour. Slowly stir in the milk, 4 tbsp at a time, and continue cooking, stirring continuously, for 1–2 minutes until smooth. Reduce the heat to low and simmer for 15 minutes, stirring occasionally, until the sauce is pale in colour and satiny in texture. Add the sauce to the chicken and ham, season with salt and pepper and stir well.
3 On a lightly floured surface, roll half the pastry into a 21 x 30cm/8¼ x 12in rectangle and cut out 12 circles, using the pastry cutter. Put 1 tsp of the chicken mixture slightly off-centre on each pastry circle, then fold over to form a semi-circle and pinch the edges together to seal. Put on a baking sheet and repeat with the remaining pastry.
4 Brush the pies with the egg yolk mixture and bake for 12–15 minutes until puffed and golden. Serve immediately.

PREPARING AHEAD: These can be made to the end of step 3 up to 2 hours in advance, covered with cling film and stored in the fridge.

151 Chicken Arosto

MAKES: 24 **PREPARATION TIME:** 10 minutes **COOKING TIME:** 35 minutes

4 boneless, skinless chicken thighs, cut into 24 x 3cm/1¼in cubes
1 tbsp olive oil

6 garlic cloves, unpeeled
2 rosemary sprigs
salt

1 Preheat the oven to 180°C/350°F/Gas 4. Put the chicken in a baking dish and drizzle the oil over. Add the garlic and rosemary and bake for 15 minutes.
2 Remove the chicken from the oven and stir to coat well in the released juices. Return to the oven and bake for a further 15 minutes until the chicken is cooked through, the juices run clear when the meat is pierced with a sharp knife and the garlic is soft. Season with salt and serve with cocktail sticks or forks.

52 Duck & Ginger Wontons

MAKES: 36 **PREPARATION TIME:** 30 minutes, plus making the duck **COOKING TIME:** 12 minutes

1 recipe quantity Crispy Duck,
  finely chopped (see page 13)
4 tbsp hoisin sauce
6cm/2½in piece root ginger, peeled
  and coarsely chopped

4 spring onions, finely sliced,
  plus extra to serve
36 wonton wrappers
125ml/4fl oz/½ cup soy sauce
  (optional), to serve

1 Put the duck, hoisin sauce, ginger and spring onions in a food processor and
  process for 1–2 minutes until the mixture forms a mince.
2 Position a wonton wrapper as a diamond on a work surface. Put 1 tbsp of the duck
  mixture across the bottom half and fold the bottom corner over the filling. Fold in
  the sides to encase the filling and roll up to form a parcel. Dab a little water on the
  end and press to seal. Repeat with the remaining wrappers.
3 Put the soy sauce in a dipping bowl and sprinkle with spring onion, then set aside.
4 Bring a large saucepan of water to a rolling boil. Put the wontons in the water,
  using a slotted spoon, and boil for 2 minutes, or until they float to the surface. Work
  in batches to avoid overcrowding the pan Remove the wontons, using a slotted
  spoon, and serve immediately with the soy sauce, if using.

PREPARING AHEAD: These can be made to the end of step 2 up to 8 hours in advance and stored
in an airtight container in the fridge.

153 Broad Bean Purée & Crispy Bacon Crostini

MAKES: 48   **PREPARATION TIME:** 30 minutes, plus making the crostini
COOKING TIME: 15 minutes

250g/9oz/scant 1½ cups shelled
  broad beans
185ml/6fl oz/¾ cup olive oil
16 rindless streaky bacon rashers,
  finely chopped

1 recipe quantity Crostini
  (see page 15)
300g/10½oz/1½ cups cream cheese
salt and freshly ground black pepper

1   To make the broad bean purée, bring a pan of salted water to the boil, add the
    beans and cook, covered, for 3 minutes until tender. Drain, transfer the beans
    to a bowl and add 170ml/5½fl oz/⅔ cup of the oil. Using a hand-held immersion
    blender, purée the broad beans for 1–2 minutes until smooth. Alternatively,
    process in a food processor until smooth.
2   Heat the remaining oil in a frying pan over a medium-high heat. Add the bacon
    and fry for 8–10 minutes until crisp. Drain on kitchen paper.
3   Spread each of the crostini with 1 heaped tsp of the cream cheese, followed by
    1 tsp of the broad bean purée. Sprinkle with a few bacon pieces, season with salt
    and pepper and serve.

154 Vietnamese Minced-Beef Patties

MAKES: 24   **PREPARATION TIME:** 20 minutes, plus 1 hour chilling and making the dip
COOKING TIME: 20 minutes

500g/1lb 2oz beef mince
2 red chillies, finely chopped
2 small handfuls coriander leaves,
  finely chopped
5cm/2in piece root ginger, peeled
  and finely grated

2 spring onions, finely chopped
2 tbsp olive oil
salt and freshly ground black pepper
1 recipe quantity Sweet Chilli Dip,
  (see page 12), to serve

1   Put the mince, chilli, coriander leaves, ginger and spring onions in a bowl, season
    with salt and pepper and mix well, using your hands.
2   Shape the mixture into 24 balls of equal size and flatten them slightly so they
    are 2cm/¾in thick. Put the patties on a plate, cover with cling film and chill for
    at least 1 hour.
3   Heat the oil in a frying pan over a medium heat. Working in batches, fry the patties
    for 2–3 minutes on each side until brown. Serve immediately with the dip.

PREPARING AHEAD: These can be made to the end of step 2 up to 1 day in advance and stored
in the fridge.

155   Pork Spring Rolls

MAKES: 24   **PREPARATION TIME:** 40 minutes, plus making the dip   **COOKING TIME:** 10 minutes

200g/7oz pork mince
1/4 red cabbage, finely chopped
1 small red chilli, finely chopped
2 spring onions, finely chopped
4cm/1 1/2in piece root ginger, peeled
   and finely grated

24 x 11cm/4 1/4in-square spring
   roll wrappers
1l/35fl oz/4 cups sunflower oil
salt and freshly ground black pepper
1 recipe quantity Sweet Chilli Dip,
   (see page 12), to serve

1   Put the mince, cabbage, chilli, spring onions and ginger in a bowl and mix well.
2   Position a spring roll wrapper as a diamond on a work surface. Put 1 tbsp of the
chicken mixture across the bottom half and fold the bottom corner over the filling.
Fold in the sides to encase the filling and roll up to form a parcel. Dab a little water
on the end and press to seal. Repeat with the remaining wrappers.
3   Heat the oil in a deep saucepan or wok to 180°C/350°F, or until a small piece of
spring roll wrapper sizzles when dropped in. Fry the spring rolls for 1–2 minutes
until golden, working in batches to avoid overcrowding the pan. Remove from the
pan, using a slotted spoon, and drain on kitchen paper. Bring the oil back to
temperature before each batch. Serve warm with the dip.

PREPARING AHEAD: These can be made to the end of step 2 up to 8 hours in advance and stored
in an airtight container in the fridge.

156   Polenta Wedges with Blue Cheese & Pancetta

MAKES: 24   **PREPARATION TIME:** 20 minutes   **COOKING TIME:** 8 minutes

190g/6 3/4oz polenta
125g/4 1/2oz blue cheese, such
   as Roquefort, broken up into
   24 small pieces

8 slices of pancetta, sliced widthways
   into thirds

1   Bring 750ml/26fl oz/3 cups water to the boil in a large saucepan. Stir in the polenta
and remove from the heat. Leave to stand, covered, for 5 minutes.
2   Line a baking sheet with greaseproof paper and spread the polenta evenly across
the sheet to 1.5cm/2/3in thick. Turn onto a board, peel off the paper and cut the
polenta into 24 wedges.
3   Preheat the grill to high. Top each polenta square with 1 piece of cheese and 1 slice
of pancetta and put them on a baking sheet. Grill for 5 minutes until the cheese
has melted and the pancetta is crispy. Serve immediately.

PREPARING AHEAD: The polenta can be made to the end of step 2 up to 8 hours in advance
and stored in an airtight container in the fridge.

157 Peppercorn Beef with Béarnaise Sauce

MAKES: 24   **PREPARATION TIME:** 15 minutes   **COOKING TIME:** 15 minutes
EQUIPMENT: 24 x 10cm/4in skewers

350g/12oz rump steak, cut into
    24 x 3mm/⅛in slices
2 tbsp black peppercorns, crushed

BÉARNAISE SAUCE
185ml/6fl oz/¾ cup white
    wine vinegar
5 shallots, finely chopped
2 thyme sprigs
1 bay leaf
4 large egg yolks
200g/7oz butter, cut into 4 pieces
1 lemon wedge
leaves from 3 tarragon sprigs

1   If using wooden skewers, soak them in cold water for at least 30 minutes before grilling. Preheat the grill to high. Roll the beef strips in the crushed peppercorns to coat completely, then thread them onto the skewers. Put the brochettes on a baking sheet and grill for 4 minutes until brown.

2   To make the béarnaise sauce, put the vinegar, shallots, thyme and bay leaf in a saucepan and bring to the boil. Continue boiling for 2 minutes, or until the liquid has reduced to 3 tbsp. Remove from the heat and strain through a sieve into a bowl, pushing with a wooden spoon to extract the maximum amount of flavour. Put the bowl on top of a saucepan of simmering water, over a medium-low heat, making sure that the bottom of the bowl does not touch the water. Stir the egg yolks and 1 piece of the butter into the bowl, whisking until the butter has melted.

3   Add the remaining pieces of butter one at a time, whisking well after each addition until melted. Squeeze in a few drops of lemon juice, add the tarragon and stir. Turn the heat off and stir for a further 2–3 minutes until the sauce is thick. Remove from the heat and serve with the brochettes.

158 Beef Skewers with Soy & Tomato Dip

MAKES: 24   **PREPARATION TIME:** 15 minutes   **COOKING TIME:** 20 minutes
EQUIPMENT: 24 x 10cm/4in skewers

120g/4oz cherry tomatoes, finely
    chopped
3 tbsp soy sauce
5 chives, finely chopped

1 tbsp olive oil
400g/14¼oz chilled beef fillet,
    sliced into 24 x 5mm/¼in slices

1   If using wooden skewers, soak them in cold water for at least 30 minutes before cooking. Put the tomatoes, soy sauce, chives and oil in a small serving bowl and mix well. Set aside until needed.

2   Thread 1 slice of beef onto each skewer.

3   Heat a griddle pan over a high heat for 4–5 minutes until smoking hot. Working in batches, cook the skewers for 1–2 minutes on each side until brown on the outside and pink in the centre. Serve immediately or at room temperature with the dip.

PREPARING AHEAD: These can be made to the end of step 2 up to 1 day in advance and stored in an airtight container in the fridge.

159 Rare Roast Beef, Tomato & Pesto Crostini

MAKES: 24   PREPARATION TIME: 20 minutes, plus making the crostini and pesto
COOKING TIME: 20 minutes

250g/9oz beef fillet
½ recipe quantity Crostini
   (see page 15)
200g/7oz/1 cup cream cheese

4 tomatoes, sliced and each
   slice halved
1 recipe quantity Pesto (see page 11)

1   Preheat the oven to 180°C/350°F/Gas 4. Take the beef out of the fridge 20 minutes
    before cooking so that it is at room temperature. Put the beef in a roasting tin and
    bake for 15–20 minutes until brown on the outside and pink in the centre, then
    remove from the oven and leave to rest for 20 minutes.
2   When ready to serve, carve the beef crossways into 24 x 3mm/⅛in slices. Spread
    each of the crostini with cream cheese, add 1 piece of the tomato and 1 slice of
    the beef. Top with 1 tsp of the pesto and serve.

PREPARING AHEAD: The beef in step 1 can be made up to 1 day in advance, wrapped in cling film
and stored in the fridge. Once sliced, it must be used within 30 minutes, otherwise it will discolour.

160 Spicy Beef Kebabs

MAKES: 24   PREPARATION TIME: 15 minutes   COOKING TIME: 20 minutes
EQUIPMENT: 24 x 10cm/4in skewers

400g/14oz beef mince
1 red chilli, roughly chopped
1 garlic clove, chopped
1 egg

1 handful coriander leaves
1 tsp salt
1 tbsp olive oil

1   If using wooden skewers, soak them in cold water for at least 30 minutes before
    frying. Put all the ingredients except the oil in a food processor and process for
    1–2 minutes until the mixture forms a fine mince.
2   Divide the mixture into 24 portions of equal size and, using your hands, shape
    the mixture into 5cm/2in logs around the pointed end of each skewer.
3   Heat the oil in a frying pan over a medium heat. Working in batches, fry
    the skewers for 3 minutes on each side until brown and cooked through, then
    serve immediately.

PREPARING AHEAD: These can be made to the end of step 2 up to 1 day in advance and stored
in an airtight container in the fridge.

161 Pear & Blue Cheese Wrapped in Parma Ham

MAKES: 24   PREPARATION TIME: 30 minutes

2 Comice pears, peeled, cored and cut
   into 12 equal pieces each
8 slices of Parma ham, cut lengthways
   into thirds

100g/3½oz blue cheese,
   cut into 24 small pieces

1   Put each pear segment on 1 strip of the Parma ham and top it with 1 piece
    of the cheese.
2   Roll up tightly, secure with a cocktail stick and serve.

162 Vitello Tonnato Crostini

MAKES: 24 **PREPARATION TIME:** 20 minutes, plus 1 hour chilling and making the crostini and mayonnaise **COOKING TIME:** 3 minutes

2 tbsp olive oil
300g/10½oz veal escalopes, cut into 2 x 1cm/½ x ¾in pieces
½ recipe quantity Crostini (see page 15)
185g/6½oz tinned tuna in olive oil, drained

1 tbsp capers, plus extra to serve
2 tinned anchovy fillets in oil, drained
juice of 1 lemon
½ recipe quantity Mayonnaise (see page 12)
a few parsley sprigs, chopped, to serve

1 Heat 1 tbsp of the oil in a wok or frying pan over a medium heat. Add the veal and fry, stirring occasionally, for 2 minutes until cooked and pale brown on all sides. Set aside and leave to cool.
2 Put the tuna, remaining oil, capers, anchovies, lemon juice and mayonnaise in a food processor and pulse for 1–2 minutes until well mixed. Transfer the tonnato to a mixing bowl, cover and chill for 1 hour.
3 Finely chop the veal, add it to the tonnato and mix well. Cover and chill in the fridge for 1 hour.
4 To assemble, put 1 tsp of the veal tonnato on each of the crostini. Top with the parsley and the remaining capers and serve.

PREPARING AHEAD: The tonnato can be made to the end of step 3 up to 2 days in advance and stored in an airtight container in the fridge.

163 Mint Lamb Kebabs

MAKES: 24 **PREPARATION TIME:** 20 minutes, plus 1 hour resting **COOKING TIME:** 5 minutes **EQUIPMENT:** 24 x 10cm/4in skewers

2 tbsp olive oil, plus extra for drizzling
4 x 80g/2¾oz lamb steaks

leaves from 4 mint sprigs
freshly ground black pepper

1 Heat the oil in a frying pan over a medium-high heat. Add the steaks and fry for 2 minutes on each side until browned, then set aside.
2 Put a large sheet of cling film, about 30cm/12in across, on a work surface and position the mint leaves in the centre so they are not overlapping. Season the steaks well with pepper and put them in a row on top of the mint leaves. Drizzle with a little oil and roll tightly in the cling film. Leave to stand for 1 hour at room temperature.
3 When ready to serve, unwrap the steaks from the cling film and mint leaves and slice each one into 6 pieces. Put each piece of steak on a skewer and serve.

PREPARING AHEAD: These can be made to the end of step 2 up to 1 day in advance and stored in an airtight container in the fridge. Leave to stand at room temperature for 20 minutes before serving.

64 Yorkshire Puddings & Roast Beef

MAKES: 24 **PREPARATION TIME:** 25 minutes, plus 30 minutes resting
COOKING TIME: 40 minutes **EQUIPMENT:** 2 x 12-hole mini-muffin tins

115g/4oz/scant 1 cup plain flour
$\frac{1}{4}$ tsp salt
2 eggs
145ml/4$\frac{3}{4}$fl oz/scant $\frac{2}{3}$ cup milk

400g/14oz rump steak
3 tbsp olive oil
2 tbsp hot mustard
salt and freshly ground black pepper

1 Preheat the oven to 200°C/400°F/Gas 6. Sift the flour and salt into a bowl,
add the eggs and stir until well combined. Add the milk and stir until smooth.
Cover the bowl with a clean tea towel and leave to rest for 30 minutes.

2 Put the steak in a roasting tin and rub with 1 tbsp of the oil. Bake for 15–20
minutes, or until cooked to your liking. Remove from the oven and leave to rest
while you make the Yorkshire puddings.

3 Put $\frac{1}{4}$ tsp of the oil into each hole of the mini-muffin tins. Put the tins on a baking
sheet and heat in the oven for 5 minutes until the oil is smoking hot. Remove
from the oven and immediately spoon 1 tbsp of the batter into each of the muffin
holes. Bake for 12 minutes until puffed and golden. Leave to cool in the tins while
you prepare the beef.

4 Slice the beef into strips that will fit neatly on top of the Yorkshire puddings.
Remove the puddings from the tins and arrange on a plate. Spoon $\frac{1}{4}$ tsp of the
mustard onto each pudding and top with 1 slice of the beef. Serve immediately.

165   Puréed Pea & Pancetta Croustades

MAKES: 24   **PREPARATION TIME:** 10 minutes, plus making the croustades
COOKING TIME: 15 minutes

8 slices of pancetta
250g/9oz/scant 1²/₃ cups peas
4 tbsp olive oil

1 recipe quantity Croustades
  (see page 14)
salt and freshly ground black pepper

1   Preheat the grill to high. Put the pancetta on a wire wrack on top of a baking
     sheet and grill for 5–7 minutes until crisp, watching carefully so it does not burn.
     Leave to cool for a few minutes and then crumble it into small pieces and set aside.
2   Bring a saucepan of water to the boil. Add the peas and boil for 5 minutes,
     or until tender, then drain. Put the peas and oil in a food processor and process
     for 1–2 minutes until smooth. Season with salt and pepper.
3   Divide the pea purée into the croustades, sprinkle with the pancetta and serve.

166 Baby New Potatoes Stuffed with Ham & Parsley Sauce

MAKES: 24   **PREPARATION TIME:** 40 minutes   **COOKING TIMES:** 35 minutes

12 baby new potatoes
30g/1oz butter
4½ tsp plain flour
375ml/13fl oz/1½ cups milk, warmed

80g/2¾oz cooked gammon,
   finely diced
1 handful parsley sprigs,
   finely chopped
salt and freshly ground black pepper

1   Put the potatoes in a saucepan, cover with water and bring to the boil. Boil for
    15 minutes, or until tender. Drain and leave to cool for a few minutes.
2   Cut each potato in half lengthways and, using a sharp knife, carefully cut out
    the centre to form a boat. The centre can be used in a recipe that calls for mashed
    potato. Put the potatoes on a serving plate and cut away a small piece from the
    bottom of any that wobble.
3   To make the sauce, melt the butter in a saucepan over a medium-low heat, then
    stir in the flour. Slowly stir in the milk, 4 tbsp at a time, and continue cooking,
    stirring continuously, for 1–2 minutes until smooth. Reduce the heat to low
    and simmer, stirring occasionally, for 15 minutes until the sauce is pale in colour
    and satiny in texture. Remove from the heat. Stir in the gammon and parsley and
    season with salt and pepper.
4   Divide the mixture into the potato boats and serve immediately.

PREPARING AHEAD: The potatoes in step 1 can be boiled up to 4 hours in advance and stored
in an airtight container in the fridge. Leave to stand at room temperature for 30 minutes before
filling and serving. The parsley sauce in step 3 can be made up to 8 hours in advance, stored
in an airtight container in the fridge and reheated in a saucepan over a low heat before serving.

167 Salami, Spinach & Gorgonzola Pizzarettes

MAKES: 24   **PREPARATION TIME:** 30 minutes, plus making the pizza dough
COOKING TIME: 16 minutes   **EQUIPMENT:** 5cm/2in plain round pastry cutter

1 tbsp olive oil
15g/½oz butter
110g/4oz baby spinach,
   washed and dried
plain flour, for rolling the dough

½ recipe quantity Pizza Dough
   (see page 15)
12 slices of Italian salami,
   finely chopped
80g/2¾oz Gorgonzola cheese,
   crumbled

1   Preheat the oven to 200°C/400°F/Gas 6. Heat the oil and butter in a large saucepan
    over a medium heat until the butter has melted. Add the spinach and cook for
    4 minutes until wilted. Transfer the spinach to a colander and squeeze out as much
    excess water as possible, then chop.
2   On a lightly floured surface, roll out the pizza dough to 2mm/¹⁄₁₆in thick and cut
    out 24 circles, using the pastry cutter, then put the circles on a baking sheet.
3   Put 1 tsp of the spinach on each circle, followed by a few pieces of the salami
    and Gorgonzola. Bake for 12 minutes until golden and the cheese has melted.
    Serve immediately.

Chorizo, Membrillo & Manchego Skewers

MAKES: 24 **PREPARATION TIME:** 15 minutes **COOKING TIME:** 5 minutes
EQUIPMENT: 24 x 10cm/4in skewers

1 tsp olive oil
250g/9oz chorizo, cut into
   24 slices
120g/4¼oz Manchego cheese,
   cut into 24 pieces

360g/12¾oz membrillo
   (quince cheese), cut into
   24 x 2.5cm/1in cubes

1   Heat the oil in a frying pan over a medium-high heat. Add the chorizo and fry
   for 1½ minutes on each side until slightly shrunken and browned.
2   Put 1 slice of the chorizo, 1 piece of the Manchego and 1 cube of the membrillo
   on each skewer and serve.

PREPARING AHEAD: These can be made up to 2 hours in advance and stored in an airtight
container in a cool, dry place..

169 Honey & Rosemary Cocktail Sausages

MAKES: 48   PREPARATION TIME: 5 minutes   COOKING TIME: 25 minutes

48 cocktail sausages
125g/4½oz/½ cup clear honey

4 rosemary sprigs
4 tbsp Dijon mustard, to serve

1   Preheat the oven to 190°C/375°F/Gas 5. Put the sausages in a roasting tin, drizzle over the honey and mix well to coat.
2   Add the rosemary sprigs and bake for 20–25 minutes until browned. Serve with the Dijon mustard for dipping.

PREPARING AHEAD: These can be made up to 8 hours in advance, covered and stored in the fridge. Reheat at 160°C/315°F/Gas 2–3 for 10–15 minutes before serving.

170 Pork Balls with Sweet & Sour Dipping Sauce

MAKES: 36   PREPARATION TIME: 35 minutes   COOKING TIME: 25 minutes

500g/1lb 2oz pork mince
leaves from 2 thyme sprigs
grated zest of 3 limes
2 tbsp olive oil
freshly ground black pepper

SWEET & SOUR DIPPING SAUCE
4 tbsp clear honey
juice of 2 limes
4 tsp soy sauce
2 chillies, finely sliced
2 spring onions, finely sliced

1   To make the sweet & sour sauce, put the honey, lime juice and soy sauce in a small bowl and mix well. Stir in the chillies and spring onions and set aside.
2   Put the pork, thyme and lime zest in a bowl, season with pepper and mix well. Shape the mixture into 36 small balls of equal size.
3   Heat the oil in a frying pan over a medium-high heat and cook the pork balls for 4 minutes, turning occasionally, until brown all over. Work in batches if necessary to avoid overcrowding the pan. Serve with the dipping sauce.

PREPARING AHEAD: The pork balls in step 2 can be made up to 1 day in advance and stored in an airtight container in the fridge. Bring to room temperature before serving.

171 Pork Satays with Peanut Dip

MAKES: 24   PREPARATION TIME: 35 minutes   COOKING TIME: 10 minutes
EQUIPMENT: 24 x 10cm/4in skewers

375g/13oz pork loin
5cm/2in piece root ginger, peeled and finely chopped
1 large red chilli, chopped
1 egg
salt and freshly ground pepper

PEANUT DIP
3 tbsp crunchy peanut butter
3 tsp clear honey
1 tsp chilli powder
3 tsp dark soy sauce
juice of 1 lime

1   If using wooden skewers, soak them in water for at least 30 minutes before cooking. Preheat the oven to 200°C/400°F/Gas 6. Put the pork, ginger, chilli and egg in a food processor. Season with salt and pepper and process for 1 minute until the mixture forms a mince.
2   Divide the mince into 24 portions of equal size and shape around the pointed end of the skewers, then put the skewers on a baking sheet.
3   Bake for 10 minutes until pale brown.
4   Meanwhile, mix together all the ingredients for the peanut dip and transfer to a serving bowl. Serve the satays with the dip.

PREPARING AHEAD: The pork satays can be made to the end of step 2 up to 1 day in advance, covered with cling film and stored in the fridge. The peanut dip in step 4 can be made up to 1 day in advance and stored in an airtight container at room temperature.

172 Parma Ham, Blue Cheese & Ricotta Toasts

MAKES: 24   **PREPARATION TIME:** 15 minutes   **COOKING TIME:** 5 minutes

6 slices of white bread,
  crusts removed
90g/3¼oz Parma ham

360g/12¾oz ricotta cheese
210g/7½oz blue cheese,
  cut into 24 slices

1 Preheat the grill to high. Cut each slice of bread into four squares. Cut the Parma ham into 24 pieces equal in size to the bread squares and put 1 piece on each bread square. Top with a scant 1 tbsp of the ricotta, followed by 1 slice of the blue cheese.

2 Put the bread squares on a grill pan and grill for 4–5 minutes until the cheese has melted and is beginning to brown. Serve warm.

173 Baby New Potatoes with Scrambled Eggs & Bacon

MAKES: 24   **PREPARATION TIME:** 25 minutes   **COOKING TIME:** 25 minutes

24 baby new potatoes
1 tbsp olive oil
6 unsmoked streaky bacon rashers,
  finely chopped

30g/1oz butter
2 eggs, beaten
salt and freshly ground black pepper

1 Put the potatoes in a saucepan, cover with water and bring to the boil. Boil for 8–10 minutes, or until tender. Drain and leave to cool for a few minutes.

2 Cut the top off of each potato and scoop out the centre, using a sharp knife, to form a boat. The centre can be used in a recipe that calls for mashed potato. Put the potatoes on a serving plate and cut away a small piece from the bottom of any that wobble.

3 Heat the oil in a frying pan over a medium-high heat. Add the bacon and cook, stirring occasionally, for 8–10 minutes until crisp.

4 Heat the butter in a saucepan over a medium-low heat until melted. Add the eggs and cook, stirring continuously, for 1–1½ minutes until they are just beginning to set. Remove from the heat.

5 Divide the scrambled eggs into the potato shells and sprinkle with the bacon. Season with salt and pepper and serve immediately.

PREPARING AHEAD: The potatoes in step 1 can be boiled up to 4 hours in advance and stored in an airtight container in the fridge. Leave to stand at room temperature for 30 minutes before filling and serving.

174 Mortadella & Pesto Crostini

MAKES: 48   **PREPARATION TIME:** 25 minutes, plus making the crostini and pesto

6 slices of mortadella, about
  250g/9oz
300g/10½oz/1½ cups cream cheese

1 recipe quantity Crostini
  (see page 15)
1 recipe quantity Pesto (see page 11)

1 Cut each slice of mortadella into 8 long strips.

2 Spread 1 heaped tsp of the cream cheese onto each of the crostini and cover with 1 strip of the mortadella.

3 Top with ½ tsp of the pesto and serve immediately.

75 Carrot Halva with Pistachio Shortbread

MAKES: 36   **PREPARATION TIME:** 15 minutes, plus making the shortbread
COOKING TIME: 25 minutes

30g/1oz unsalted butter
4 large carrots, peeled and
   coarsely grated
200g/7oz tinned condensed milk

seeds from 55g/2oz/¼ cup
   cardamom pods, shelled
80g/2¾oz/scant ⅔ cup raisins
1 recipe quantity Pistachio
   Shortbread (see page 110)

1   Melt the butter in a saucepan over a medium-low heat. Add the carrots and cook,
    stirring occasionally, for 5 minutes, or until soft.
2   Add the condensed milk and cardamom seeds and cook, stirring occasionally,
    for a further 20 minutes until the liquid has almost all evaporated. Stir in the raisins.
3   Put 1 tsp of the halva on each of the shortbread and serve.

PREPARING AHEAD: The carrot halva can be made to the end of step 2 up to 1 day in advance
and stored in an airtight container in the fridge. Reheat and then leave to cool to room temperature
before serving.

76 Chocolate Tartlets

MAKES: 24   **PREPARATION TIME:** 10 minutes, plus making the tartlet cases
COOKING TIME: 15 minutes

125ml/4fl oz/½ cup double cream
4 tbsp milk
175g/6oz plain chocolate, chopped
1 egg

55g/2oz crystallized ginger,
   finely chopped
½ recipe quantity sweet Tartlet Cases,
   blind-baked (see page 14)
cocoa powder, for dusting

1   Preheat the oven to 170°C/325°F/Gas 3. Put the cream and milk in a saucepan
    and bring to the boil, then set aside. Put the chocolate in a heatproof bowl over
    a saucepan of simmering water, making sure the bottom of the bowl does not
    touch the water. Stir for 5 minutes, or until the chocolate has melted.
2   Beat the egg into the cream mixture and strain through a sieve into the melted
    chocolate. Mix well, then stir in the ginger.
3   Divide the filling into the tartlet cases, put them on a baking sheet and bake
    for 6–8 minutes until a thin crust has formed over the top. Remove from the oven
    and leave to cool.
4   Dust with cocoa powder and serve.

PREPARING AHEAD: These can be made to the end of step 3 up to 6 hours in advance and stored
in an airtight container in a cool, dry place. Leave to stand at room temperature for 30 minutes
before dusting with the cocoa powder and serving.

177 Brandy Snap Baskets with Ginger Cream

MAKES: 24   **PREPARATION TIME:** 20 minutes   **COOKING TIMES:** 15 minutes
EQUIPMENT: 2 x 12-hole deep mini-muffin tins

80g/2¾oz unsalted butter, plus extra
  for greasing (optional)
80g/2¾oz/¼ cup golden syrup
90g/3¼oz/heaped ⅓ cup
  caster sugar
75g/2½oz/heaped ½ cup plain flour

1 tsp ground ginger
55g/2oz crystallized ginger,
  finely chopped
100g/3½oz/½ cup crème fraîche
24 mint leaves
icing sugar, for dusting

1 Preheat the oven to 180°C/350°F/Gas 4. Grease two or three baking sheets with butter or line them with baking parchment. Put the butter, syrup and caster sugar in a saucepan and heat over a low heat until the butter has melted. Stir in the flour and ground ginger, then remove from the heat and put 8–12 teaspoonfuls of the mixture onto each baking sheet, spacing them well apart.

2 Bake for 10–12 minutes until golden, then remove from the oven. Leave the brandy snaps to cool for 3 minutes until cool enough to handle but still soft, then, working quickly, ease each one off the baking sheet, using a palette knife or spatula, and press them into the muffin holes. The brandy snaps will turn crisp when cool.

3 Put the crystallized ginger and crème fraîche in a bowl and mix well.

4 When ready to serve, divide the crème fraîche mixture into the brandy snap baskets, top each one with 1 mint leaf and dust with icing sugar, then serve.

PREPARING AHEAD: The brandy snap baskets can be made to the end of step 2 up to 2 days in advance and stored in an airtight container at room temperature.

178 Pistachio Shortbread

MAKES: 36   **PREPARATION TIME:** 15 minutes, plus 1 hour chilling   **COOKING TIME:** 10 minutes
EQUIPMENT: 4cm/1½in plain round pastry cutter

125g/4½oz/1 cup plain flour,
  plus extra for rolling
70g/2½oz butter
60g/2¼oz/½ cup icing sugar

50g/1¾oz /⅓ cup shelled
  pistachio nuts
1 egg yolk

1 Put the flour and butter in a food processor and process for 1 minute until the mixture resembles breadcrumbs. Add the sugar, pistachio nuts and egg yolk and process for a further 1 minute until well combined.

2 Turn the dough out onto a work surface and shape into a log. Wrap in cling film and chill for 1 hour.

3 Preheat the oven to 180°C/350°F/Gas 4. On a lightly floured surface, roll the dough out to 5mm/¼in thick and cut out 36 circles, using the pastry cutter. Put the biscuits on a baking sheet and bake for 10 minutes until golden. Transfer to a cooling rack and leave to cool completely, then serve.

PREPARING AHEAD: These can be made up to 8 hours in advance and stored in an airtight container at room temperature.

179 # Chocolate Fondue

SERVES: 24   **PREPARATION TIME:** 5 minutes   **COOKING TIME:** 5 minutes

200g/7oz plain chocolate, chopped
2 tbsp golden syrup
3 tbsp milk

1 tbsp whisky
24 physalis, about 150g/5oz
24 strawberries, about 400g/14oz

1   Put the chocolate in a heatproof bowl that will fit over a saucepan. Add the syrup, milk and whisky. Put the bowl over a saucepan of simmering water, making sure the bottom of the bowl does not touch the water, and stir for 5 minutes, or until well mixed and the chocolate has melted.

2   To prepare the physalis, peel the papery pods back to form a handle and expose the orange fruit, then arrange them and the strawberries on a serving plate. Put the chocolate fondue in a serving bowl and put it in the centre of the serving plate and serve immediately.

PREPARING AHEAD: The fondue in step 1 can be made up to 4 hours in advance and stored in an airtight container in a cool, dry place or in the fridge.

Hazelnut Clusters

MAKES: 24   **PREPARATION TIME:** 10 minutes, plus 1 hour chilling   **COOKING TIME:** 15 minutes

100g/3½oz/scant ¾ cup
  blanched hazelnuts
4 tbsp caster sugar

100g/3½oz plain chocolate,
  coarsely chopped

1   Preheat the oven to 200°C/400°F/Gas 6. Line a baking sheet with greaseproof
    paper and spread the nuts over it. Toast the nuts for 5–6 minutes until pale brown.

2   Put the sugar and 2 tbsp water in a saucepan and heat over a low heat, stirring
    occasionally, until the sugar has dissolved. Bring the mixture to the boil and boil
    for 5 minutes until beginning to thicken and turn golden brown. Remove from
    the heat and quickly stir in the nuts to coat. Return to the heat and cook for
    a further 30 seconds so the caramel remains liquid, then turn the mixture out onto
    the greaseproof paper and spread it into a single layer. While still warm, shape the
    nuts into 24 small clusters of 3, using two teaspoons. Leave to cool and set.

3   Put the chocolate in a heatproof bowl over a saucepan of simmering water,
    making sure the bottom of the bowl does not touch the water. Heat for 5 minutes,
    stirring, until the chocolate has melted. Line a large plate with greaseproof paper.
    Dip each nut cluster into the chocolate to coat completely, then transfer it to the
    plate. When the chocolate is too low for dipping, either use a teaspoon or pour
    the remaining chocolate over the nuts. Chill for 1 hour, or until hard. Serve at
    room temperature.

PREPARING AHEAD: These can be made up to 3 days in advance and stored in an airtight
container in the fridge.

81 Raspberries on Caramelized Pastry

MAKES: 24   PREPARATION TIME: 25 minutes   COOKING TIME: 17 minutes
EQUIPMENT: 5cm/2in plain round pastry cutter

plain flour, for rolling the pastry and
   flouring the baking sheet
250g/9oz ready-to-roll puff pastry
2 tbsp icing sugar, plus extra for
   sweetening and dusting

160ml/5¼fl oz/scant ⅔ cup
   double cream
200g/7oz raspberries

1 Preheat the oven to 200°C/400°F/Gas 6. On a lightly floured surface, roll the
   pastry into a 20 x 30cm/8 x 12in rectangle. Cut out 24 circles, using the pastry
   cutter, and put them on a lightly floured baking sheet. Cover with a piece
   of baking parchment and then with a second baking sheet to weigh down the
   pastry. Bake for 15 minutes until pale brown. Remove from the oven and remove
   the top baking sheet and parchment.
2 Preheat the grill to high. Sprinkle ¼ tsp of the icing sugar onto each pastry circle
   and grill for 1–2 minutes until the sugar has melted and turned light brown. Watch
   closely so the sugar does not burn.
3 Put the cream in a mixing bowl and whip, using a whisk or hand-held electric
   mixer, for 1 minute, or until soft peaks form. Sweeten to taste with icing sugar.
4 Spoon some of the whipped cream onto each caramelized pastry circle and top
   with 3 raspberries. Dust with icing sugar and serve.

PREPARING AHEAD: The pastry circles can be made to the end of step 2 up to 8 hours in advance
and stored in an airtight container at room temperature.

182 Treacle Tartlets

MAKES: 24   PREPARATION TIME: 20 minutes, plus making the tartlet cases
COOKING TIME: 8 minutes

325ml/11fl oz/scant 1⅓ cups
   golden syrup
juice and finely grated zest of 1 lemon

100g/3½oz/1 cup breadcrumbs
½ recipe quantity sweet Tartlet Cases,
   blind-baked (see page 14)

1 Preheat the oven to 180°C/350°F/Gas 4. Put the golden syrup and lemon juice and
   zest in a saucepan and heat over a low heat for 2 minutes until smooth and runny.
2 Divide the breadcrumbs into the tartlet cases and pour the golden syrup mixture
   over the top to fill. Bake for 8 minutes until golden.
3 Remove from the oven and leave the tartlets to cool for at least 10 minutes so the
   syrup mixture can set, then serve.

PREPARING AHEAD: These can be made up to 1 day in advance and stored in an airtight container
in a cool, dry place.

CHAPTER 4

LATE-NIGHT DRINKS

Sometimes, the best night out is a night in. Inviting friends over

for a casual late-night get-together is an excellent way to unwind,

catch up and linger over good food, good drink and good

conversation. In this chapter, you'll find world tapas recipes that

are perfect for lounging around with 6–8 people. From Cheese

Fondue and Lamb Koftas to Crispy Salted Pork Belly and Banana

& Coconut Ice Cream, this is food to complement the comfortable,

familiarity found among friends.

The recipes for these light bites are all easy and delicious.

Some recipes, such as Mackerel Escabesche and Caponata, can

be prepared completely ahead of time, while dishes like Creamy

Mushroom Crêpes and Crab on Globe Artichoke Leaves simply

need to be assembled at the last minute. Dishes such as Sarong

Prawns, Chickpea Patties and Sicilian Rice Balls can be ready and

waiting to be cooked as guests arrive.

Whether you're eating around the kitchen table or off your lap

on the sofa, this chapter will help you create a fabulous night in.

STEAK BÉARNAISE & CHIPS *(SEE PAGE 137)*

183 Cheese Fondue

SERVES: 6–8   PREPARATION TIME: 10 minutes   COOKING TIME: 20 minutes
EQUIPMENT: fondue set

1 tbsp olive oil
2 garlic cloves, flattened
125ml/4fl oz/½ cup white wine
1 tsp Kirsch or cherry liqueur
200g/7oz Emmental cheese, grated

365g/13oz Gruyère cheese, grated
1 tbsp Dijon mustard
1 French baguette, sliced
15 slices of salami (optional)
12–16 cornichons (gherkins), optional

1   Heat the oil in the fondue saucepan over a medium heat. Add the garlic and fry, stirring, for 2 minutes until soft and aromatic but not brown. Add the wine and Kirsch and continue cooking, stirring occasionally, for 2 minutes until well mixed. Remove the garlic and stir in the cheeses and mustard. Reduce the heat to low and cook, stirring occasionally, for 10–15 minutes until the cheese has melted.
2   When the cheese is ready, set the fondue saucepan over the fondue-set flame and serve with the bread and the salami and cornichons, if using.

184 Spinach & Ricotta Eggs

MAKES: 12   PREPARATION TIME: 15 minutes   COOKING TIME: 11 minutes

6 eggs, at room temperature
½ tsp white wine vinegar
180g/6¼oz baby spinach,
   washed and dried

70g/2½oz/⅓ cup ricotta cheese
1 tsp anchovy essence
salt and freshly ground black pepper

1   Bring a saucepan of water to the boil. Add the eggs and vinegar and boil for 6 minutes, then drain and leave to stand until cool enough to handle, then peel.
2   Bring 2 tbsp water to the boil in a large saucepan and add the spinach. Cook for 3–5 minutes until wilted. Transfer to a colander and squeeze out as much excess water as possible. Chop the spinach and put it in a bowl with the ricotta and anchovy essence. Mix well and season with salt and pepper.
3   Just before serving, slice the eggs in half lengthways. Scoop out the yolks and crumble them into a small bowl. Fill each egg half with the spinach and ricotta mixture, sprinkle with the egg yolk and season with pepper. Serve immediately.

PREPARING AHEAD: The eggs can be boiled and peeled up to 1 day in advance and stored, covered, in cold water in the fridge. Do not cut the eggs until ready to use or they will discolour. Remove the yolks right before stuffing the eggs or the whites will discolour.

185 Asparagus & Egg Mimosa

SERVES: 6   PREPARATION TIME: 10 minutes   COOKING TIME: 8 minutes

1 egg, at room temperature
½ tsp white wine vinegar
24 asparagus spears
juice of ½ lemon

1 tsp mustard
3 tbsp olive oil
country bread, sliced, to serve

1   Bring a saucepan of water to the boil. Add the egg and vinegar and boil for 6 minutes, then drain and leave to stand until cool enough to handle, then peel.
2   Bring a large saucepan of water to the boil and cook the asparagus for 1 minute until it starts to turn tender. Drain immediately and transfer to a serving dish.
3   Put the lemon juice and mustard in a small bowl and mix well, then add the olive oil and stir until smooth.
4   Pour the dressing over the asparagus and grate the hard-boiled egg over the top. Serve immediately with the bread.

PREPARING AHEAD: The egg can be boiled and peeled up to 1 day in advance and stored, covered, in water in the fridge.

186 Thick-Cut Chips & Mayonnaise

SERVES: 6   PREPARATION TIME: 5 minutes, plus making the mayonnaise
COOKING TIME: 15 minutes

6 large potatoes, unpeeled
1 litre/35fl oz/4 cups sunflower oil

2 recipe quantities Mayonnaise
(see page 12)

1   Cut the potatoes in half lengthways, then cut each half into 5 or 6 long chips.
2   Heat the oil in a deep saucepan or wok to 190°C/375°F, or until a piece of potato
    floats and sizzles when dropped in. Fry the potatoes for 5–7 minutes until golden,
    working in batches to avoid overcrowding the pan. Remove from the pan, using
    a slotted spoon and drain on kitchen paper. Bring the oil back to temperature
    before each batch. Serve with the mayonnaise.

187 Green Beans & Coconut

SERVES: 6   PREPARATION TIME: 5 minutes   COOKING TIME: 5 minutes

1 tsp olive oil
2 tsp garam masala
1 garlic clove, finely chopped
1 small red chilli, finely chopped
250g/9oz green beans, trimmed

250ml/9fl oz/1 cup coconut milk
1 handful coriander leaves,
    coarsely chopped
6 pitta or naan breads, halved,
    to serve

1   Heat the olive oil in a frying pan over a medium heat. Add the garam masala,
    garlic and chilli and cook for 2 minutes, stirring occasionally, until well mixed
    and aromatic.
2   Add the beans and stir well to coat. Stir in the coconut milk and bring to the boil.
    Boil for 3 minutes until almost all the liquid has evaporated. Sprinkle with the
    coriander leaves and serve immediately with the bread.

188 Indian Eggs

MAKES: 12   PREPARATION TIME: 15 minutes   COOKING TIME: 15 minutes

6 eggs, at room temperature
1/2 tsp white wine vinegar
2 tbsp olive oil
1/2 onion, finely sliced
1 tsp cumin seeds

1 tsp ground coriander
2 tomatoes, finely chopped
2 small red chillies, finely chopped
12 coriander leaves, to serve
salt and freshly ground black pepper

1   Bring a saucepan of water to the boil. Add the eggs and vinegar and boil for
    6 minutes, then drain and leave to stand until cool enough to handle, then peel.
2   Heat the olive oil in a frying pan over a medium heat. Add the onion, cumin and
    ground coriander and fry, stirring occasionally, for 2 minutes until the onion begins
    to soften and turn translucent. Add the tomatoes and cook for a further 2 minutes
    until softened, then stir in the chillies and continue cooking for 4 minutes. Remove
    from the heat.
3   Slice the eggs in half lengthways. Scoop the yolks out into the onion mixture and
    mash, using a fork. Season with salt and pepper. Divide the mixture into each egg
    white half, top with 1 coriander leaf and serve.

PREPARING AHEAD: The eggs can be boiled and peeled up to 1 day in advance and stored,
covered, in cold water in the fridge. Do not cut the eggs until ready to use or they will discolour.

189 Rosemary Focaccia

SERVES: 6–8 **PREPARATION TIME:** 25 minutes, plus 1½ hours rising **COOKING TIME:** 15 minutes

500g/1lb 2oz/4 cups strong white
    bread flour, plus extra for kneading
2 tsp dried active yeast
2 tsp salt
2 tsp caster sugar

100ml/3½fl oz/scant ¼ cup olive oil,
    plus extra for greasing
3 rosemary sprigs, cut into thirds
a pinch coarse salt
1 tbsp balsamic vinegar

1   Sift the flour into a bowl. Add the yeast, salt, sugar and 3 tbsp of the oil and
    250ml/9fl oz/1 cup lukewarm water and mix together for 4–5 minutes until the
    dough comes away from the sides of the bowl. On a lightly floured surface, knead
    the dough for 10 minutes until smooth and elastic. Put the dough in a clean bowl,
    cover with a clean, damp tea towel and leave to rise in a warm place for 1 hour
    until doubled in size.
2   Grease a baking sheet with oil. Knock back the dough and knead on a lightly
    floured surface for a further 5 minutes until smooth. Roll the dough into a 2cm/
    ¾in-thick rectangle and put it on the baking sheet. Make a series of symmetrical
    indentations over the surface, using your fingertips. Stick the rosemary springs into
    the top and sprinkle with the salt. Leave to rest for a further 30 minutes to allow
    the focaccia to develop the air it needs before baking. Preheat the oven to
    190°C/375°F/Gas 5.
3   Put the focaccia in the oven and carefully close the door so as not to let all the air
    escape. Bake for 15 minutes until golden. Meanwhile, put the remaining oil and
    balsamic vinegar in a small bowl, mix well and set aside.
4   Cut the focaccia into strips and serve with the balsamic mixture for dipping.

190 Flatbread Stuffed with Halloumi

MAKES: 8 **PREPARATION TIME:** 20 minutes, plus 2 hours rising **COOKING TIME:** 15 minutes

1 tsp dried active yeast
550g/1lb 4oz/4½ cups plain flour,
   plus extra for kneading and rolling
   the dough

2 tbsp caster sugar
200g/7oz halloumi cheese, sliced
4½ tsp olive oil
coarse salt

1 Put the yeast and 125ml/4fl oz/½ cup lukewarm water in a bowl and stir until the yeast has dissolved. Add 100g/3oz/scant 1 cup of the flour and mix to form a paste. Leave the starter to stand at room temperature for 1½ hours.
2 Mix the sugar and 185ml/6fl oz/¾ cup lukewarm water into the starter. Add the remaining flour and mix until the dough comes away from the sides of the bowl. Knead on a lightly floured surface for 10 minutes until smooth and elastic. Cover with a clean damp tea towel and leave to rise at room temperature for 30 minutes.
3 Preheat the oven to 180°C/350°F/Gas 4. Divide the dough into 8 pieces of equal size and roll each one into an oval, about 5mm/¼in thick. Put the flatbreads on a baking sheet and bake for 10 minutes.
4 Remove the breads from the oven and split each one along one side. Stuff each bread with about 25g/1oz of the halloumi. Put the breads flat on the baking sheet, drizzle with the oil and sprinkle with salt. Return to the oven and bake for a further 3–4 minutes until the halloumi has warmed through. Remove from the oven, slice each flatbread in half and serve immediately.

191 Tomato & Ginger Jam with Goat's Cheese

SERVES: 6–8 **PREPARATION TIME:** 5 minutes **COOKING TIMES:** 15 minutes

400g/14oz tinned peeled and
   chopped tomatoes
55g/2oz/¼ cup crystallized stem
   ginger, coarsely chopped
1 tsp salt

180g/6¼oz/heaped ¾ cup caster
   sugar
250g/9oz soft goat's cheese
24 cheese biscuits, to serve

1 Put the tomatoes, ginger, salt and sugar in a large saucepan and heat over a low heat, stirring occasionally, for 5 minutes until the sugar has dissolved.
2 Increase the heat to high and bring the mixture to a boil. Boil for 10 minutes, stirring occasionally to ensure the jam does not burn. The jam is ready when most of the liquid has evaporated. Serve with the goat's cheese and biscuits.

PREPARING AHEAD: The jam can be made up to 5 days in advance and stored in an airtight container in the fridge.

192 Bruschetta with Red & Yellow Cherry Tomatoes

MAKES: 12 **PREPARATION TIME:** 15 minutes, plus 1–2 hours marinating

12 red cherry tomatoes, quartered
12 yellow cherry tomatoes, quartered
1 tbsp olive oil
12 slices of ciabatta

1 small garlic clove, peeled
1 handful marjoram or basil leaves,
   chopped
salt and freshly ground black pepper

1 Put the tomatoes and oil in a bowl, season with salt and pepper and mix well. Cover and leave to marinate at room temperature for 1–2 hours.
2 Rub the slices of ciabatta with the garlic clove. Heat a ridged griddle pan over a high heat for 5 minutes until smoking hot, then cook the bread for 2–3 minutes on each side until toasted and marked.
3 Spoon the tomato mixture evenly onto the bruschetta, sprinkle with the marjoram and serve.

193 Creamy Mushroom Crêpes

MAKES: 12   **PREPARATION TIME:** 20 minutes, plus 1 hour resting
COOKING TIME: 1 hour

250ml/9fl oz/1 cup milk
15g/½oz unsalted butter
150g/5½oz/scant 1¼ cups plain flour
a pinch salt
1 egg, beaten
4 tsp olive oil

200g/7oz button mushrooms,
  coarsely chopped
4 tbsp white wine
125ml/4fl oz/½ cup double cream
55g/2oz ham, thinly sliced
freshly ground black pepper

1 Put the milk and butter in a saucepan and heat over a medium heat for
   2–3 minutes until the butter has melted.
2 Sift the flour and salt into a bowl. Stir in the egg and 2 tbsp of the milk mixture,
   then add the remaining milk and stir until smooth. Cover with a clean tea towel
   and leave to stand at room temperature for 1 hour.
3 Heat 1 tbsp of the oil in a frying pan over a medium heat. Add the mushrooms
   and cook, stirring occasionally, for 5 minutes until soft. Stir in the wine and cook
   for 3 minutes until the liquid has almost completely evaporated. Add the cream
   and ham and cook for a further 2–3 minutes until thick and bubbling. Season
   to taste with salt and pepper.
4 Heat the remaining oil in a 15cm/6in frying pan over a low heat. Remove the pan
   from the heat, add 1 tbsp of the batter and tilt the pan from side to side until the
   base is evenly covered. Return to the heat and cook for 1–2 minutes on each side
   until the crêpe begins to brown. Transfer to a plate and repeat with the remaining
   batter, adding more oil to the pan as needed.
5 Put 1 tbsp of the mushroom mixture slightly off centre on 1 crêpe. Fold the crêpe
   in half and then in half again to form a small triangle, then secure with a cocktail
   stick. Repeat with the remaining crêpes and filling, then serve.

194 Sweet-Glazed Carrots

SERVES: 6   **PREPARATION TIME:** 5 minutes   **COOKING TIME:** 35 minutes

400g/14oz carrots, peeled and cut
  in half lengthways
5 tbsp caster sugar

60g/2¼oz butter
2 tbsp chopped parsley

1 Put the carrots, sugar and 750ml/26fl oz/3 cups water in a saucepan. Bring to the
   boil, then reduce the heat to medium and simmer for 10 minutes until the carrots
   start to soften.
2 Add the butter and cook for a further 20 minutes until the water has evaporated
   and the carrots are glazed and tender. Sprinkle with the parsley and serve hot.

195 Asparagus & Mangetout with Garlic

SERVES: 6–8   **PREPARATION TIME:** 5 minutes   **COOKING TIME:** 5 minutes

250g/9oz asparagus, cut into
  6cm/2½in pieces
250g/9oz mangetout

3 tbsp olive oil
3 garlic cloves, flattened
salt

1 Bring a saucepan of water to the boil. Add the asparagus and mangetout and cook
   for 1 minute. Drain immediately and transfer to a bowl.
2 Heat the oil in a frying pan over a medium heat. Add the garlic, and cook, stirring,
   for 20 seconds until warmed, then pour over the vegetables. Mix well, season with
   salt and serve warm.

96 Iman Biyaldi

MAKES: 16 **PREPARATION TIME:** 15 minutes, plus 30 minutes resting **COOKING TIME:** 40 minutes

2 small aubergines, sliced lengthways
  into 8 pieces each
1 tbsp salt
4 tsp olive oil, plus extra as needed
½ onion, finely sliced
1 garlic clove, flattened

¼ tsp sweet paprika
¼ tsp allspice
400g/14oz tinned peeled
  and chopped tomatoes
4 tsp tomato purée
2 tbsp chopped parsley

1 Put the aubergines in a colander, sprinkle with the salt and leave to rest in the sink
   for 30 minutes. Rinse under cold water and then pat dry with kitchen paper. Heat
   1 tbsp of the oil in a frying pan over a high heat. Working in batches, fry the
   aubergine for 2–3 minutes on each side until brown, then drain on kitchen paper.
2 Add the remaining 1 tsp oil to the pan. Add the onion and fry, stirring occasionally,
   for 4–5 minutes until soft. Add the garlic and fry for a further 2 minutes. Stir in the
   paprika, allspice, tomatoes and tomato purée and cook for 6 minutes until
   thickened. Remove from the heat and leave to cool.
3 Spread the onion and tomato mixture over each aubergine strip. Roll and secure
   with a cocktail stick. Sprinkle with the parsley and serve.

PREPARING AHEAD: The aubergines and filling can be made to the end of step 2 up to 8 hours
 in advance and stored in separate airtight containers in the fridge until ready to assemble. Leave
 to stand at room temperature for 20 minutes before assembling and serving.

197 Potato Pie

SERVES: 6   PREPARATION TIME: 20 minutes   COOKING TIME: 1 hour 10 minutes
EQUIPMENT: small funnel

plain flour, for rolling the pastry
500g/1lb 2oz ready-to-roll puff pastry
1 egg
125ml/4fl oz/½ cup double cream,
   plus extra as needed

1 garlic clove, finely chopped
350g/12½oz potatoes, peeled and
   cut into 2mm/¹⁄₁₆in slices
1 egg yolk beaten with 1 tbsp milk
salt and freshly ground black pepper

1. Preheat the oven to 180°C/350°F/Gas 4. On a lightly floured surface, roll out the pastry to 3mm/⅛in thick. Put a 25cm/10in round plate on the pastry and use it as a guide to cut a circle out of the pastry. Put the pastry circle on a lightly floured baking sheet. Gather the trimmings and roll them into a 23cm/9in square and set aside.
2. Put the egg, cream and garlic in a mixing bowl and beat well. Season with salt and pepper and set aside.
3. Starting in the centre of the pastry circle, arrange the potatoes in concentric rings, making a spiral pattern and leaving a 4cm/1½in border around the edge of the pastry. Make 4 evenly spaced incisions in the border and brush around the edge with the egg yolk mixture, then fold the border over the potatoes. Carefully but firmly place the square of pastry over the top and press down the edges to seal.
4. Using a small, sharp knife, make a small hole in the centre of the pie, large enough to fit the end of the funnel. Put the funnel in the hole and slowly pour the cream mixture into the pie.
5. Bake for 30 minutes. If any cream leaks from the bottom during baking, remove the pie from the oven and brush some more of the egg yolk mixture onto the leaking area. If necessary, pour more cream into the pie, then return it to the oven.
6. Reduce the oven temperature to 150°C/300°F/Gas 2 and bake for a further 30–40 minutes. Remove from the oven and leave to cool and set for 15 minutes. Serve hot or cold.

198 Roast Pepper & Pesto Mozzarella Skewers

MAKES: 16   PREPARATION TIME: 20 minutes, plus 30 minutes marinating and making the pesto
COOKING TIME: 30 minutes   EQUIPMENT: 16 x 10cm/4in skewers

16 bocconcini (mozzarella balls),
   3cm/1¼in round
½ recipe quantity Pesto (see page 11)
2 red peppers

16 pitted black olives
1 small bunch basil leaves,
   coarsely chopped

1. Preheat the oven to 180°C/350°F/Gas 4. Put the mozzarella and pesto in a bowl, mix gently to coat, then chill, covered, in the fridge for 30 minutes.
2. Meanwhile, put the whole peppers in a baking dish and bake for 25–30 minutes until the skins are wrinkled and the peppers are soft. Leave to cool for a few minutes and, when cool enough to handle, remove the skin and cut the peppers in half. Remove the stalks and seeds and slice each of the peppers into 8 thin strips, about 10cm/4in long.
3. Fold 1 pepper strip into thirds and thread it onto a skewer to form an 's' shape. Add 1 olive and 1 mozzarella ball. Repeat with the remaining skewers. Sprinkle the skewers with the basil and serve.

99 Sicilian Rice Balls

MAKES: 18 **PREPARATION TIME:** 10 minutes **COOKING TIME:** 55 minutes

1 litre/35fl oz/4 cups vegetable stock
1 tbsp olive oil
15g/½oz butter
1 onion, finely chopped
1 garlic clove, finely chopped

200g/7oz/scant 1 cup arborio rice
100g/3½oz/heaped ¾ cup plain flour
1l/35fl oz/4 cups sunflower oil
salt and freshly ground black pepper

1 Put the stock in a saucepan and bring to the boil, then turn the heat off. Meanwhile, heat the olive oil and butter in a frying pan over a medium heat until the butter has melted. Add the onion and fry stirring occasionally, until soft. Add the garlic and fry for a further 1 minute, then stir in the rice.
2 Cook the rice, stirring continuously, for 2–3 minutes until it begins to turn translucent, then add 2–3 ladlefuls of the hot stock and continue stirring. When the stock has been almost completely absorbed by the rice, add another 2–3 ladlefuls of stock. Continue cooking the risotto in this way over a medium heat, stirring continuously, for 25 minutes, or until the rice is soft and has absorbed the stock. The rice should have a slightly chewy bite. If more liquid is required after all the stock is absorbed, use boiled water. Take care not to overcook the risotto or it will be soggy and porridge-like. Season with salt and pepper and leave to cool.
3 Roll the cooled risotto into 18 balls of equal size and roll in the flour to coat.
4 Heat the sunflower oil in a deep saucepan or wok to 180°C/350°F. Carefully add the rice balls, working in batches to avoid overcrowding the pan, and fry for 2–3 minutes until golden. Remove, using a slotted spoon, and drain on kitchen paper. Serve immediately.

200 Herbed Lentil Patties

MAKES: 18 **PREPARATION TIME:** 25 minutes **COOKING TIME:** 40 minutes

100g/3½oz/heaped ½ cup green
  lentils
1 red chilli
1 shallot
2 tbsp olive oil

a few coriander leaves
100g/3½oz/heaped ¾ cup plain flour
2 tbsp sunflower oil
salt
mango chutney, to serve

1 Put the lentils, chilli, shallot, olive oil and coriander leaves in a food processor and process for 1 minute until well combined. Transfer to a saucepan and cover with water. Bring to the boil and cook, stirring occasionally, for 30 minutes until the lentils are tender. Add more water during cooking if the mixture becomes too dry.
2 Drain the lentils and leave to cool for a few minutes. When cool enough to handle, shape the mixture into 18 x 3cm/1¼in patties, about 1cm/½in thick.
3 Roll the patties in the flour to coat and set aside until ready to cook. Heat 1 tbsp of the sunflower oil in a frying pan over a medium-high heat. Working in batches, fry the patties for 30 seconds–1 minute on each side until brown. Remove, using a slotted spoon, season with salt and serve with mango chutney.

PREPARING AHEAD: These can be made to the end of step 2 up to 4 hours in advance, covered and stored in the fridge.

201 Chickpea Patties

MAKES: 18 **PREPARATION TIME:** 15 minutes, plus making the salsa
COOKING TIME: 15 minutes

450g/1lb tinned chickpeas, drained
   and rinsed
1 garlic clove, coarsely chopped
1 handful coriander leaves
4–5 tbsp olive oil

1 egg, beaten
50g/1³⁄₄oz/¹⁄₂ cup breadcrumbs
salt and freshly ground black pepper
1 recipe quantity Salsa Verde
   (see page 11)

1 Put the chickpeas, garlic, coriander leaves and 2 tbsp of the oil in a food processor and process for 2–3 minutes until smooth. Shape the mixture into 18 small balls of equal size and gently flatten them. Dip each patty in the egg and coat in the breadcrumbs.
2 Heat 1 tbsp of the oil in a frying pan over a high heat. Working in batches, fry the patties for 2 minutes on each side until golden and heated through. Remove from the oil, using a slotted spoon, and transfer to a serving plate. Repeat with the remaining patties, adding more oil to the pan as needed. Serve hot with the salsa.

202 Roast Tikka Potatoes

SERVES: 6–8 **PREPARATION TIME:** 10 minutes **COOKING TIME:** 1 hour

4 potatoes, peeled and quartered
   lengthways
1 tbsp olive oil

¹⁄₂ tsp garam masala
salt

1 Preheat the oven to 180°C/350°F/Gas 4. Put the potatoes in a baking dish and drizzle with the olive oil. Sprinkle over the garam masala and salt and toss to coat.
2 Bake for 45 minutes–1 hour, or until the potatoes are tender. Serve immediately.

203 Potato Harra Fried with Chickpeas & Spices

SERVES: 6 **PREPARATION TIME:** 10 minutes, plus making the parathas
COOKING TIME: 20 minutes

6 potatoes, peeled and halved
   lengthways
2 tbsp olive oil
2 garlic cloves, peeled and crushed
1 tsp turmeric
1 tsp black mustard seeds
1 tsp cayenne pepper

seeds from 12 cardamom pods
2 tbsp pine nuts
400g/14oz tinned chickpeas,
   drained and rinsed
1 recipe quantity Spinach & Paneer
   Parathas (see page 50), to serve

1 Put the potatoes in a large saucepan, cover with water and bring to the boil. Boil for 10 minutes, or until tender, then drain.
2 Heat the oil in a frying pan over a medium heat. Add the garlic, turmeric, mustard seeds, cayenne pepper, cardamom seeds and pine nuts and cook, stirring continuously, for 1 minute until aromatic.
3 Add the chickpeas and cook, stirring occasionally, for a further 2 minutes. Add the boiled potatoes and cook, stirring, for 3 minutes until warmed through and coated in the spices. Serve with the parathas.

204 Patatas Bravas

SERVES: 6–8 **PREPARATION TIME:** 15 minutes **COOKING TIME:** 35 minutes

1 tbsp olive oil
1 small onion, finely chopped
1 garlic clove, finely chopped
6 potatoes, quartered lengthways

1 tsp hot paprika
1 small handful parsley,
   finely chopped

1 Heat the oil in a frying pan over a medium heat. Add the onion and cook, stirring occasionally, for 5 minutes until soft. Add the garlic and cook for a further 1 minute, then add the potatoes and stir until completely coated in the onion and garlic.
2 Cover the potatoes with 500ml/17fl oz/2 cups water and bring to the boil. Reduce the heat to medium-low and simmer for 20 minutes until the potatoes are cooked, then increase the heat and bring to a boil. Boil for 5 minutes until the liquid has almost completely evaporated.
3 Add the paprika and stir until the potatoes are evenly coated. Sprinkle with the parsley and serve.

205 Caponata

SERVES: 6   **PREPARATION TIME:** 20 minutes, plus overnight resting and making the focaccia
COOKING: 50 minutes

1 tbsp olive oil
1 onion, finely sliced
2 celery sticks, diced
1 aubergine, cut into cubes
2 garlic cloves, flattened
280g/10oz tomatoes, chopped

2 tbsp tomato purée
250ml/9fl oz/1 cup red wine
2 tbsp balsamic vinegar
1 tsp salt
1 recipe quantity Rosemary Focaccia
   (see page 118), to serve

1   Heat the oil in a non-aluminium saucepan with a lid. Add the onions, cover with
    the lid and cook, stirring occasionally, for 7 minutes until soft. Add the celery and
    cook for a further 2 minutes, then add the aubergine, garlic, tomatoes and tomato
    purée and cook, stirring occasionally, for 2 minutes.
2   Stir in the wine, scraping all the bits off the base of the pan. Stir in the balsamic
    vinegar and salt, then reduce the heat to low and cook for 40 minutes. Remove
    from the heat and leave to cool completely. Chill, covered, in the fridge overnight.
    Serve warmed or at room temperature with the focaccia.

206 Whitebait & Salsa Verde

SERVES: 12 **PREPARATION TIME:** 5 minutes, plus making the salsa **COOKING TIME:** 15 minutes

450g/1lb whole whitebait
150g/5½oz/scant 1¼ cups plain flour
2 tsp paprika or cayenne pepper

1l/35fl oz/4 cups sunflower oil
1 recipe quantity Salsa Verde
   (see page 11)

1   Put the whitebait in a colander and rinse under cold running water for 1 minute, then pat dry with a clean tea towel. Put the flour and cayenne pepper in a bowl and mix well. Roll the whitebait in the flour to coat.
2   Heat the oil in a deep saucepan or wok to 180°C/350°F. Carefully drop 10–14 pieces of the whitebait into the oil, working in batches to avoid overcrowding the pan. Fry for 1–2 minutes until brown and crispy. Remove, using a slotted spoon, and drain on kitchen paper. Repeat with the remaining fish, bringing the oil back to temperature before each batch. Serve immediately with the salsa verde.

207 Sardine, Sweet Red Pepper & Lemon Toasts

MAKES: 16 **PREPARATION TIME:** 15 minutes **COOKING TIME:** 5 minutes

120g/4¼oz tinned sardines in oil,
   drained
4 slices of bread
90g/3oz/⅓ cup cream cheese
1 large handful parsley,
   finely chopped

juice of 1 lemon
8 mini sweet red peppers,
   finely sliced
freshly ground black pepper

1   Cut each sardine in half along the backbone, using a sharp knife. Remove the backbone and cut each fillet in half.
2   Lightly toast the bread and cut each slice into quarters.
3   Put the cream cheese, parsley and lemon juice in a food processor and process for 30 seconds until smooth. Spread 1 tsp of the mixture on each toast, add 1 piece of sardine and 2–3 slices of the sweet pepper, season with pepper and serve.

208 Smoked Mackerel Pâté

SERVES: 8 **PREPARATION TIME:** 5 minutes

150g/5½oz smoked mackerel fillets,
   skin removed
200g/7oz/heaped ¾ cup
   crème fraîche

juice of 1 lemon
freshly ground black pepper
6 slices of warm bread or toast,
   quartered, to serve

1   Put the mackerel, crème fraîche and lemon juice in a food processor and process for 2–3 minutes until the mixture forms a coarse paste.
2   Season with pepper and serve with the bread or toast.

PREPARING AHEAD: This can be made up to 1 day in advance and stored in an airtight container in the fridge.

209 Cod Empanadas

MAKES: 24 **PREPARATION TIME:** 25 minutes **COOKING TIME:** 35 minutes
EQUIPMENT: 9cm/3½in plain round pastry cutter

2 tbsp olive oil
1 onion, finely chopped
400g/14oz tinned chopped tomatoes
200g/7oz tinned haricot or canellini
    beans, drained and rinsed

175g/6oz skinless cod fillet
plain flour, for rolling the pastry
500g/1lb 2oz ready-to-roll puff pastry
1 egg yolk, beaten with 1 tbsp milk
salt and freshly ground black pepper

1   Preheat the oven to 180°C/350°F/Gas 4. Heat 1 tbsp of the oil in a frying pan
    over a medium-low heat. Add the onion, cover and cook, stirring occasionally,
    for 5 minutes until translucent.
2   Add the tomatoes and cook for 5 minutes until the liquid has reduced by half. Stir
    in the beans, remove from the heat, season with salt and pepper and leave to cool.
3   Rub the remaining 1 tbsp of oil over the cod fillet, put in a roasting tin and bake for
    10 minutes. Remove from the oven and set aside to cool for 10–15 minutes. Break
    the cod into flakes, transfer to a bowl and season with salt.
4   On a lightly floured surface, roll out the pastry into a 46cm/18in square. Cut out
    24 circles, using the pastry cutter. Put 1½ tsp of the flaked cod slightly off centre
    on each circle and top with 1 tbsp of the bean mixture. Fold the pastry in half, press
    the edges together and press with a fork to seal.
5   Put the empanadas on a baking sheet and brush with the egg yolk mixture. Bake
    for 15 minutes until puffed and golden, then serve.

210 Mackerel Escabesche

SERVES: 6–8 **PREPARATION TIME:** 15 minutes, plus 40 minutes cooling
COOKING TIME: 10 minutes

2 tsp white wine vinegar
160ml/5¼fl oz/⅔ cup white wine
juice and zest of 1 orange
1 tsp caster sugar
1 large garlic clove, thinly sliced
¼ tsp coriander seeds
2 bay leaves
½ onion, thinly sliced
1 carrot, thinly sliced

½ fennel bulb, thinly sliced
100ml/3½fl oz/⅓ cup plus 2 tbsp
    olive oil
2 mackerel fillets
1 small handful parsley,
    coarsely chopped
1 small handful dill, coarsely chopped
salt and freshly ground black pepper
bread, to serve

1   Put the vinegar, wine, orange juice, sugar, garlic, coriander and bay leaves
    in a saucepan and bring to the boil. Add the onion, carrot and fennel and boil
    for a further 5 minutes until the vegetables begin to soften. Remove from the heat
    and leave to cool for 10 minutes.
2   Heat 2 tbsp of the oil in a frying pan. Add the mackerel fillets, skin-side down,
    and fry for 2 minutes until the skin begins to turn grey. Remove from the heat.
3   Transfer the vegetables to a serving dish, using a slotted spoon. Leave the liquid
    in the saucepan. Put the mackerel skin-side down on top of the vegetables.
4   Bring the vegetable liquid to the boil and spoon half of the liquid over the
    mackerel. Carefully turn the fillets over and drizzle with the remaining oil and
    cooking liquid. Turn again so that the mackerel is skin-side down. Leave to cool
    for 30 minutes.
5   Sprinkle over the parsley and dill and season with salt and pepper. Serve
    with bread.

PREPARING AHEAD: This can be made to the end of step 4 up to 1 day in advance, covered
and stored in the fridge. Leave to stand at room temperature for 20 minutes before serving.

11 Crab on Globe Artichoke Leaves

MAKES: 18   **PREPARATION TIME:** 10 minutes   **COOKING TIME:** 35 minutes

1 globe artichoke
100g/3½oz white crab meat

juice of 1 lime, plus wedges to serve
freshly ground black pepper

1   Bring a large saucepan of water to the boil. Add the artichoke and boil for 25–30 minutes until cooked and a leaf can be pulled off easily. Transfer the artichoke to a bowl of cold water, leave to stand for 5 minutes, then drain.
2   Remove 18 regular-shaped large leaves from the artichoke and put them on a serving plate, flesh-side up.
3   Put the crab meat and lime juice in a bowl, mix well and season with pepper. Put 1 tsp of the crab mixture on the end of each artichoke leaf and serve with the lime wedges.

212 Squid Stuffed with Pine Nut & Raisin Rice

MAKES: 12 **PREPARATION TIME:** 20 minutes, plus 30 minutes soaking
COOKING TIME: 35 minutes

70g/2¹/₂oz/heaped ¹/₂ cup raisins
90g/3¹/₄oz/scant ¹/₂ cup basmati rice
30g/1oz/scant ¹/₄ cup pine nuts
2 tbsp olive oil
¹/₂ onion, finely chopped
1 tsp cinnamon

1 large handful parsley,
  finely chopped
juice of ¹/₂ lemon, plus ¹/₂ lemon,
  cut into wedges
12 small squid, cleaned, dried
  and tentacles discarded

1   Put the raisins and 125ml/4fl oz/¹/₂ cup boiling water in a heatproof bowl and leave
    to soak for 30 minutes. Bring a large saucepan of water to the boil. Add the rice and
    cook for 10–12 minutes until tender. Drain and set aside.
2   Meanwhile, put the pine nuts in a dry frying pan and heat over a medium heat,
    stirring occasionally, for 2–3 minutes until beginning to brown, then set aside.
3   Heat 1 tbsp of the oil in a frying pan over a medium heat. Add the onion and fry,
    stirring occasionally, for 5 minutes until soft. Add the raisins and soaking liquid,
    pine nuts and cinnamon and cook for a further 5 minutes until most of the liquid
    evaporates. Remove from the heat and stir in the rice, parsley and lemon juice.
4   Fill each squid with 2 tbsp of the rice mixture. Thread a cocktail stick through the
    open end of the squid to close.
5   Heat the remaining 1 tbsp of the oil in a frying pan and fry the squid for 2 minutes
    on each side until cooked through, working in batches to avoid overcrowding the
    pan. Squeeze the lemon wedges over the squid and serve immediately.

PREPARING AHEAD: These can be made to the end of step 3 up to 8 hours in advance, covered
and stored in the fridge. Leave at room temperature for 20 minutes before cooking.

213 Sarong Prawns

MAKES: 16   **PREPARATION TIME:** 20 minutes, plus making the dip   **COOKING TIME:** 10 minutes

75g/2³/₄oz/heaped ¹/₂ cup plain flour
¹/₂ tsp cayenne pepper
¹/₂ tsp ground coriander
2 eggs
¹/₄ tsp freshly ground black pepper
60g/2¹/₄oz vermicelli or very thin
  rice noodles

16 peeled uncooked king prawns,
  about 225g/8oz
1l/35fl oz/4 cups sunflower oil
1 recipe quantity Sweet Chilli Dip
  (see page 12), to serve

1   Sift the flour, cayenne pepper and coriander into a mixing bowl. Add the eggs and pepper and stir until smooth.
2   Put the noodles in a heatproof bowl, cover with boiling water and leave to soak for 3 minutes until soft, then drain. Separate the noodles into 16 equal portions and space them out in straight lines on a clean tea towel.
3   Heat the oil in a deep saucepan or wok to 180°C/350°F. Dip each prawn into the batter and then roll it as tightly as possible in a portion of the noodles. Repeat with the remaining prawns.
4   Working in batches to avoid overcrowding the pan, carefully drop 4 of the noodle-wrapped prawns into the oil and fry for 2 minutes until golden and crispy. Remove from the oil, using a slotted spoon, and drain on kitchen paper. Serve with the dip.

214 Tapenade Squid Parcels

MAKES: 6   **PREPARATION TIME:** 15 minutes   **COOKING TIME:** 5 minutes

6 small squid, cleaned, dried and
  tentacles discarded
150g/5¹/₂oz/scant 1¹/₄ cups plain flour
1 egg, beaten
50g/1³/₄oz/¹/₂ cup breadcrumbs
1l/35fl oz/4 cups sunflower oil

TAPENADE
2 tbsp capers
90g/3¹/₄oz/³/₄ cup pitted black olives
8 tinned anchovy fillets in oil, drained
1 tbsp olive oil
juice of ¹/₂ lemon

1   To make the tapenade, put the capers, olives, anchovies, oil and lemon juice in a food processor and process for 1–2 minutes until the mixture forms a thick paste. Alternatively, grind all the ingredients together using a pestle and mortar.
2   Fill the squid with the tapenade and thread a cocktail stick through the open end to close.
3   Roll each squid in the flour, dip it in the egg and then roll it in the breadcrumbs to coat.
4   Heat the oil in a deep saucepan or wok to 180°C/ 350°F. Working in batches to avoid overcrowding the pan, carefully drop a few of the squid into the oil and fry for 30 seconds–1 minute until crispy and golden. Remove, using a slotted spoon, and serve immediately.

PREPARING AHEAD: The tapenade can be made up to 1 day in advance and stored in an airtight container in the fridge. The squid can be made to the end of step 2 up to 8 hours in advance, covered and stored in the fridge. Leave at room temperature for 20 minutes before cooking.

215 Chicken Liver Pâté

SERVES: 8 **PREPARATION TIME:** 10 minutes **COOKING TIME:** 7 minutes

125g/4½oz butter
2 garlic cloves, finely chopped
250g/9oz chicken livers, trimmed
  and halved

3 tbsp sherry, brandy or port
salt and freshly ground black pepper
1 baguette, sliced, to serve

1   Heat half of the butter in a frying pan over a low heat. Add the garlic and cook
    for 1–2 minutes until softened but not browned. Add the chicken livers, increase
    the heat slightly and fry for 5 minutes until grey-brown on the outside but slightly
    pink in the middle. Transfer to a food processor, using a slotted spoon.
2   Heat the same frying pan over a medium heat. Add the sherry and, using
    a wooden spoon, scrape any bits off the base of the pan and stir well. Add the
    liquid to the chicken livers and season with salt and pepper.
3   Melt the remaining butter in a saucepan. Turn the food processor on and add all
    but 2 tbsp of the butter in a slow, steady stream, processing for 2–3 minutes until
    smooth. Transfer the pâté to a serving dish and smooth the surface. Pour the
    remaining 2 tbsp melted butter over the top and leave to cool completely. Cover
    and store in the fridge until ready to serve. Serve with the bread.

PREPARING AHEAD: This can be made up to 3 days in advance and stored in an airtight container
in the fridge.

216 Savoy Cabbage & Chicken Parcels

MAKES: 12 **PREPARATION TIME:** 20 minutes, plus 30 minutes cooling
COOKING TIME: 25 minutes

4 Savoy cabbage leaves
½ tsp olive oil, for brushing
6 slices of pancetta, halved crossways

2 boneless, skinless chicken breasts,
  about 140g/5oz each
salt and freshly ground black pepper

1   Preheat the oven to 180°C/350°F/Gas 4. Bring a large saucepan of water to the boil.
    Cut the stem out of each cabbage leaf in a 'v' shape and discard. Boil the leaves
    for 1 minute, then remove from the water, using a slotted spoon, and drop them
    in a bowl of cold water. Put the leaves between two clean tea towels and pat dry.
2   Put two 23 x 33cm/9 x 13in pieces of foil on a work surface and brush with the oil.
    On one piece of foil, put 2 cabbage leaves with the core ends overlapping slightly,
    then put 6 pancetta halves across the centre. Put 1 of the chicken breasts on the
    pancetta and fold the bottom of the leaves over the filling, then roll up tightly and
    wrap in the foil. Repeat with the other piece of foil to make a second parcel.
3   Poke 6 holes down each side of the parcels, using a skewer, and put them in
    a baking dish. Fill the baking dish with enough water to cover the holes, then bake
    for 20 minutes until cooked through. Remove from the oven, carefully drain the
    water from the dish and leave the parcels to cool for 30 minutes.
4   Remove the foil and put the chicken parcels on a cutting board. Trim away the
    untidy ends and then slice each parcel into 6 pieces of equal size, using a sharp
    knife. Serve immediately.

PREPARING AHEAD: These can be made to the end of step 2 up to 8 hours in advance and stored
in the fridge. Leave at room temperature for 20 minutes before baking.

217   Ginger Chicken, Mushroom & Aubergine Skewers

MAKES: 12   **PREPARATION TIME:** 25 minutes, plus 1 hour resting   **COOKING TIME:** 20 minutes
EQUIPMENT: 12 x 15cm/6in skewers

1 aubergine, cut into 12 equal-sized chunks
1 tbsp salt
4 tbsp sunflower oil, plus extra as needed
3 large open-capped field mushrooms, quartered

1 large boneless, skinless chicken breast, about 200g/7oz, chopped into bite-sized chunks
3cm/1¼in piece root ginger, peeled and finely chopped
30g/1oz/scant ⅓ cup breadcrumbs
1 handful parsley, chopped
2 lemons, quartered, to serve

1   Put the aubergine in a colander and sprinkle with the salt. Put a saucer on top of the aubergine and leave to stand for 1 hour.
2   Squeeze the aubergine to extract as much water as possible. Heat the oil in a frying pan over a medium heat. Add the aubergine and fry, stirring occasionally, for 5 minutes until golden on all sides. Transfer to a plate, using a slotted spoon, and set aside.
3   Add the mushrooms to the oil remaining in the pan and fry for 3–5 minutes until beginning to brown and soften. Transfer to another plate, using a slotted spoon, and set aside.
4   Add the chicken pieces and ginger to the oil remaining in the pan and fry for 8 minutes until cooked through and the juices run clear when pricked with a sharp knife. Transfer to another plate, using a slotted spoon, and set aside.
5   Add an additional 1 tbsp of oil to the pan, if necessary. Stir in the breadcrumbs and fry for 1 minute until beginning to brown. Add the aubergine and continue cooking, stirring continuously, for a further 1–2 minutes until the breadcrumbs are golden and the aubergine is well coated. Remove the pan from the heat.
6   To assemble, spear 1 piece of aubergine onto a skewer, followed by 1 mushroom and 1 piece of chicken. Sprinkle with the parsley and any breadcrumbs left in the pan and serve with the lemon wedges for squeezing.

218   Pollo Sorpresa

MAKES: 12   **PREPARATION TIME:** 25 minutes   **COOKING TIME:** 12 minutes

45g/1½oz butter
1 garlic clove, peeled and quartered
1 small handful parsley leaves
1 boneless, skinless chicken breast, about 185g/6½oz

75g/2½oz/heaped ½ cup plain flour
1 large egg, beaten
100g/3½oz/1 cup breadcrumbs
4 tbsp sunflower oil
salt and freshly ground black pepper

1   Put the butter, garlic and parsley in a food processor and process for 1 minute until the butter is soft.
2   Cut the chicken breast lengthways into 12 slices and, using a rolling pin, flatten each piece. Spread ½ tsp of the garlic butter over each piece of chicken and roll into small parcels.
3   Season the flour with salt and pepper and roll each chicken parcel in it, then dip the chicken in the egg and roll in the breadcrumbs to coat.
4   Heat the oil in a 25cm/10in frying pan over a medium-high heat until hot. Working in batches, add the chicken and fry for 2 minutes on each side until golden. Remove the parcels from the pan, using a slotted spoon, and transfer to a serving plate. Sprinkle with salt, if desired, and serve immediately.

219 Chicken & Guacamole Wraps

MAKES: 12   **PREPARATION TIME:** 15 minutes   **COOKING TIME:** 8 minutes

1 large boneless, skinless chicken
  breast, about 200g/7oz
olive oil, for brushing
2 tortilla wraps, 25cm/10in round
salt and freshly ground black pepper

GUACAMOLE
1 avocado, halved and stoned
85g/3oz cherry tomatoes, quartered
1 tbsp olive oil
juice of ½ lemon

1   To make the guacamole, scoop the avocado flesh into a bowl and mash, using
    a fork. Add the tomatoes, oil and lemon juice. Mix well and set aside.
2   Heat a ridged griddle pan over a high heat. Lightly brush the chicken with oil, then
    cook for 3–4 minutes on each side until cooked through and the juices run clear
    when pricked with a sharp knife. Transfer to a plate and leave to rest for 5 minutes,
    then cut into 10 slices of equal size.
3   Spread half the guacamole onto 1 wrap, then put 5 chicken pieces across the
    bottom half and season with salt and pepper. Fold the left and right sides over
    the filling, then roll up tightly. Repeat with the other wrap. Slice each wrap into
    6 pieces and serve.

PREPARING AHEAD: The guacamole in step 1 can be made up to 2 hours in advance and stored
in an airtight container in the fridge.

220 Chicken Liver, Mushroom & Bacon Kebabs

MAKES: 16   **PREPARATION TIME:** 15 minutes   **COOKING TIME:** 12 minutes
EQUIPMENT 16 x 10cm/4in skewers

200g/7oz chicken livers
8 rindless streaky bacon rashers,
　halved crossways

5 closed-cap white mushrooms,
　each cut into 3–4 slices
1 tbsp olive oil

1　Preheat the oven to 180°C/350°F/Gas 4. Put the chicken livers in a colander and
　wash under cold water. Remove any white or black bits, using a small sharp knife.
　Slice the livers into 3cm/1¼in chunks and roll each piece in a strip of the bacon.
2　Put a mushroom slice on a board and put the chicken liver parcel on top,
　then carefully pierce through the centre with a skewer. Repeat with the
　remaining ingredients.
3　Put the kebabs on a baking sheet and brush the mushroom with the oil.
　Bake for 12 minutes until brown and cooked through, then serve.

221 Griddled Chicken Breast Pittas with Tsatsiki

MAKES: 8   **PREPARATION TIME:** 20 minutes, plus 30 minutes resting
COOKING TIME: 13 minutes

½ cucumber, halved lengthways,
　deseeded and finely chopped
1 small garlic clove, finely chopped
125ml/4fl oz/½ cup natural yogurt
leaves from 3 mint sprigs,
　finely chopped

1 large boneless, skinless chicken
　breast, about 200g/7oz
olive oil, for brushing
8 mini pitta breads
salt and freshly ground black pepper

1　To make the tsatsiki, put the cucumber, garlic, yogurt and mint in a bowl and mix
　thoroughly. Season with salt and pepper and leave to stand for 30 minutes.
2　Meanwhile, preheat the oven to 130°C/250°F/Gas 1 and heat a ridged griddle pan
　over a high heat. Lightly brush the chicken with oil, then cook for 3–4 minutes on
　each side until cooked through and the juices run clear when pricked with a sharp
　knife. Transfer to a plate and leave to rest for 5 minutes, then cut into 8 slices.
3　Put the pitta breads on a baking sheet and warm them in the oven for 5 minutes.
　Split the breads open and fill each one with 1 slice of the chicken and 1 tbsp of the
　tsatsiki, then serve.

222 Pan-Fried Quail

SERVES: 6   **PREPARATION TIME:** 10 minutes   **COOKING TIME:** 15 minutes

2 large quail, about 175g/6oz each
3 tbsp olive oil

¼ tsp salt
freshly ground black pepper

1　Preheat the oven to 180°C/350°F/Gas 4. Cut each quail in half down the backbone,
　using a pair of kitchen scissors, then use a knife to remove the legs and cut the
　breasts in half.
2　Put the quail pieces in a mixing bowl, add 1 tbsp of the oil and toss to coat, then
　season liberally with pepper.
3　Heat the remaining 2 tbsp oil in a frying pan over a medium-high heat for
　2 minutes until smoking. Add the quail, sprinkle with the salt and fry for 3 minutes
　on each side until beginning to brown. Transfer to a baking dish and bake for
　7 minutes until cooked through and the juices run clear when pierced with a sharp
　knife. Serve hot.

223 Spicy Beef Toasts

MAKES: 12   PREPARATION TIME: 10 minutes   COOKING TIME: 10 minutes, plus grilling

1 tsp cumin seeds
1/2 tsp ground nutmeg
1 tsp ground cinnamon
1 tsp ground ginger
1 tsp cayenne pepper
1 tbsp olive oil
1 onion, finely chopped
2 garlic cloves, finely chopped

250g/9oz beef mince
80ml/2 1/2 fl oz/1/3 cup white wine
1 tbsp tomato purée
1 egg
125ml/4fl oz/1/2 cup double cream
1 tbsp finely grated Parmesan cheese
6 slices of toast, halved
freshly ground black pepper

1   In a small bowl, mix together the cumin, nutmeg, cinnamon, ginger and cayenne pepper and set aside.
2   Heat the olive oil in a saucepan over a medium heat. Add the onion and cook, stirring occasionally, for 4 minutes until soft, then add the garlic and cook, stirring, for a further 1 minute until soft. Add the spice mix and stir until combined. Add the mince and cook, stirring, for 5 minutes until brown.
3   Add the wine and, using a wooden spoon, scrape any bits off the base of the pan, add the tomato purée and stir well. Cook for 3 minutes until well combined, then remove from the heat and season with salt and pepper.
4   Preheat the grill to high. Put the egg, cream and Parmesan in a bowl and mix well. Put the toasts on a baking sheet and divide the spicy beef mixture over them. Top each toast with 1 tsp of the egg mixture and grill for 5 minutes until brown and the egg is cooked. Serve immediately.

224 Meat Fondue & Sauces

SERVES: 6   PREPARATION TIME: 15 minutes, plus making the mayonnaise, Béarnaise sauce and guacamole   EQUIPMENT: fondue set and metholated spirits

1 recipe quantity Mayonnaise
   (see page 12)
2 tbsp milk
1 recipe quantity Béarnaise Sauce
   (see page 137)
1 recipe quantity Guacamole
   (see page 134)
750ml/26fl oz/3 cups grapeseed oil
900g/2lb rump steak, cut into
   2.5cm/1in cubes
salt and freshly ground black pepper

TOMATO SALSA
175g/6oz cherry tomatoes
1 garlic clove
1 large red chilli, deseeded
1 tbsp olive oil
1/2 tsp salt
1 tbsp clear honey

1   To make the salsa, put all the ingredients in a food processor and process for 30–45 seconds until well mixed but still coarse. Set aside until needed.
2   Put the mayonnaise in a bowl, add the milk and stir well, then set aside until needed, no longer than 1 hour unrefrigerated.
3   Just before serving, make the Béarnaise sauce and put it in a bowl. Put the guacamole in another bowl and position both bowls and the fondue set where everyone has easy access to it.
4   Put the grapeseed oil in the fondue pot and heat to 160°C/300°F on the hob. Light the fondue burner and transfer the pot of oil to the stand above the burner. Invite your guests to spear and cook their own meat in the hot oil and season it with salt and pepper. Serve with the Béarnaise sauce, salsa, mayonnaise and guacamole for dipping.

PREPARING AHEAD: The salsa in step 1 can be made up to 4 hours in advance and stored in an airtight container in the fridge. The steak can be cut into cubes and tossed in a little olive oil up to 8 hours in advance and stored in an airtight container in the fridge.

225 Steak Béarnaise & Chips

MAKES: 24 **PREPARATION TIME:** 5 minutes **COOKING TIME:** 35 minutes

2 large potatoes, cut into
   24 x 5mm/¼in slices
1l/35fl oz/4 cups sunflower oil
300g/10½oz rump steak

BÉARNAISE SAUCE
125ml/4fl oz/½ cup white
   wine vinegar
3 shallots, finely chopped
1 thyme sprig
1 bay leaf
3 egg yolks
140g/5oz butter, cut into 4 pieces
1 lemon wedge
leaves from 2 tarragon sprigs

1 Pat the potatoes dry with a clean tea towel. Heat the oil in a large deep saucepan or wok to 200°C/400°F. Add the potatoes and cook for 5–6 minutes until golden brown and cooked through. Work in batches to avoid overcrowding the pan. Remove from the pan, using a slotted spoon, and drain on kitchen paper.
2 Heat ½ tsp of the oil in a frying pan over a high heat until smoking hot. Add the steak and cook for 2 minutes on each side until brown, then leave to rest.
3 To make the Béarnaise sauce, put the vinegar, shallots, thyme and bay leaf in a saucepan. Bring to the boil and boil for 2 minutes, or until the mixture has reduced to 2 tbsp. Remove from the heat and strain the liquid through a sieve into a bowl that will sit comfortably on top of a saucepan. Press the mixture with a wooden spoon to extract as much flavour as possible.
4 Put the bowl over a saucepan of simmering water over a medium heat, but do not allow the bottom of the bowl to touch the water. Stir in the egg yolks and 1 piece of the butter. Whisk until the butter has melted. Repeat with the remaining pieces of butter, whisking until smooth. Squeeze in a few drops of lemon juice, add the tarragon and stir. Turn the heat off and stir for a further 2–3 minutes until thick.
5 Cut the steak into thin strips and put 1–2 strips on each potato slice. Top with 1 tsp of the Béarnaise sauce and serve immediately.

226 Lamb Chops with Babaganoush

MAKES: 12 **PREPARATION TIME:** 5 minutes, plus making the babaganoush
COOKING TIME: 8 minutes

12 French-trimmed lamb mini-chops
1 garlic clove
2 tbsp olive oil, for brushing

leaves from 2 thyme sprigs
1 recipe quantity Babaganoush
   (see page 44)

1 Preheat the grill to high. Rub each side of the lamb chops with the garlic clove, brush with the oil and sprinkle over the thyme leaves.
2 Put a grill rack over a baking tray and put the lamb on top of it. Grill for 3–4 minutes on each side until brown on the outside but still slightly pink in the centre. Remove from the heat and leave to rest for 5 minutes. Serve with the babaganoush.

227 Lamb Koftas

MAKES: 24   **PREPARATION TIME:** 10 minutes, plus 1 hour chilling and making the dip
COOKING TIME: 35 minutes

1 tbsp olive oil
½ onion, finely chopped
1 tsp cumin seeds
½ tsp cayenne pepper
250g/9oz lamb mince
4 tbsp natural yogurt

leaves from 1 mint sprig, chopped,
  plus 24 leaves to serve
2 tbsp sunflower oil
1 recipe quantity Mint & Yogurt Dip
  (see page 11)
salt and freshly ground black pepper

1   Heat the olive oil in a frying pan over a medium heat. Add the onion, cumin
   seeds and cayenne pepper and fry, stirring occasionally, for 5 minutes until the
   onion has softened.
2   Put the mince, onion mixture, yogurt and chopped mint in a bowl. Season with
   salt and pepper, mix well and cover with cling film. Chill for 1 hour.
3   Shape the mixture into 24 small balls of equal size.
4   Heat the sunflower oil in a frying pan over a medium heat. Add the koftas and
   fry, turning occasionally, for 10 minutes until brown all over. Work in batches
   to avoid overcrowding the pan. Top each kofta with 1 tsp of the dip and serve
   with the mint leaves.

PREPARING AHEAD: These can be made to the end of step 3 up to 1 day in advance and stored
in an airtight container in the fridge. Leave at room temperature for 20 minutes before cooking.

228 Veal & Spanish Ham Serranitos

MAKES: 16   **PREPARATION TIME:** 20 minutes, plus 10 minutes resting
COOKING TIME: 5–10 minutes

250g/9oz veal escalopes
3 tbsp olive oil, plus extra as needed
100g/3½oz Serrano ham,
   very thinly sliced

100g/3½oz Manchego cheese,
   very thinly sliced
1 baguette, cut into 32 very thin slices
16 Padrón peppers (optional)

1   Wrap the veal in a piece of cling film and beat it flat, using a wooden spoon or rolling pin. Heat 1 tsp of the oil in a frying pan over a high heat until it begins to smoke. Add the veal and cook for 30 seconds on each side. Remove from the heat and leave to rest in the pan for 10 minutes.
2   Cut the veal and the ham slices into 16 pieces equal in size to the baguette slices. Cut the Manchego slices into 32 pieces equal in size to the baguette slices.
3   Put 1 slice of the cheese on each of 16 baguette slices. Top with 1 piece of the ham, then 1 piece of the veal and another slice of the cheese. Cover with the remaining baguette slices.
4   Heat 1 tbsp of the oil in a frying pan. Add the peppers, if using, and cook, stirring occasionally, for 3 minutes until brown and blistered on all sides, then set aside.
5   Heat 1 tbsp of the oil in a frying pan. Working in batches, carefully fry the sandwiches for 1–2 minutes on each side until brown, adding more oil to the pan as needed. Spear 1 pepper, if using, onto the top of each of the serranitos with a cocktail stick and serve.

229 Pork & Cabbage Terrine

SERVES: 12   **PREPARATION TIME:** 20 minutes   **COOKING TIME:** 35 minutes
EQUIPMENT: 900g/2lb terrine

2 tbsp olive oil
1 onion, finely chopped
1 large garlic clove
8 thyme sprigs
500g/1lb 2oz pork mince

50g/1¾oz tinned anchovy fillets
   in oil, drained
⅓ cup capers, finely chopped
2 tbsp grated horseradish
1 Savoy cabbage, leaves separated
freshly ground black pepper

1   Preheat the oven to 190°C/375°F/Gas 5. Heat the olive oil in a frying pan over a medium-high heat. Add the onion and cook, stirring occasionally, for 5 minutes until soft. Add the garlic and thyme and cook, stirring, for 1 minute until aromatic.
2   Put the mince in a mixing bowl and stir in the onion mixture. In a small bowl, mix together the anchovies, capers and horseradish and season with pepper. Add to the pork mixture and stir well.
3   Bring a large saucepan of water to the boil. Cut the stem out of each cabbage leaf in a 'v' shape and cook for 1 minute in the boiling water, working in batches to avoid overcrowding the pan. Remove the leaves from the water, using a slotted spoon, put them between two clean tea towels and pat dry.
4   Line the base and sides of the terrine with the cabbage leaves, leaving some to extend over the top. Press the pork mixture tightly into the terrine, fold the cabbage leaves over the top to cover and then cover the terrine with foil.
5   Put the terrine in a roasting tin and add enough water to come halfway up the sides of the terrine. Bake for 25 minutes until slightly shrunken and firm. Remove from the oven and carefully tilt the terrine sideways to drain the juices, then leave to cool and set for 30 minutes.
6   Turn the terrine out onto a board and, using a very sharp knife, cut into 12 slices and serve.

230 Fried Lamb with Hummus & Pine Nuts

SERVES: 6   **PREPARATION TIME:** 15 minutes   **COOKING TIME:** 9 minutes

85ml/2¾fl oz/⅓ cup plus 1 tsp
  olive oil
150g/5½oz lamb steak, halved
410g/14½oz tinned chickpeas,
  drained and rinsed
2 tbsp tahini
1 garlic clove, coarsely chopped

juice of 1 lemon
50g/1¾oz/⅓ cup pine nuts
a pinch paprika
1 small handful parsley, chopped
salt and freshly ground black pepper
6 pitta breads, sliced, to serve

1   Preheat the oven to 130°C/250°F/Gas 1. Heat ½ tsp of the oil in a frying pan over
a medium-high heat. Add the steak and fry for 2 minutes on each side until brown.
Remove from the heat and set aside.

2   Put the chickpeas, tahini, garlic, lemon juice, 4 tbsp of the oil and 4 tbsp water
in a food processor and process for 2–3 minutes until smooth. Season with salt
and pepper, transfer to a serving bowl and drizzle with the remaining 2 tbsp oil.

3   Put the pitta breads on a baking sheet and heat in the oven for 5 minutes until
warm. Meanwhile, put the pine nuts in a dry frying pan and heat over a medium
heat for 2–3 minutes until beginning to brown. Sprinkle the hummus with the
paprika, parsley and pine nuts, slice the steaks thinly and serve with the breads.

PREPARING AHEAD: The hummus in step 2 can be made up to 1 day in advance and stored
in an airtight container in the fridge.

231 Dolmades

MAKES: 24   **PREPARATION TIME:** 30 minutes, plus 20 minutes soaking
COOKING TIME: 1 hour 15 minutes

225g/8oz vine leaves in brine
100g/3½oz/½ cup long grain rice
1 tbsp olive oil
1 onion, finely chopped

250g/9oz lamb mince
1 handful parsley, finely chopped
juice of 1 lemon
salt and freshly ground black pepper

1   Separate the vine leaves and put them in a large heatproof bowl. Cover with
boiling water and leave to soak for 20 minutes. Meanwhile, bring 500ml/17fl oz/
2 cups water to the boil in a saucepan. Add the rice and cook for 15 minutes until
cooked, then drain.

2   While the rice is cooking, heat the oil in a frying pan over a medium heat.
Add the onion and fry, stirring occasionally, for 10 minutes until soft, then transfer
to a bowl. Mix in the cooked rice, mince, parsley and lemon juice and season with
salt and pepper.

3   Drain the vine leaves and select 24 good unbroken ones, then line the base
of a saucepan with the remaining leaves.

4   Put 1 leaf, smooth-side down and with stalk nearest you, on a cutting board. Put
1 tbsp of the rice mixture just above the stalk and fold the bottom of the leaf over
it. Fold the sides over the filling, then roll upwards to form a small parcel. Transfer
the dolmade to the leaf-lined saucepan and repeat with the remaining leaves and
filling, tightly packing them into the saucepan.

5   Cover the dolmades with water and cover with a plate to keep them from floating
during cooking. Bring to the boil, then reduce the heat to low and simmer,
covered, for 1 hour.

6   Carefully remove the dolmades, using a slotted spoon, and transfer to a plate.
Leave to cool for 20 minutes. Serve warm or cold.

232 Ham & Mushroom Calzones

MAKES: 16   **PREPARATION TIME:** 25 minutes, plus making the pizza dough
COOKING TIME: 20 minutes   **EQUIPMENT:** 9cm/3½in plain round pastry cutter

15g/½oz butter
150g/5½oz button mushrooms,
  chopped
80g/2¾oz ham, finely sliced
plain flour, for rolling the dough

½ recipe quantity Pizza Dough
  (see page 15)
80g/2¾oz mozzarella cheese,
  coarsely chopped
2 tbsp olive oil

1   Preheat the oven to 200°C/400°F/Gas 6. Heat the butter in a frying pan over
   medium heat until melted. Add the mushrooms and fry, stirring occasionally, for
   5–7 minutes until beginning to brown. Stir in the ham and remove from the heat.
2   On a lightly floured surface, roll the pizza dough out into a 36cm/14¼in square
   and cut out 16 circles using the pastry cutter.
3   Add the mozzarella to the mushroom mixture and mix well. Put 2 tsp of the
   mixture slightly off-centre on each dough circle and fold in half, pressing the edges
   together to seal. Put the calzones on a baking sheet.
4   Brush the calzones with the oil and bake for 12 minutes until golden. Leave to cool
   for 5 minutes, then serve.

PREPARING AHEAD: The filling can be made to the end of step 1 up to 2 hours in advance, covered
and stored at room temperature.

233 Leek & Bacon Feuillettes

MAKES: 24 **PREPARATION TIME:** 15 minutes **COOKING TIME:** 25 minutes
EQUIPMENT: 2 x 12-hole mini-muffin tins, 5.5cm/2¼in plain round pastry cutter

1 tbsp olive oil
1 large leek, finely chopped
8 rindless, unsmoked streaky bacon
   rashers, finely chopped

2 tbsp white wine
4 tbsp double cream
plain flour, for rolling the pastry
250g/9oz ready-to-roll puff pastry

1   Preheat the oven to 180°C/350°F/Gas 4. Heat the oil in a frying pan over a medium
    heat. Add the leek and fry, stirring occasionally, for 5 minutes until soft. Add the
    bacon and cook for a further 3 minutes until the bacon is cooked but not crispy.
2   Add the white wine and, using a wooden spoon, scrape any bits off the base
    of the pan and stir well. Cook for 1 minute until the liquid has almost completely
    evaporated, then add the cream and cook, stirring, for a further 1 minute until
    bubbling. Remove from the heat and leave to cool.
3   On a lightly floured surface, roll the pastry into a 30 x 30cm/12 x 12in square and
    cut out 24 circles, using the pastry cutter. Gently press the pastry circles into
    the bases of two 12-hole mini-muffin tins. Put 1 tsp of the leek and bacon mixture
    in each and press down a little so it does not fall out during cooking when the
    pastry puffs up.
4   Bake the feuillettes for 12 minutes until puffed and lightly golden, then serve.

PREPARING AHEAD: The leek and bacon mixture can be made to the end of step 2 up to 4 hours
in advance and stored in an airtight container in the fridge. Leave to stand at room temperature
for 30 minutes before baking.

234 Baked Chicory & Ham

SERVES: 6   **PREPARATION TIME:** 10 minutes   **COOKING TIME:** 40 minutes

4¹/₂ tsp olive oil
3 heads of chicory, halved lengthways
¹/₄ tsp salt
3 slices ham
30g/1oz Parmesan cheese, grated

WHITE SAUCE
30g/1oz butter
4¹/₂ tsp plain flour
500ml/17fl oz/2 cups milk

1 Preheat the oven to 180°C/350°F/Gas 4. To make the sauce, melt the butter in a saucepan over a medium heat then stir in the flour. Slowly stir in the milk, 4 tbsp at a time and continue cooking, stirring continuously, for 1–2 minutes until smooth. Reduce the heat to low and simmer for 15 minutes, stirring occasionally, until the sauce is pale in colour and satiny in texture.
2 Heat the oil in a frying pan over a medium heat. Add the chicory, cut-side down, and sprinkle with the salt. Cook for 8 minutes, turning halfway through, until brown and beginning to soften. Remove from the pan and put the halves back together, then wrap each pair in 1 slice of the ham.
3 Put the wrapped chicory in a baking dish. Pour the sauce over and sprinkle with the Parmesan.
4 Bake for 10 minutes until golden and bubbling. Cut each head of chicory crossways into 6 slices and serve.

PREPARING AHEAD: This can be made to the end of step 3 up to 2 hours in advance, covered and stored in the fridge. Leave to stand at room temperature for 20 minutes before baking.

235 Frittata

SERVES: 8   **PREPARATION TIME:** 10 minutes   **COOKING TIME:** 45 minutes

500g/1lb 2oz new potatoes, quartered
1 tbsp olive oil
1 onion, thinly sliced
150g/5¹/₂oz smoked streaky bacon, finely chopped

140g/5oz/scant ¹/₂ cup peas
6 eggs, beaten
30/1oz Parmesan cheese, grated
salt and freshly ground black pepper

1 Put the potatoes in a saucepan, cover with water and bring to the boil. Boil for 8–10 minutes until tender, then drain and set aside.
2 Preheat the oven to 180°C/350°F/Gas 4. Heat the oil in a 25cm/10in ovenproof frying pan over a medium heat. Add the onion and cook, stirring occasionally, for 5 minutes until soft. Stir in the bacon and cook, stirring, for a further 5 minutes until cooked through. Add 4 tbsp water and, using a wooden spoon, scrape any bits off the base of the pan and stir well.
3 Add the peas and cook for a further 3 minutes, then add the potatoes and cook for 2 minutes, stirring, until well combined. Season well with salt and pepper and remove from the heat.
4 Add the eggs and Parmesan and put the frying pan in the oven. Bake for 15–20 minutes until the eggs have set. Cut the frittata into 8 wedges and serve straight from the frying pan, warm or cold.

PREPARING AHEAD: This can be made up to 4 hours in advance, covered and stored at room temperature.

236 Chorizo, Red Pepper & Manchego Empanadas

MAKES: 12   PREPARATION TIME: 30 minutes   COOKING TIME: 50 minutes
EQUIPMENT: 8cm/3¼in plain round pastry cutter

1 red pepper
20cm/8in chorizo sausage,
   finely diced
plain flour, for rolling the pastry

250g/9oz ready-to-roll puff pastry
30g/1oz Manchego cheese, grated
1 egg yolk, beaten with 1 tbsp milk

1   Preheat the oven to 180°C/350°F/Gas 4. Put the whole pepper in a baking dish and bake for 20–30 minutes until the skin is wrinkled and the pepper is soft. Leave to cool for 10 minutes or until cool enough to handle, then remove the skin, stalk and seeds and chop coarsely.
2   Meanwhile, heat a frying pan over a high heat. Add the chorizo and fry, stirring occasionally, for 3–4 minutes until beginning to shrink, then remove from the heat and leave to cool.
3   On a lightly floured surface, roll the pastry into a 25 x 32cm/10 x 12¾in rectangle and cut out 12 circles, using the pastry cutter. Put the Manchego, chorizo and pepper in a bowl and mix well. Put 1 tbsp of the mixture slightly off centre on each pastry circle. Fold the pastry over the filling, pinching the edges closed to seal. Put the empanadas on a baking sheet and brush with the egg yolk mixture. Bake for 12–15 minutes until golden and puffed. Serve immediately.

237 Merguez & White Bean Stew

SERVES: 6   PREPARATION TIME: 10 minutes   COOKING TIME: 20 minutes

4 tsp olive oil
350g/12oz merguez sausage, sliced
1 onion, finely sliced
1 garlic clove, finely chopped
4 tbsp red wine

250g/9oz tinned butter beans,
   drained and rinsed
400g/14oz tinned tomatoes
1 tsp caster sugar
salt and freshly ground black pepper
ciabatta bread, sliced, to serve

1   Heat 1 tsp of the oil in a frying pan over a high heat. Add the merguez and fry, stirring occasionally, for 15 minutes, or until cooked through.
2   Meanwhile, heat the remaining oil in another frying pan over a medium heat. Add the onion and cook for 5 minutes until soft. Stir in the garlic and cook for a further 1 minute. Add the wine and, using a wooden spoon, scrape any bits off the base of the pan and stir well. Add the beans, tomatoes and sugar and stir well. Reduce the heat to low and cook for 10 minutes until the liquid has almost completely evaporated.
3   Stir in the merguez, including the juices released during cooking. Season with salt and pepper and serve with bread.

238 Crispy Salted Pork Belly

SERVES: 8   **PREPARATION TIME:** 15 minutes   **COOKING TIME:** 1 hour

350g/12oz pork belly
1 tbsp olive oil

1 tsp salt
Dijon mustard, to serve

1   Preheat the oven to 190°C/375°F/Gas 5. Using a sharp knife, score the pork belly by making several deep criss-cross incisions through the skin to the meat, spacing the cuts 2.5cm/1in apart. Put the pork, skin-side up, in a colander and pour 1l/35fl oz/4 cups boiling water over the top. Leave to stand for 3–4 minutes to enable the skin to crisp up in the oven, then pat dry with a clean tea towel.
2   Rub the oil and salt over the scored skin and put the pork, skin-side up, in a baking dish. Bake for 45 minutes, then reduce the temperature to 150°C/ 300°F/Gas 2 and bake for a further 15 minutes until soft and cooked through with a crispy skin. Remove from the oven and leave to rest for 15 minutes, then, using the criss-cross incisions as guides, cut 16 squares of crackling and meat. Serve immediately with the mustard.

239 Roast Shallots & Lardons

SERVES: 6   **PREPARATION TIME:** 10 minutes   **COOKING TIME:** 50 minutes

185g/6½oz shallots, peeled
200g/7oz lardons
5 sage leaves, torn

3 tbsp olive oil
100g/3½oz/1 cup breadcrumbs
salt and freshly ground black pepper

1   Preheat the oven to 180°C/350°F/Gas 4. Bring a saucepan of water to the boil and boil the shallots for 5 minutes until they begin to soften. Drain well.
2   Put the shallots, lardons and sage leaves in a baking dish, add 2 tbsp of the oil and season with salt and pepper, then toss until coated. Roast for 45 minutes until the onions are soft and the lardons cooked through.
3   Meanwhile, heat the remaining 1 tbsp of the oil in a frying pan over a medium heat. Add the breadcrumbs and fry, stirring, for 4 minutes until golden brown. Sprinkle the breadcrumbs over the lardons, season with salt and pepper and serve.

240 White Asparagus & Ham Fritters

MAKES: 24   **PREPARATION TIME:** 20 minutes   **COOKING TIME:** 8 minutes

125g/4½oz/1 cup plain flour
1 tsp dried active yeast
80ml/2½fl oz/⅓ cup ale
1 tbsp olive oil
120g/4¼oz Manchego cheese,
   thinly sliced

12 white asparagus spears,
   about 210g/7½oz bottled,
   halved crossways
12 thin slices of Serrano ham, halved
1l/35fl oz/4 cups sunflower oil
100g/3½oz/1 cup breadcrumbs

1   Put the flour and yeast in a mixing bowl, add the ale, oil and 80ml/2½fl oz/⅓ cup lukewarm water and stir until smooth. Set the batter aside.
2   Cut the Manchego slices so that they are the same size as the halved asparagus spears. Put 1 piece of the asparagus and 1 slice of cheese on each slice of ham and roll tightly to form parcels.
3   Heat the oil in a deep saucepan or wok to 180°C/350°F/Gas 4. Dip the parcels in the batter, then roll them in the breadcrumbs to coat. Fry the parcels for 2 minutes until golden, working in batches to avoid overcrowding. Serve hot.

241　Baby Bubble & Squeaks

MAKES: 18　**PREPARATION TIME:** 20 minutes　**COOKING TIME:** 40 minutes

500g/1lb 2oz potatoes, peeled
1/2 Savoy cabbage, about 250g/9oz,
　finely sliced
30g/1oz butter, plus extra as needed
2 tbsp olive oil, plus extra as needed

6 unsmoked streaky bacon rashers,
　finely chopped
18 parsley leaves
salt and freshly ground black pepper

1　Put the potatoes in a saucepan, cover with water and bring to the boil. Boil for
　15–20 minutes until tender, then drain and transfer to a mixing bowl. Mash the
　potatoes, using a fork, and set aside.
2　Bring a saucepan of water to the bowl. Add the cabbage and boil for 3 minutes
　until soft. Drain and add to the mashed potatoes.
3　Heat 15g/1/2oz of the butter and 1 tbsp of the oil in a frying pan over a medium
　heat. Add the bacon and fry for 5 minutes until cooked through. Add to the
　potatoes, then season with salt and pepper.
4　Using your hands, shape rounded teaspoonfuls of the mixture into 2.5cm/1in
　patties. Heat the remaining oil and butter in a frying pan over a medium heat.
　Working in batches, fry the patties for 2 minutes on each side until golden, adding
　more butter and oil to the pan as needed. Top each patty with a parsley leaf and
　serve immediately.

242　Deep-Fried Pork & Manchego Meatballs

MAKES: 16　**PREPARATION TIME:** 20 minutes　**COOKING TIME:** 45 minutes

4 tsp olive oil
1/2 onion, finely chopped
1 carrot, peeled and finely chopped
250g/9oz pork mince
1 tbsp spicy paprika
1/4 tsp salt
30g/1oz butter

41/2 tsp plain flour
375ml/13fl oz/11/2 cups milk
60g/21/4oz Manchego cheese, grated
1l/35fl oz/4 cups sunflower oil
30g/1oz/scant 1/3 cup breadcrumbs
salt and freshly ground black pepper

1　Preheat the oven to 180°C/350°F/Gas 4. Heat the olive oil in a frying pan over
　a medium heat, add the onion and carrot and fry, stirring occasionally, for
　10 minutes until soft.
2　Put the mince and paprika in a mixing bowl, add the onion mixture and stir well,
　then set aside.
3　Melt the butter in a saucepan over a low heat, then stir in the flour. Slowly add the
　milk, 4 tbsp at a time, stirring continuously, for 1–2 minutes until smooth. Reduce
　the heat to low and simmer for 15 minutes, stirring occasionally, until the sauce is
　pale in colour and satiny in texture.
4　Add the Manchego and 2 tbsp of the sauce to the pork mixture and mix well.
　Shape the mixture into 16 meatballs of equal size, using your hands, and put them
　on a baking sheet. Bake for 15 minutes until dark brown. Leave to cool to room
　temperature on the baking sheet.
5　Heat the sunflower oil in a deep saucepan or wok to 180°C/350°F. Dip the
　meatballs in the remaining white sauce and roll in the breadcrumbs. Fry for
　30 seconds–1 minute until golden and crisp, working in batches to avoid
　overcrowding the pan. Season with salt and pepper and serve immediately.

243 Cantucci Biscuits

MAKES: 24 **PREPARATION TIME:** 15 minutes **COOKING TIME:** 35 minutes

1 egg
90g/3¼oz/heaped ⅓ cup
    caster sugar

100g/3½oz/⅔ cup whole
    shelled almonds
100g/3½oz/scant ¾ cup plain flour
¼ tsp baking powder

1   Preheat the oven to 160°C/315°F/Gas 2–3 and line a baking sheet with baking
    parchment. Put the egg and sugar in a bowl and whisk for 2 minutes until pale
    and a ribbon forms when drizzled over the mixture. Gently fold in the almonds,
    flour and baking powder until well combined.
2   Transfer the mixture to the baking sheet and shape it into a 25 x 10cm/10 x 4in log.
    Bake for 15 minutes until pale brown, then remove from the oven and, using
    a sharp knife, immediately cut the log in half lengthways, then cut crossways
    to make 24 biscuits, each about 2.5cm/1in thick. Lay the cantucci flat on the baking
    sheet and bake for a further 20 minutes, turning them over after 10 minutes.
    Remove and leave to cool, then serve.

    PREPARING AHEAD: These can be made up to 5 days in advance and stored in an airtight
    container at room temperature.

244 Banana & Coconut Ice Cream

SERVES: 6–8   PREPARATION TIME: 10 minutes, plus 30 minutes freezing
COOKING TIME: 5 minutes   EQUIPMENT: ice-cream machine, small ice-cream scoop

180g/6¼oz/scant 1 cup caster sugar
2 tbsp cardamom pods, crushed
2 ripe bananas, peeled

250ml/9fl oz/1 cup coconut milk
8 flat-bottomed wafer cups

1 Put the sugar, cardamom pods and 250ml/9fl oz/1 cup water in a saucepan and heat over a low heat, stirring occasionally, for 5 minutes until the sugar has dissolved. Increase the heat to high and bring to the boil. Boil for 5 minutes until the mixture turns syrupy. Remove from the heat and leave to cool.
2 Put the bananas and coconut milk in a food processor and process for 2 minutes until smooth. Remove the cardamom pods from the sugar syrup and stir the syrup into the banana mixture.
3 Churn the mixture in an ice-cream machine according to the manufacturer's instructions. Working quickly, put 1 scoop of ice cream on each cone and serve immediately.

PREPARING AHEAD: The ice cream can be made up to 1 week in advance and stored in a freezerproof container in the freezer.

245 Chocolate Biscuit Cake

SERVES: 8   PREPARATION TIME: 10 minutes, plus 2 hours chilling   COOKING TIME: 5 minutes
EQUIPMENT: 20cm/8in square baking tray

200g/7oz dark chocolate,
   coarsely chopped
165g/5¾oz/½ cup golden syrup

100g/3½oz unsalted butter, chopped,
   plus extra for greasing
100g/3½oz rich tea biscuits, crushed

1 Lightly grease the tray and line it with greaseproof paper, ensuring the paper hangs over the sides. Put the chocolate, golden syrup and butter in a heatproof bowl and rest it over a saucepan of simmering water, making sure the bottom of the bowl does not touch the water. Stir for 3 minutes, or until smooth and the chocolate and butter have melted.
2 Put the biscuits in a bowl and pour the chocolate mixture over, then mix well. Pour the biscuit mixture into the tray and chill in the fridge for 2 hours until hard.
3 Remove from the fridge, turn onto a board and peel off the paper. Cut the biscuit cake into 16 squares and serve immediately

PREPARING AHEAD: This can be made up to 1 week in advance and stored in an airtight container in the fridge.

246 Bakewell Tartlets

MAKES: 24   PREPARATION TIME: 10 minutes, plus making the tartlet cases
COOKING TIME: 12 minutes

50g/1¾oz/½ cup flaked almonds
50g/1¾oz unsalted butter, softened
50g/1¾oz caster sugar
1 egg

½ recipe quantity sweet Tartlet Cases,
   blind-baked (see page 14)
4 tbsp raspberry jam

1 Preheat the oven to 170°C/325°F/Gas 3. Put the almonds, butter, sugar and egg in a food processor and process for 2 minutes until well mixed and smooth.
2 Put the tartlet cases on a baking sheet and put ½ tsp of the jam in each one. Add 1 heaped tsp of the almond mixture and bake for 10–12 minutes until light brown and set. Serve warm or cold.

247 Honey Ice Cream Balls Rolled in Crushed Nuts

SERVES: 12 **PREPARATION TIME:** 15 minutes, plus 1 hour 40 minutes freezing
COOKING TIME: 15 minutes **EQUIPMENT:** ice-cream machine, small ice-cream scoop

300ml/10½fl oz/scant 1¼ cups milk
300ml/10½fl oz/scant 1¼ cups
   double cream
250g/9oz/scant 1 cup clear honey
4 egg yolks, beaten

60g/2¼oz/scant ½ cup pine nuts
55g/2oz/heaped ⅓ cup, hazelnuts,
   roasted and chopped
12 waffle cones

1 Put the milk, cream and honey in a saucepan and slowly bring to the boil over
a low heat, stirring until the honey dissolves. Put the egg yolks in a large heatproof
mixing bowl and add the milk mixture, stirring until well combined. Return the
mixture to the saucepan and cook over a very low heat, stirring continuously,
for 10 minutes until thick. Remove from the heat and leave to cool completely.
2 Transfer the mixture to an ice-cream machine and churn according to the
manufacturer's instructions, then put the ice-cream in the freezer for 1 hour.
3 Put the nuts in a food processor and pulse for 1–2 minutes until they resemble
coarse breadcrumbs, then transfer to a small bowl.
4 Working quickly, put 1 scoop of ice cream on each cone, roll it in the nuts
and serve immediately.

PREPARING AHEAD: The ice cream can be made up to 1 week in advance and stored
in a freezerproof container in the freezer.

CHAPTER 5

PARTIES & CELEBRATIONS

From birthdays and anniversaries to graduations and other special milestones, there's no better way to celebrate than by bringing your family and friends together for a big party. Catering for, and pleasing, such a large crowd may seem intimidating at first, but the mouthwatering recipes in this chapter make it easy. Just make sure you organize some reliable help ahead of time for before, during and after the event *(see page 9)*. Many of the recipes in this chapter, such as Chicken, Pancetta & Sage Involtini, Celeriac Remoulade Crostini and Wessex Lamb Pasties are designed to serve large numbers; others are easily doubled. And with a world of flavours on offer, everyone will be happy. Serve up succulent Beef Empanadas and Coriander Prawn Balls on Lemongrass Skewers alongside Spiced Lamb Pinchos with Mint-Egg Mayonnaise and Potato Parathas. Include a few classic party favourites, such as Honey-Glazed Spare Ribs and Spicy Chicken Wings, too. Top the occasion off with a spread of irresistible sweet treats, such as Baklava, Mint Chocolate Chip Ice Cream and Raspberry Meringues, and your reputation as party-giver extraordinaire will be clinched.

SPINACH & PINE NUT FILO PARCELS *(SEE PAGE 157)*

248 Mushrooms Stuffed with Spinach & Gorgonzola

MAKES: 12   **PREPARATION TIME:** 10 minutes   **COOKING TIME:** 20 minutes

1 tbsp olive oil
10g/¼oz butter
125g/4½oz baby spinach,
  washed and dried

12 open-cap mushrooms,
  stems discarded
85g/3oz Gorgonzola cheese,
  crumbled

1 Preheat the oven to 180°C/350°F/Gas 4. Heat the oil and butter in a large saucepan over a medium heat until the butter has melted. Add the spinach and cook for 3–5 minutes until wilted. Transfer to a colander and press down with a saucer to squeeze out as much excess water as possible.
2 Put the mushrooms, open-side up, on a baking sheet. Put 1 tsp of the spinach in each mushroom and top with a small piece of Gorgonzola.
3 Bake for 15 minutes until the cheese is melted and bubbling. Serve immediately.

PREPARING AHEAD: These can be made to the end of step 2 up to 2 hours in advance, covered with cling film and stored in the fridge.

249 Falafel

MAKES: 24   **PREPARATION TIME:** 15 minutes   **COOKING TIME:** 12 minutes

820g/1lb 13oz tinned chickpeas,
  drained and rinsed
2 garlic cloves
1 tsp ground coriander
1 tsp ground cumin
2 tbsp olive oil
150g/5½oz/scant 1¼ cups plain flour

2 eggs
1 tsp salt
zest of 1 lemon
160ml/5¼fl oz/scant ⅔ cup
  sunflower oil
1 tsp black sesame seeds

1 Put all the ingredients, except the sunflower oil and sesame seeds, in a food processor and process for 2 minutes until the mixture forms a coarse mash. Shape the mixture into 24 balls of equal size.
2 Heat half of the sunflower oil in a frying pan. Working in batches, fry the falafel for 2–3 minutes on each side, adding more oil to the pan as needed.
3 Sprinkle the sesame seeds over and serve.

PREPARING AHEAD: These can be made to the end of step 1 up to 8 hours in advance, covered with cling film and stored in the fridge.

250 Cheesy Choux Buns

MAKES: 24   **PREPARATION TIME:** 15 minutes   **COOKING TIME:** 12 minutes

45g/1½oz butter
70g/2½oz/heaped ½ cup plain flour
2 eggs, beaten
1 tbsp Dijon mustard

80g/2¾oz mature Cheddar cheese,
  grated
80g/2¾oz Gruyère cheese, grated
1l/35fl oz/4 cups sunflower oil

1 Melt the butter in a saucepan over a low heat. Add 125ml/4fl oz/½ cup water and bring to the boil. Sift in the flour and stir until the mixture forms a ball and comes away from the sides of the pan. Remove from the heat and cool for 5 minutes.
2 Add the egg a little at a time to the dough, mixing until thoroughly incorporated before adding more. Put the mustard and cheese in a bowl and mix until it forms a sticky paste. Add the paste to the choux dough and mix well.
3 Heat the oil to 180°C/350°F, or until a sprinkle of flour sizzles when dropped in. Drop 24 teaspoonfuls of the choux pastry into the oil and fry for 2 minutes until golden, working in batches to avoid overcrowding the pan. Remove from the pan, using a slotted spoon, and drain on kitchen paper. Bring the oil back to temperature before each batch. Serve hot.

251 Caramelized Onion & Blue Cheese Pizzarettes

MAKES: 24 **PREPARATION TIME:** 20 minutes, plus making the pizza dough
COOKING TIME: 25 minutes **EQUIPMENT:** 5cm/2in plain round pastry cutter

15g/¹⁄₂oz butter
1 tbsp olive oil
1 onion, finely sliced
plain flour, for rolling the dough

¹⁄₂ recipe quantity Pizza Dough
 (see page 15)
100g/3¹⁄₂oz blue cheese,
 cut into 24 slices

1 Preheat the oven to 200°C/400°F/Gas 6. Heat the butter and oil in a frying pan over a low heat until the butter has melted. Add the onion, increase the heat to medium-low and fry, stirring occasionally, for 20 minutes until sweet, soft and golden brown.
2 On a lightly floured surface, roll out the pizza dough to 2mm/¹⁄₁₆in thick and cut out 24 circles, using the pastry cutter, then put the circles on a baking sheet.
3 Put 1 tsp of the caramelized onion on each pizza base and top with 1 slice of the blue cheese. Bake for 3 minutes until the cheese has melted, then serve.

PREPARING AHEAD: The onions in step 1 can be made up to 4 hours in advance and stored in an airtight container at room temperature.

252 Cherry Tomatoes Filled with Herby Cream Cheese

MAKES: 36 **PREPARATION TIME:** 30 minutes

36 large cherry tomatoes
1 handful chives, finely chopped
1 large handful dill, finely chopped
250g/9oz/1¹⁄₄ cups cream cheese

1 tbsp Dijon mustard
salt and freshly ground black pepper

1 Slice the top off each cherry tomato and carefully scoop out and discard the seeds, using a small spoon. Put the tomatoes on a serving plate and cut away a small piece from the bottom of any that wobble.
2 Put the chives, dill, cream cheese and mustard in a bowl and mix well. Season with salt and pepper, then set aside.
3 When ready to serve, divide the herby cream cheese into the tomatoes and serve.

PREPARING AHEAD: The herby cream cheese in step 2 can be made up to 4 hours in advance and stored in an airtight container in the fridge.

253 Welsh Rarebit Bites

MAKES: 24 **PREPARATION TIME:** 15 minutes **COOKING TIMES:** 15 minutes
EQUIPMENT: 4cm/1¹⁄₂in fluted round pastry cutter

6 slices of white bread
4 tbsp milk
2 tsp Dijon mustard
1 tsp paprika

125g/4¹⁄₂oz/1 cup grated cheese,
 such as mature Cheddar,
 red Leicester or other
 strong-flavoured hard cheese
1 egg yolk
1 handful parsley, finely chopped
salt and freshly ground black pepper

1 Preheat the oven to 170°C/325°F/Gas 3. Cut out 4 circles from each slice of bread, using the pastry cutter, and put them on a baking sheet. Bake for 5 minutes, or until lightly toasted.
2 Put the milk, mustard and paprika in a saucepan and heat over a low heat, stirring until well mixed. Add the cheese and cook, stirring, for 2–3 minutes until the mixture forms a paste. Remove from the heat and beat in the egg yolk.
3 Divide the mixture over the toast circles and bake for 5 minutes until bubbling and slightly brown. Sprinkle with the parsley, season with salt and pepper and serve.

254 Avocado & Tomato Piadini

MAKES: 24   **PREPARATION TIME:** 30 minutes   **COOKING TIME:** 30 minutes

300g/10½oz/scant 2½ cups plain
   flour, plus extra for kneading
   and rolling the dough
1½ tsp salt
30g/1oz butter, diced
1 avocado

12 cherry tomatoes, quartered
1 spring onion, finely sliced
48 tarragon leaves
juice of ½ lemon
salt and freshly ground black pepper

1   Put the flour, salt and butter in a large mixing bowl. Add 185ml/6fl oz/¾ cup lukewarm water and mix together until the mixture forms a dough. Turn the dough out onto a lightly floured surface and knead for 10 minutes until elastic.

2   Roll the piadini dough into a log about 2.5cm/1in in diameter, then cut it into 2cm/1in-thick pieces and, on a lightly floured surface, roll each one into a 12cm/4¾in circle.

3   Heat a heavy frying pan over a medium-high heat for 3–4 minutes until hot. Put 1–2 dough circles in the dry pan and cook for 1 minute until the surface bubbles slightly and dark brown spots appear on the underside, then turn over and cook for a further 1 minute. Repeat with the remaining dough circles.

4   Halve the avocado lengthways, remove the stone and scoop the flesh into a bowl, then mash it into a coarse paste, using a fork.

5   Spread each of the piadini bases with a little of the avocado and top with 2 pieces of the tomato, 1 slice of the spring onion, 2 tarragon leaves and 1 drop of lemon juice. Season with salt and pepper and serve.

255 Potato Parathas

MAKES: 36   **PREPARATION TIME:** 45 minutes   **COOKING TIME:** 1 hour 10 minutes

200g/7oz potatoes, peeled
1 tbsp olive oil
1 onion, thinly sliced
2 tsp garam masala

150g/5½oz/scant 1¼ cups plain flour,
   plus extra for rolling the dough
1 tsp sunflower oil
salt

1   Put the potatoes in a saucepan, cover with water and bring to the boil. Boil for 15–20 minutes until tender, then drain. Transfer to a large bowl and set aside.

2   Heat the olive oil in a frying pan over a medium-low heat. Add the onion and cook, stirring occasionally, for 10 minutes until very soft and beginning to turn brown. Stir in the garam masala and fry for a further 1 minute.

3   Lightly mash the potato, then add the onion. Mix well and season with salt.

4   Put the flour, sunflower oil and 80ml/2½fl oz/⅓ cup water in a bowl and mix together, using your hands. Add an additional 1–2 tbsp of water if the mixture is too dry. Knead the dough for 2 minutes until smooth, then divide it into 12 pieces of equal size. Roll each piece into a 3cm/1¼in ball. Roll the potato and onion mixture into 12 slightly smaller balls.

5   Press an indentation in the centre of each dough ball, using your thumb. Put 1 potato ball in this indentation, then bring the edges of the dough up and over the potato and press it together to seal. Flatten the balls slightly in your palms, then, on a well floured surface, roll them into 10cm/4in circles. Transfer the rolled-out parathas to a plate until ready to cook.

6   Heat a heavy frying pan over a high heat for 3–4 minutes until hot. Put 2–3 parathas in the pan and cook for 1–2 minutes until the underside begins to brown and blister. Lightly brush the top with olive oil and season with salt, then turn it over and cook for a further 1–2 minutes until brown and blistered. Transfer to a plate and repeat with the remaining parathas.

7   Cut each of the parathas into 3 pieces and serve immediately.

256 Mozzarella & Tomato Piadini

MAKES: 18 **PREPARATION TIME:** 40 minutes **COOKING TIME:** 30 minutes

300g/10½oz/scant 2½ cups plain
   flour, plus extra for kneading
   and rolling
1½ tsp salt
30g/1oz butter, diced
1 large garlic clove
3 tbsp olive oil

18 red cherry tomatoes, halved
18 yellow cherry tomatoes, halved
180g/6¼oz mozzarella cheese,
   cut into 36 small slices
18 small basil leaves
salt and freshly ground black pepper

1 Put the flour, salt and butter in a large mixing bowl. Add 185ml/6fl oz/¾ cup
   lukewarm water and mix together until the mixture forms a dough. Turn the
   dough out onto a lightly floured surface and knead for 10 minutes until elastic.
2 Roll the piadini dough into a log about 2.5cm/1in in diameter, then cut it into
   2cm/1in-thick pieces and, on a lightly floured surface, roll each one into a
   12cm/4¾in circle.
3 Heat a heavy frying pan over a medium-high heat for 3–4 minutes until hot. Put
   1–2 dough circles in the dry pan and cook for 1 minute until the surface bubbles
   slightly and dark brown spots appear on the underside, then turn over and cook
   for a further 1 minute. Transfer to a baking sheet and repeat with the remaining
   dough circles.
4 Preheat the grill to high. Rub one side of each of the piadini bases with the garlic
   clove and then brush with a little of the oil. Top with 2 pieces each of the red and
   yellow cherry tomatoes and 2 slices of the mozzarella. Grill for 4–5 minutes until
   the mozzarella has melted and is bubbling. Season with salt and pepper, top with
   1 basil leaf and serve.

PREPARING AHEAD: The piadini dough can be made up to 2 hours in advance, covered
and stored in the fridge. The cooked piadini bases can also be made up to 2 hours in advance
and stored in an airtight container until needed.

257 Celeriac Remoulade Crostini

MAKES: 48   **PREPARATION TIME:** 25 minutes, plus making the mayonnaise and crostini

500g/1lb 2oz celeriac, peeled and
  finely grated
juice of ½ lemon
1 recipe quantity Mayonnaise
  (see page 12)

1 tbsp Dijon mustard
1 recipe quantity Crostini
  (see page 15)
1 handful parsley, finely chopped
salt and freshly ground black pepper

1   Put the celeriac, lemon juice, mayonnaise and mustard in a bowl and mix well.
    Season with salt and pepper.
2   Put 1 tbsp of the remoulade on each of the crostini, sprinkle with parsley and
    pepper and serve.

PREPARING AHEAD: The celeriac remoulade in step 1 can be made up to 8 hours in advance
and stored in an airtight container in the fridge.

258 Olive & Tomato Tartlets

MAKES: 24 **PREPARATION TIME:** 25 minutes **COOKING TIME:** 30 minutes
EQUIPMENT: 2 x 12-hole mini-muffin tins, 5cm/2in plain round pastry cutter

1 tbsp olive oil
1 onion, finely sliced
2 garlic cloves, coarsely chopped
185g/6^1/$_2$oz cherry tomatoes, halved
150g/5^1/$_2$oz/1^1/$_4$ cups pitted black
    olives, chopped

2 tbsp capers
4 tbsp sweet sherry
plain flour, for rolling the pastry
500g/1lb 2oz ready-to-roll puff pastry

1   Preheat the oven to 180°C/350°F/Gas 4. Heat the oil in a frying pan over a medium heat. Add the onion and cook, stirring occasionally, for 4 minutes until soft and translucent. Add the garlic and cook for a further 1 minute, then add the tomatoes, olives and capers and continue cooking, stirring occasionally, for 3 minutes until well mixed and warmed through. Add the sherry, increase the heat a little and cook for 5–6 minutes until most of the liquid has evaporated.
2   On a lightly floured surface, roll the pastry into a 20 x 30cm/8 x 12in rectangle and cut out 24 circles, using the pastry cutter. Gently press the circles into the bases of the mini-muffin tins and fill with 1 tbsp of the tomato mixture.
3   Bake for 12–15 minutes until puffed and golden. Serve immediately.

259 Spinach & Pine Nut Filo Parcels

MAKES: 36 **PREPARATION TIME:** 45 minutes, plus 30 minutes soaking
COOKING TIME: 35 minutes

40g/1^1/$_2$oz/^{1}/$_3$ cup raisins
100g/3^1/$_2$oz butter
250g/9oz baby spinach, washed
    and dried
40g/1^1/$_2$oz/^{1}/$_4$ cup pine nuts

30g/1oz/^{1}/$_4$ cup chopped hazelnuts
90g/3oz feta cheese
12 filo pastry sheets
375ml/13fl oz/1^1/$_2$ cups sunflower oil,
    plus extra as needed

1   Put the raisins in a heatproof bowl, cover with boiling water and leave to soak for 30 minutes, then drain. Meanwhile, heat 15g/^{1}/$_2$oz of the butter in a large saucepan over a medium heat. Add the spinach and cook for 3–5 minutes until wilted. Transfer to a colander and press down with a saucer to squeeze out as much excess water as possible, then chop finely and put in a large mixing bowl.
2   Put the pine nuts and hazelnuts in a dry frying pan and toast lightly over a medium heat for 3 minutes until they begin to brown. Add the nuts and drained raisins to the spinach, crumble in the cheese and mix well.
3   Melt the remaining butter in a small saucepan over a low heat. Put 1 sheet of filo pastry on a work surface and keep the rest covered with a clean damp tea towel while you work. Brush the pastry with a little of the melted butter, then cover with a second filo sheet and butter again. Cut the filo lengthways into 6 long strips.
4   Position 1 pastry strip vertically in front of you. Put 1 tbsp of the filling at the bottom end of the pastry, leaving a little space between the edges of the pastry and the filling. Fold the bottom-right corner of the pastry diagonally up over the filling to form a triangle, then fold the lower left-hand corner up the left edge, keeping the triangular shape. Continue folding until you reach the end of the pastry and the filling is enclosed. Repeat with the remaining pastry and filling.
5   Heat the oil in a deep saucepan or wok until a small piece of pastry sizzles when dropped in. Fry the parcels for 1–2 minutes on each side until golden brown, working in batches to avoid overcrowding the pan. Remove from the pan, using a slotted spoon, and drain on kitchen paper. Repeat with the remaining parcels, adding more oil to the pan if necessary. Serve hot.

PREPARING AHEAD: These can be made to the end of step 4 up to 6 hours in advance, covered and stored in the fridge.

260   Crab Cakes

MAKES: 18   **PREPARATION TIME:** 5 minutes, plus making the potatoes
COOKING TIME: 10 minutes

2 potatoes, peeled and quartered
150g/5½oz crab meat, about
   1 dressed crab
1 egg
1 handful parsley, finely chopped

10 chives, finely chopped
1 egg yolk, beaten
75g/2½oz/heaped ½ cup plain flour
2 tbsp sunflower oil
salt and freshly ground black pepper

1   Put the potatoes in a saucepan, cover with water and bring to the boil. Boil for 10–15 minutes until tender, then drain.
2   Put the potatoes and crab in a mixing bowl and mash together. Stir in the egg and mix well. Add the parsley and chives, season with salt and pepper and chill in the fridge for 20 minutes. Shape the mixture into 18 balls of equal size and flatten slightly.
3   Roll each crab cake in the egg yolk, then roll in the flour to coat.
4   Heat 1 tbsp of the oil in a frying pan over a medium heat. Working in batches, fry the crab cakes for 2 minutes on each side until cooked, adding more oil to the pan as needed. Serve immediately.

PREPARING AHEAD: These can be made to the end of step 2 up to 8 hours in advance, covered with cling film and stored in the fridge.

261   Scampi

MAKES: 24   **PREPARATION TIME:** 10 minutes, plus making the mayonnaise
COOKING TIMES: 10 minutes

150g/5½oz/scant 1¼ cups plain flour
24 peeled king prawns
2 eggs, beaten
100g/3½oz/1 cup breadcrumbs
1l/35fl oz/4 cups sunflower oil

salt and freshly ground black pepper
2 lemons, cut into wedges, to serve
1 recipe quantity Mayonnaise
   (see page 12), to serve

1   Put the flour in a bowl and season with salt and pepper. Roll each prawn in the flour to coat, then dip in the egg and roll in the breadcrumbs to coat. Put the coated prawns on a plate until ready to fry.
2   Heat the oil in a deep saucepan or wok to 180°C/350°F, or until a few breadcrumbs sizzle when dropped in. Fry the scampi for 1–2 minutes until golden brown, working in batches to avoid overcrowding the pan. Remove from the pan, using a slotted spoon, and drain on kitchen paper. Bring the oil back to temperature before each batch.
3   Squeeze 1 lemon wedge over the scampi and serve immediately with the mayonnaise and remaining lemon wedges.

262 Coriander Prawn Balls on Lemongrass Skewers

MAKES: 24   **PREPARATION TIME:** 20 minutes   **COOKING TIME:** 5 minutes
EQUIPMENT: 30cm/12in steamer basket

300g/10½oz peeled, cooked prawns
2 lemongrass stalks,
   coarsely chopped, plus 24 stalks
   for skewering

2 spring onions, coarsely chopped
2 handfuls coriander leaves
2 tsp fish sauce

1   Put the prawns, lemongrass, spring onions, coriander and fish sauce in a food processor and process for 2 minutes until the mixture forms a coarse paste.
2   Shape the mixture into 24 small balls of equal size and put 1 ball on each lemongrass skewer.
3   Put the skewers in a steamer over a saucepan of boiling water. Cover and steam for 5 minutes until the prawn balls are white and cooked through, then serve.

263 Eastern Squid

MAKES: 24   PREPARATION TIME: 20 minutes   COOKING TIME: 30 minutes

6 tbsp olive oil
1 onion, finely chopped
1 large red chilli, deseeded and
    finely chopped
120g/4¼oz shiitake mushrooms,
    finely chopped
400g/14oz pork mince

1 large handful coriander leaves,
    finely chopped
juice and zest of 2 lemons
24 small squid, cleaned, dried
    and tentacles removed
salt and freshly ground black pepper

1   Heat 1 tbsp of the oil in a frying pan over a medium-low heat Add the onion and chilli and fry, stirring occasionally, for 5 minutes until soft. Add an additional 3 tbsp oil and the mushrooms and fry, stirring, for a further 5 minutes until soft. Stir in the mince and cook for 2 minutes until browned. Stir in the coriander leaves and lemon juice and zest, remove from the heat and season with salt and pepper.
2   Stuff the squid with the pork mixture and secure each opening with a cocktail stick.
3   When ready to serve, heat the remaining 2 tbsp of the oil in a frying pan. Add the squid, a few at a time, and fry for 2 minutes on each side. Serve immediately.

PREPARING AHEAD: These can be made to the end of step 2 up to 8 hours in advance, covered with cling film and stored in the fridge.

264 Prawn, Egg & Ham Croquettes

MAKES: 24   PREPARATION TIME: 20 minutes   COOKING TIME: 35 minutes

2 eggs, at room temperature
½ tsp white wine vinegar
30g/1oz butter
4½ tsp plain flour
375ml/13fl oz/1½ cups milk

150g/5½oz small peeled,
    cooked prawns
90g/3oz Parma ham, finely chopped
60g/2¼oz/1 cup fresh breadcrumbs
375ml/13fl oz/1½ cups sunflower oil

1   Bring a saucepan of water to the boil. Add the eggs and vinegar and boil for 6 minutes, then drain and leave to stand until cool enough to handle.
2   Melt the butter in a saucepan over a medium-low heat, then stir in the flour. Slowly stir in the milk, 4 tbsp at a time, and continue cooking, stirring continuously, for 1–2 minutes until smooth. Reduce the heat to low and simmer for 15 minutes, stirring occasionally, until the sauce is pale in colour and satiny in texture.
3   Peel the eggs and grate them into a bowl. Add the prawns, Parma ham, breadcrumbs and white sauce and mix well. Shape the mixture into 18 balls of equal size.
4   Heat the oil in a frying pan over a medium heat, or until a few breadcrumbs sizzle when dropped in. Working in batches, fry the croquettes for 1–2 minutes on each side until golden and crispy. Remove from the pan, using a slotted spoon, and drain on kitchen paper. Serve immediately.

PREPARING AHEAD: The eggs can be boiled and peeled up to 1 day in advance and stored, covered, in cold water in the fridge. Do not cut the eggs until ready to use or they will discolour. The croquettes can be made to the end of step 3 up to 8 hours in advance, covered with cling film and stored in the fridge.

265 Fish Goujons

MAKES: 24   PREPARATION TIME: 15 minutes   COOKING TIME: 25 minutes

400g/14oz haddock, cut into
   24 x 5cm/2in-long strips
300g/10½oz/scant 2½ cups
   plain flour
4 eggs, beaten

235g/8½oz/2⅓ cups breadcrumbs
375ml/13fl oz/1½ cups sunflower oil
125ml/4fl oz/½ cup tartar sauce,
   to serve

1   Roll the haddock strips in the flour, then in the eggs and finally in the breadcrumbs
   to coat. Transfer to a plate.
2   Heat the oil in a pan over a medium-high heat until a few breadcrumbs sizzle
   when dropped in. Working in batches, fry the haddock for 3 minutes on each side
   until golden and crispy. Serve with the tartar sauce.

266 Fritto Misto

SERVES: 24   PREPARATION TIME: 15 minutes   COOKING TIME: 25 minutes

300g/10½oz peeled cooked prawns
250ml/9fl oz/1 cup milk
250g/9oz/2 cups semolina flour,
   seasoned with salt

750g/1lb 10oz small squid, cleaned,
   tentacles reserved, and each cut
   into 3 or 4 pieces
1l/35fl oz/4 cups sunflower oil
4 lemons cut into wedges, to serve

1   Dip 1 prawn in the milk, then roll it in the semolina flour to coat and set aside
   on a plate. Repeat with the remaining prawns and the squid pieces and tentacles.
2   Heat the oil in a deep saucepan or wok to 180°C/350°F, or until a pinch of flour
   sizzles when dropped in. Working in batches to avoid overcrowding the pan,
   fry the prawns and squid in batches for 3–4 minutes until beginning to brown.
   Remove from the pan, using a slotted spoon, and drain on kitchen paper. Serve
   with lemon wedges for squeezing.

267 Cod, Egg & Caper Croquettes

MAKES: 24   PREPARATION TIME: 30 minutes   COOKING TIME: 45 minutes

300g/10½oz potatoes, quartered
1 egg, at room temperature
½ tsp white wine vinegar
300g/10½oz cod fillet
1l/35fl oz/4 cups milk

2 tbsp double cream
2 tsp capers, chopped
15g/½oz parsley, finely chopped
2 tbsp olive oil
salt and freshly ground black pepper

1   Put the potatoes in a saucepan, cover with water and bring to the boil. Boil for
   10–15 minutes until tender, then drain. Meanwhile, bring a saucepan of water
   to the boil. Add the egg and vinegar and boil for 6 minutes, then drain and leave
   to stand until cool enough to handle, then peel.
2   Put the cod fillet in a deep frying pan and cover with the milk. Bring to a very low
   simmer over a low heat and gently poach for 5 minutes. Remove from the heat,
   take the fish out of the milk, using a slotted spoon, and peel off the skin.
3   Mash the potatoes and cream together in a bowl. Break the cod into the potatoes.
   Chop the egg, add it to the bowl along with the capers and parsley and mix well.
   Season with salt and pepper and shape the mixture into 24 patties of equal size.
4   Heat 1 tbsp of the oil in a frying pan over a medium heat. Working in batches, fry
   the croquettes for 3 minutes on each side until golden, adding more oil to the pan
   as needed. Remove, using a slotted spoon, and drain on kitchen paper. Serve hot.

PREPARING AHEAD: These can be made to the end of step 3 up to 8 hours in advance, covered
with cling film and stored in the fridge. The egg in step 1 can be boiled and peeled up to 1 day
in advance and stored, covered, in cold water in the fridge. Do not cut it until ready to use or it
will discolour.

268 Spicy Cod & Coriander Fishcakes

MAKES: 24   **PREPARATION TIME:** 25 minutes, plus making the dip   **COOKING TIME:** 25 minutes
EQUIPMENT: 5cm/2in plain round pastry cutter

450g/1lb skinless cod or coley fillets
4 spring onions, coarsely chopped
1 small red chilli, deseeded and
   coarsely chopped
1 handful coriander leaves and
   stems, coarsely chopped, plus
   extra to serve

6 tbsp olive oil, plus extra as needed
salt and freshly ground black pepper
2 recipe quantities Sweet Chilli Dip
   (see page 12), to serve

1 Put the fish, spring onions, chilli, coriander and 4 tbsp of the oil in a food processor.
   Season with salt and pepper and process for 2 minutes until the mixture forms
   a paste.
2 Turn the mixture onto a clean work surface and flatten it into a 1cm/½in-thick
   disk. Cut out 24 fishcakes, using the pastry cutter.
3 Heat the remaining oil in a frying pan. Working in batches, fry the fishcakes for
   3–4 minutes on each side until golden, adding more oil to the pan as needed.
   Remove from the pan and drain on kitchen paper. Serve immediately with the dip.

PREPARING AHEAD: These can be made to the end of step 2 up to 8 hours in advance, covered
with cling film and stored in the fridge.

269 Salmon en Croûtes

MAKES: 24   **PREPARATION TIME:** 35 minutes   **COOKING TIME:** 15 minutes
EQUIPMENT: 8cm/3¹/₄in plain round pastry cutter

1 tbsp olive oil, plus extra for greasing
365g/12³/₄oz skinless salmon fillets
4 tbsp capers
20 chives, chopped
juice and grated zest of 1 lemon

plain flour, for rolling the pastry
500g/1lb 2oz ready-to-roll puff pastry
1 egg yolk, beaten with 1 tbsp milk
freshly ground black pepper

1 Preheat the oven to 180°C/350°F/Gas 4 and lightly grease a baking sheet. Put the
salmon, capers, chives and lemon juice and zest in a food processor and process
for 15 seconds until roughly chopped.
2 On a lightly floured surface, roll half the pastry into a 24 x 32cm/9¹/₂ x 12³/₄in
rectangle and cut out 12 circles, using the pastry cutter. Put 1 tbsp of the salmon
mixture slightly off centre on 1 pastry circle, then fold over to form a semi-circle.
Press the edges together to seal and transfer to the baking sheet. Repeat with the
remaining pastry and filling.
3 Brush the pies with the egg yolk mixture and bake for 12–15 minutes until puffed
and golden. Serve immediately.

PREPARING AHEAD: These can be made to the end of step 2 up to 8 hours in advance, covered
with cling film and stored in the fridge.

270 Salmon Fishcakes

MAKES: 18   **PREPARATION TIME:** 20 minutes, plus 20 minutes resting and making the salsa
COOKING TIME: 20 minutes

375g/13oz skinless salmon fillets
1 large handful tarragon leaves
3 garlic cloves, finely chopped
3 small red chillies, deseeded and
    coarsely chopped

2 tbsp olive oil
2 tbsp sunflower oil
1 recipe quantity Salsa Verde
    (see page 11)

1 Put the salmon, tarragon, garlic, chillies and olive oil in a food processor. Process for
1 minute until well mixed, then transfer to a bowl, cover and chill for 20 minutes.
2 Shape the mixture into 18 patties of equal size.
3 Heat the sunflower oil in a frying pan. Working in batches, fry the fishcakes for
3–4 minutes on each side until golden. Remove from the pan and drain on kitchen
paper. Top each fish cake with ½ tsp of the salsa verde and serve immediately.

PREPARING AHEAD: These can be made to the end of step 2 up to 8 hours in advance, covered
with cling film and stored in the fridge.

271 Calamari with Tartar Sauce

MAKES: 24   **PREPARATION TIME:** 15 minutes   **COOKING TIME:** 20 minutes

120g/4¹/₄oz small squid, cleaned,
    dried and tentacles discarded
150g/5¹/₂oz/scant 1¹/₄ cups plain flour
1 egg, beaten
55g/2oz/heaped ¹/₂ cup breadcrumbs

1l/35fl oz/4 cups sunflower oil
1 lemon, cut into 4 wedges, to serve
125ml/4fl oz/¹/₂ cup tartar sauce,
    to serve

1 Cut the squid into 24 rings, then roll them first in the flour, then in the egg
and finally in the breadcrumbs to coat. Put the coated squid on a plate.
2 Heat the oil in a deep saucepan or wok to 180°C/350°F, or until a few breadcrumbs
sizzle when dropped in. Working in batches, fry the calamari for 4 minutes until
golden, then remove, using a slotted spoon, and drain on kitchen paper. Bring the
oil back to temperature before each batch. Serve with the lemon and tartar sauce.

272 Anchovy & Egg Mayonnaise Tartlets

MAKES: 24 PREPARATION TIME: 25 minutes, plus making the tartlet cases and mayonnaise
COOKING TIME: 8 minutes,

4 eggs, at room temperature
1/2 tsp white wine vinegar
4 tinned anchovy fillets in oil, drained
  and chopped
1 recipe quantity Mayonnaise
  (see page 12)

1/2 recipe quantity savoury Tartlet
  Cases, baked (see page 14)
8 chives, finely chopped
freshly ground black pepper

1 Bring a saucepan of water to the boil. Add the eggs and vinegar and boil for
   6 minutes, then drain and leave to stand until cool enough to handle, then peel.
2 Put the eggs and anchovies in a bowl and mash together, using a fork. Add the
   mayonnaise and mix well. Divide the mixture into the tartlet cases, sprinkle with
   the chives and season with pepper. Serve within 1 hour of assembling.

PREPARING AHEAD: The eggs can be boiled and peeled up to 1 day in advance and stored,
covered, in cold water in the fridge. Do not cut the eggs until ready to use or they will discolour.

273 Squid, Chorizo & Black Olives

SERVES: 12 PREPARATION TIME: 20 minutes   COOKING TIME: 25 minutes

2 tbsp olive oil
3 shallots, thinly sliced
3 garlic cloves, finely chopped
6 tomatoes, coarsely chopped
185g/6^1/2oz/1^1/2 cups pitted black
  olives, chopped

4 tbsp sweet sherry
185g/6^1/2oz chorizo, finely chopped
300g/10^1/2oz small squid,
  cleaned, bodies sliced and
  tentacles left whole
bread, sliced, to serve

1 Heat 1 tbsp of the oil in a frying pan over a medium-low heat. Add the shallots and
   cook, stirring occasionally, for 4 minutes until soft and translucent. Stir in the garlic
   and cook for a further 1 minute until soft. Add the tomatoes, olives and sherry
   and cook for a further 4 minutes until the tomatoes have softened, then set aside.
2 Heat the remaining 1 tbsp oil in a pan over a medium heat. Add the chorizo and
   fry, stirring occasionally, for 3 minutes until cooked on all sides. Add the chorizo
   to the olive mixture, using a slotted spoon. Drain the fat, reheat the pan and cook
   the squid for 2 minutes until cooked through and white.
3 Add the squid to the tomato and chorizo mixture, mix well and serve with bread.

274 Snails with Tarragon Butter

MAKES: 18 PREPARATION TIME: 5 minutes   COOKING TIME: 15 minutes

125g/4^1/2oz butter, diced
2 garlic cloves
1 small handful tarragon leaves

18 tinned snails and shells, drained
1 baguette, sliced, to serve

1 Preheat the oven to 180°C/350°F/Gas 4. Put the butter, garlic and tarragon in a food
   processor and process for 1 minute until soft and well mixed.
2 Put 1 snail in each shell. Spread a little of the herbed butter over the opening of
   each shell and put them in a baking dish. If snails in shells are not available, simply
   put the snails in the baking dish and gently mix in the butter mixture.
3 Bake for 15 minutes until the butter is bubbling. Leave to cool for 5 minutes, then
   serve with the bread.

275 # White Fish & Chicken with Aioli
& Seasonal Vegetables

SERVES: 12   **PREPARATION TIME:** 30 minutes   **COOKING TIME:** 50 minutes

350ml/12fl oz/scant 1½ cups olive oil
12 boneless, skinless chicken thighs,
  halved
6 garlic cloves, crushed to a pulp
6 very fresh egg yolks
6 tbsp sunflower oil
juice of 1 lemon

12 baby new potatoes
12 young bunch carrots, green tops
  trimmed to 1cm/½in
450g/1lb firm white fish
120g/4¼oz asparagus or green beans
12 radishes
salt and freshly ground black pepper

1   Preheat the oven to 180°C/350°F/Gas 4. Heat 2 tbsp of the olive oil in a frying
    pan over a medium-high heat. Add the chicken and cook for 5 minutes, turning
    occasionally, until brown on all sides. Transfer to a baking dish and bake for
    30 minutes, then turn the chicken thighs over and bake for a further 10 minutes
    until cooked through and the juices run clear when the meat is pierced with
    a sharp knife.
2   Meanwhile, put the potatoes in a saucepan, cover with water and bring to the
    boil. Boil for 15–20 minutes until tender, then drain. Meanwhile, boil the carrots
    in another saucepan for 10–15 minutes, or until tender.
3   While the chicken and vegetables are cooking, put the garlic and egg yolks in
    a large bowl and whisk until thick and creamy. Gradually add half of the remaining
    olive oil, 1 tbsp at a time, until well mixed. Add the remaining olive oil and the
    sunflower oil in a thin steady stream, whisking continuously, until thick and glossy.
    Stir in the lemon juice and season with salt and pepper. If the mixture curdles,
    simply put another egg yolk in a clean bowl and slowly and gradually whisk in the
    curdled mixture until amalgamated and thick. Transfer the aioli to a serving bowl.
4   Put the fish in a frying pan and cover with water. Slowly bring to a simmer over a
    low heat and cook for 5 minutes until white yet still firm. Set aside to cool slightly,
    then remove the skin and break the fish into chunks in a bowl.
5   Bring a large saucepan of water to the boil. Add the asparagus and cook for
    2 minutes, then drain. Serve the fish, chicken and vegetables with the aioli.

276 Chicken & Bacon Brochettes on Rosemary Skewers

MAKES: 18   **PREPARATION TIME:** 45 minutes, plus making the dip   **COOKING TIME:** 20 minutes

18 rosemary sprigs, each about
15cm/6in long
18 unsmoked streaky bacon rashers,
halved crossways

6 boneless, skinless chicken
breasts, about 125g/4½oz each,
cut into 36 x 2cm/¾in cubes
1 recipe quantity Mint & Yogurt Dip
(see page 11), to serve

1   Preheat the grill to high. Strip all but the top 1cm/½in of leaves off the rosemary sprigs and reserve for use in another recipe. Wrap the tips of the sprigs in foil.
2   Wrap 1 strip of bacon around each piece of chicken, then thread 2 of the wrapped chicken pieces onto each rosemary skewer.
3   Grill for 8–10 minutes on each side until cooked through. Discard the foil tips and serve with the dip.

277 Chicken, Pancetta & Sage Involtini

MAKES: 18   **PREPARATION TIME:** 20 minutes   **COOKING TIME:** 18 minutes

3 boneless, skinless chicken breasts,
about 125g/4½oz each, cut into
18 pieces of equal size

18 slices of pancetta
18 sage leaves

1   Preheat the oven to 180°C/350°F/Gas 4. Put 1 slice of pancetta on a work surface, then put 1 piece of chicken at one end. Top with 1 sage leaf, then roll the chicken and sage tightly in 1 slice of the pancetta. Secure each of the involtini with a cocktail stick and put them in a baking dish
2   Bake for 18 minutes until cooked through. Serve immediately.

PREPARING AHEAD: These can be made to the end of step 1 up to 1 day in advance and stored in an airtight container in the fridge. Leave at room temperature for 20 minutes before baking.

278 Garlic Chicken Thighs

MAKES: 24   **PREPARATION TIME:** 5 minutes   **COOKING TIME:** 30 minutes

2 tbsp olive oil
4 garlic cloves, whole in their skins

6 boneless, skinless chicken thighs
salt

1   Preheat the oven to 170°C/325°F/Gas 3. Put the oil in a frying pan over a medium heat. Add the garlic cloves and cook, stirring continuously, for 2 minutes. Add the chicken and season with salt. Fry for 8 minutes, then turn, season the other side with salt and fry for a further 8 minutes until brown on all sides.
2   Transfer to a baking dish and bake for 10 minutes until cooked through and the juices run clear when the meat is pierced with a sharp knife. Cut the thighs into quarters and serve.

279 Honey & Lemon Chicken Drumsticks

MAKES: 18   **PREPARATION TIME:** 5 minutes, plus 1 hour marinating
COOKING TIME: 35 minutes

juice and grated zest of 3 lemons
125ml/4fl oz/½ cup clear honey

18 chicken drumsticks
salt and freshly ground black pepper

1 Mix the lemon juice, zest and honey together in a bowl. Add the chicken and mix
   well to coat. Cover and leave to marinate at room temperature for 1 hour.
2 Preheat the oven to 180°C/350°F/Gas 4. Put the chicken in a roasting tin and bake
   for 20 minutes. Remove from the oven and baste by spooning the cooking juices
   in the bottom of the tin over the chicken. Return to the oven and bake for a further
   15 minutes until cooked through and the juices run clear when the meat is pierced
   with a sharp knife. Season with salt and pepper and serve immediately.

280 Turkey & Cranberry Toasts

MAKES: 24   **PREPARATION TIME:** 20 minutes   **COOKING TIME:** 35 minutes
EQUIPMENT: 4cm/1½in plain round pastry cutter

150g/5½oz cranberries
75g/2½oz/scant ⅓ cup caster sugar
280g/10oz turkey breast
30g/1oz butter

2 tbsp olive oil
1 tbsp brandy
8 slices of white bread
salt and freshly ground black pepper

1 Put the cranberries, sugar and 4 tbsp water in a large saucepan over a medium-low
   heat. Cook for 10 minutes, stirring occasionally, until the cranberries have begun
   to pop but have not collapsed. Transfer to a bowl and set aside until needed.
2 Preheat the oven to 160°C/315°F/Gas 2–3. Lightly season the turkey with salt. Heat
   the butter and oil in a frying pan over a medium heat until the butter has melted.
   Add the turkey and cook for 10 minutes on each side until brown. Add the brandy
   and cook for 1–2 minutes until the liquid has almost completely evaporated.
3 Cut 3 circles out of each slice of bread, using the pastry cutter, and put them
   on a baking sheet. Bake for 10 minutes, or until lightly toasted. Meanwhile, cut
   the turkey breast into very thin 4cm/1½in pieces. Dip one side of each toast
   in the juice left from cooking the turkey and top with a slice of meat and 1 tsp
   of the cranberry sauce. Season with pepper and serve immediately.

PREPARING AHEAD: The cranberry sauce can be made up to 2 weeks in advance, covered
and stored in the fridge.

281 Tarragon Chicken Sandwiches

MAKES: 24 PREPARATION TIME: 20 minutes, plus making the chicken and mayonnaise

⅓ recipe quantity Boiled Chicken, about 200g/7oz, shredded (see page 12)
1 large handful tarragon leaves, chopped

1 recipe quantity Mayonnaise (see page 12)
12 slices of white or brown bread
salt and freshly ground black pepper

1 Put the chicken, tarragon and mayonnaise in a bowl, mix well and season with salt and pepper.
2 Spread the chicken mixture over 6 slices of the bread, then cover with the remaining 6 slices, pressing down gently to seal the edges.
3 Just before serving, cut off the crusts, cut each sandwich into 4 squares and serve.

PREPARING AHEAD: These can be made to the end of step 2 up to 4 hours in advance, wrapped in cling film and stored in the fridge.

282 Pesto, Mozzarella & Chicken Goujons

MAKES: 24 PREPARATION TIME: 25 minutes, plus making the pesto
COOKING TIME: 20 minutes

125g/4½oz mozzarella cheese, cut into 24 small cubes
1 recipe quantity Pesto (see page 11)
2 boneless, skinless chicken breasts, about 140g/5oz each, cut into 12 strips each and flattened

2 eggs, beaten
200g/7oz/2 cups breadcrumbs
4 tbsp sunflower oil

1 Put the mozzarella and pesto in a bowl and mix well.
2 Put 1 piece of mozzarella in the centre of each chicken strip and roll to form a tight ball. Dip each ball in the egg, then roll in breadcrumbs to coat.
3 Heat the oil in a frying pan over a medium-high heat until a few breadcrumbs sizzle when dropped in. Working in batches, fry the goujons for 3–4 minutes on each side until golden, then spear them onto cocktail sticks and serve.

283 Spicy Chicken Wings

MAKES: 18 PREPARATION TIME: 5 minutes, plus 1 hour marinating
COOKING TIME: 30 minutes

3 tsp cayenne pepper
3 tsp salt

4½ tsp olive oil
18 chicken wings

1 Put the cayenne pepper, salt and oil in a baking dish and mix well. Add the chicken wings and turn until evenly coated. Leave to marinate, covered, in the fridge for 1 hour.
2 Preheat the oven to 200°C/400°F/Gas 6. Bake for 30 minutes until the wings are golden and the juices run clear when the meat is pierced with a sharp knife. Serve immediately.

284 Chicken Tikka Skewers

MAKES: 24   **PREPARATION TIME:** 20 minutes, plus 1–12 hours marinating and making the dip
COOKING TIME: 15 minutes   **EQUIPMENT:** 24 x 10cm/4in skewers

5 boneless, skinless chicken breasts, about 140g/5oz each, cut into 48 x 4cm/1½in cubes
1 recipe quantity Mint & Yogurt Dip (see page 11), to serve
2 lemons, cut into wedges, to serve

MARINADE
2.5cm/1in piece root ginger, peeled and coarsely chopped
1 garlic clove
4½ tsp tomato purée
1 tsp ground cumin
1 tsp ground coriander
juice of ½ lemon
250ml/9fl oz/1 cup natural yogurt
1 tbsp sunflower oil

1   Put all the marinade ingredients together in a food processor and process for 1 minute until well combined. Transfer to a bowl, add the chicken and stir to coat. Leave to marinate, covered, in the fridge, for at least 1 hour and up to 12 hours.
2   If using wooden skewers, soak them in cold water for at least 30 minutes before grilling. Preheat the grill to high. Put 2 cubes of the chicken on each skewer and put them on a grill rack above a grill pan. Grill the skewers for 15 minutes, turning halfway through, until brown and cooked through. Serve with the dip and lemon wedges.

285 Mini Beef Burgers with Caramelized Onion

MAKES: 24 **PREPARATION TIME:** 20 minutes, plus 1 hour chilling **COOKING TIME:** 45 minutes
EQUIPMENT: 4cm/1½in plain round pastry cutter

450g/1lb beef mince
1 egg
1 tsp salt
1 handful parsley, finely chopped
15g/½oz butter

4 tbsp olive oil
1 onion, finely sliced
8 slices of white bread
2 tbsp Dijon mustard, to serve

1   Put the beef, egg, salt and parsley in a bowl and mix well. Turn the mixture out onto a board and shape into a 2cm/¾in-thick square. Cut out 24 burgers, using the pastry cutter, reshaping the mixture as needed. Transfer to a plate, cover with cling film and chill for 1 hour so the burgers will hold their shape when they are cooked.
2   Heat the butter and 1 tbsp of the oil in a frying pan over a medium-low heat until the butter has melted. Add the onion and cook, stirring occasionally, for 15–20 minutes until sweet, soft and golden brown.
3   Preheat the oven to 180°C/350°F/Gas 4. Cut 24 circles from the bread, using the cleaned pastry cutter and put them on a baking sheet, then brush with a little of the remaining oil and bake for 10 minutes until golden and toasted.
4   Heat the remaining 1 tbsp oil in a frying pan over a medium-high heat. Working in batches, fry the burgers for 2–3 minutes on each side, or until cooked to your liking. Put each burger on a toast circle, top with ¼ tsp of the mustard, followed by 1 tsp of the caramelized onion and serve immediately.

PREPARING AHEAD: These can be made to the end of step 1 up to 8 hours in advance, covered with cling film and stored in the fridge.

286 Wessex Lamb Pasties

MAKES: 24 **PREPARATION TIME:** 35 minutes **COOKING TIME:** 35 minutes
EQUIPMENT: 7cm/2¾in plain round pastry cutter

225g/8oz potatoes, peeled
4½ tsp olive oil, plus extra
  for greasing
½ onion, finely chopped
1 tsp ground cumin
1 carrot, peeled and grated

1 handful parsley, chopped
125g/4½oz lamb mince
500g/1lb 2oz ready-to-roll puff pastry
plain flour, for rolling the pastry
1 egg, beaten with 1 tbsp milk
salt and freshly ground black pepper

1   Put the potatoes in a saucepan, cover with water and bring to the boil. Boil for 15–20 minutes until tender, then drain and set aside. Meanwhile, heat the oil in a frying pan over a medium heat. Add the onion and cumin and cook, stirring occasionally, for 5 minutes until the onions have softened.
2   Coarsely chop the potatoes and mix them with the carrot and parsley in a mixing bowl. Add the onion and lamb mince, season with salt and pepper and mix well.
3   Preheat the oven to 180°C/350°F/Gas 4 and lightly grease a baking sheet. Cut the pastry block in half. On a lightly floured surface, roll half of the pastry into a 30 x 22cm/12 x 8½in rectangle and cut out 12 circles, using the pastry cutter. Put 1 tbsp of the filling slightly off-centre on each pastry circle, then brush the edge with water, fold the pastry in half and press down to seal. Transfer to the baking sheet and repeat with the other half of the pastry and the remaining filling.
4   Brush the pasties with the egg yolk mixture and bake for 12–15 minutes until golden brown, then serve.

PREPARING AHEAD: These can be made to the end of step 3 up to 6 hours in advance, covered with cling film and stored in the fridge before brushing with the egg and baking.

287 Shish Barek with Yogurt

MAKES: 48   **PREPARATION TIME:** 30 minutes, plus 30 minutes soaking the raisins and making the dip
COOKING TIME: 45 minutes

60g/2oz/½ cup raisins
2 tbsp olive oil
1 onion, finely chopped
1 garlic clove, finely chopped
500g/1lb 2oz beef mince
1 tsp salt
1 tbsp paprika
1 tsp ground cinnamon
½ tsp ground nutmeg

½ tsp cumin seeds
1 tsp ground coriander
70g/2½oz/scant ½ cup pine nuts
16 filo pastry sheets
90g/3¼oz butter, melted
375ml/13fl oz/1½ cups sunflower oil,
   plus extra as needed
1 recipe quantity Mint & Yogurt Dip
   (see page 11)

1 Put the raisins in a heatproof bowl and cover with boiling water. Leave to soak for 30 minutes, then drain.
2 Heat the oil in a frying pan over a medium-low heat. Add the onion and cook, stirring occasionally, for 5 minutes until soft. Add the garlic and cook for a further 3 minutes until soft. Stir in the mince and cook, stirring occasionally, for 5 minutes until brown. Add the salt, paprika, cinnamon, nutmeg, cumin and coriander and continue to cook, stirring well, for 2–3 minutes. Stir in the raisins, remove from the heat and leave to cool.
3 Put the pine nuts in a dry frying pan and toast over a medium-low heat for 2–3 minutes, stirring continuously, until just beginning to brown, then stir them into the mince mixture.
4 Put 1 sheet of filo pastry on a work surface and keep the rest covered with a clean damp tea towel while you work. Brush the pastry with a little of the melted butter, then cover with a second filo sheet and butter again. Cut the filo lengthways into 6 long strips.
5 Position 1 pastry strip vertically in front of you. Put 2 tbsp of the filling at the bottom end of the pastry, leaving a little space between the edges of the pastry and the filling. Fold the bottom-right corner of the pastry diagonally up over the filling to form a triangle, then fold the lower left-hand corner up the left edge, keeping the triangular shape. Continue folding until you reach the end of the pastry and the filling is enclosed. Repeat with the remaining pastry and filling.
6 Heat the oil in a deep saucepan or wok until a small piece of pastry sizzles when dropped in. Fry the parcels for 1–2 minutes on each side until golden brown, working in batches to avoid overcrowding the pan. Remove from the pan, using a slotted spoon, and drain on kitchen paper. Repeat with the remaining parcels, adding more oil to the pan if necessary. Serve warm with the dip.

288 Antipasti Platter

SERVES: 12   **PREPARATION TIME:** 10 minutes

360g/12¾oz/2 cups mixed olives
12 sun-dried tomatoes
425g/15oz selection of cured
   meats, such as salami, bresaola,
   mortadella and Parma ham
6 bottled artichoke hearts, halved

185g/6½oz bocconcini
   (mozzarella balls)
2 loaves of Italian bread, such
   as ciabatta, focaccia or Pugliese,
   sliced to serve

1 Arrange all the ingredients on a large serving platter.
2 Serve with the bread.

289 Beef Empanadas

MAKES: 12 **PREPARATION TIME:** 25 minutes **COOKING TIME:** 25 minutes
EQUIPMENT: 8cm/3¼in plain round pastry cutter

1 tbsp olive oil
1 onion, finely chopped
3 garlic cloves, crushed
½ tsp ground nutmeg
1 tsp ground cinnamon
1 tsp ground ginger
1 tsp cayenne pepper

250g/9oz beef mince
80ml/2½fl oz/⅓ cup white wine
1 tbsp tomato purée
plain flour, for rolling the pastry
250g/9oz ready-to-roll puff pastry
1 egg yolk, beaten with 1 tbsp milk
salt and freshly ground black pepper

1 Preheat the oven to 180°C/350°F/Gas 4. Heat the oil in a frying pan over a medium heat. Add the onion and cook, stirring occasionally, for 5 minutes until soft. Add the garlic and cook, stirring, for a further 1 minute. Stir in the spices, add the mince and cook, stirring occasionally, for 2 minutes until brown. Add the wine and stir well. Stir in the tomato purée, season with salt and pepper, then leave to cool.

2 On a lightly floured surface, roll the pastry into a 32 x 24cm/12¾ x 9 ½in rectangle and cut out 12 circles, using the pastry cutter. Put 1 heaped tbsp of the beef mixture slightly off centre on each circle and fold the pastry in half, pressing the edges closed to seal. Put the empanadas on a baking sheet.

3 Brush with the egg yolk mixture, then bake for 15 minutes until puffed and golden. Serve warm.

PREPARING AHEAD: These can be made to the end of step 2 up to 4 hours in advance, covered with cling film and stored in the fridge before brushing with the egg and baking.

90 Beef en Croûtes

MAKES: 24   PREPARATION TIME: 30 minutes   COOKING TIME: 25 minutes

2 tsp olive oil, plus extra
   for greasing
plain flour, for rolling the pastry
250g/9oz ready-to-roll puff pastry
10g/¼oz butter
½ onion, finely chopped

100g/3½oz button mushrooms,
   finely chopped
1 large handful parsley leaves,
   finely chopped
250g/9oz beef fillet
2 tbsp Dijon mustard
1 egg yolk, beaten with 1 tbsp milk

1 Preheat the oven to 200°C/400°F/Gas 6 and lightly grease a baking sheet.
   On a lightly floured surface, roll the pastry into a 36 x 24cm/14 x 9½in rectangle
   and, using a sharp knife, cut out 24 x 6cm/2½in squares.
2 Heat the butter and half of the oil in a frying pan over a medium-low heat. Add the
   onion and fry, stirring occasionally, for 5 minutes until soft. Add the mushrooms
   and cook, stirring occasionally, for a further 8 minutes until brown and soft. Stir
   in the parsley and cook for 1 minute until well combined. Remove from the heat
   and transfer to a bowl.
3 Clean the frying pan and heat the remaining oil over a high heat. Add the beef
   and cook for 30 seconds on each side until brown on the outside but still raw
   on the inside. Cut the seared beef into 1cm/½in-thick slices. Spread each puff
   pastry square with a little of the mustard, cover with 1 tsp of the mushroom
   mixture, then top with 1 piece of the beef. Fold the edges of the pastry around
   the filling and press down to seal the edges. Put the parcels on the baking sheet.
4 Brush with the egg yolk mixture. Bake for 10 minutes until puffed and golden.
   Serve immediately.

PREPARING AHEAD: These can be made to the end of step 3 up to 4 hours in advance, covered
with cling film and stored in the fridge before being brushed with the egg and baked.

291 Wiener Schnitzels

MAKES: 24   PREPARATION TIME: 10 minutes   COOKING TIME: 25 minutes

200g/7oz veal escalopes
150g/5½oz/scant 1¼ cups plain flour
   seasoned with salt
2 eggs, beaten

100g/3½oz/1 cup breadcrumbs
1 tbsp olive oil
2 lemons, cut into wedges

1 Wrap the meat in a sheet of cling film and beat it flat, using a rolling pin. Remove
   the cling film and cut the veal into 24 bite-sized pieces. Dip the veal pieces in the
   flour to coat, then dip them in the eggs and roll in the breadcrumbs to coat.
2 Heat the oil in a frying pan over a medium-high heat. Working in batches, fry the
   schnitzels for 3 minutes on each side until pale brown. Squeeze the lemon wedges
   over the top and serve immediately.

292 Spiced Lamb Pinchos with Mint-Egg Mayonnaise

MAKES: 24 **PREPARATION TIME:** 15 minutes, plus 1 hour marinating and making the mayonnaise
COOKING TIME: 20 minutes

1 egg, at room temperature
1/2 tsp white wine vinegar
1 tsp cumin seeds
1 tsp turmeric
1 tsp paprika
1/4 tsp salt
2 tbsp olive oil
450g/1lb lamb leg or shoulder,
   cut into 24 x 2.5cm/1in cubes

1 tsp capers, finely chopped
1 handful mint leaves,
   coarsely chopped
juice of 1/2 lemon
1/2 recipe quantity Mayonnaise
   (see page 12)
freshly ground black pepper

1 Bring a saucepan of water to the boil. Add the egg and vinegar and boil for
6 minutes, then drain and leave to stand until cool enough to handle.
2 In a large bowl, mix together the cumin, turmeric, paprika, salt and oil, then
add the lamb and rub the mixture all over the lamb. Leave to marinate, covered,
at room temperature for 1 hour.
3 Peel and roughly chop the egg. Put it in a mixing bowl and stir in the capers, mint,
lemon juice and mayonnaise. Season with salt and pepper and set aside until
needed; refrigerate if for more than 30 minutes.
4 Preheat the grill to high. Transfer the lamb to a baking dish and grill for 10 minutes
until brown. Serve warm with the mint-egg mayonnaise with cocktail sticks.

PREPARING AHEAD: The egg mayonnaise in step 3 can be made up to 8 hours in advance
and stored in an airtight container in the fridge.

293 Lamb Pittas with Caramelized Onions & Pine Nuts

MAKES: 18 **PREPARATION TIME:** 20 minutes **COOKING TIME:** 30 minutes

30g/1oz butter
2 tbsp olive oil
2 small onions, thinly sliced
450g/1lb lamb steak

9 pitta breads
6 tbsp natural yogurt
1 large handful watercress
salt and freshly ground black pepper

1 Preheat the oven to 190°C/375°F/Gas 5. Heat the butter and 1 tbsp of the oil
in a frying pan over a medium-low heat until the butter has melted. Add the
onions and cook, stirring occasionally, for 15–20 minutes until sweet, soft and
golden brown.
2 Meanwhile, heat the remaining 1 tbsp oil in a frying pan over a high heat.
Add the lamb and cook for 2–3 minutes on each side until brown. Put the lamb
in a baking dish and bake for 10 minutes. Remove from the oven and leave to rest
for 5 minutes, then slice into 36 x 5mm/1/4in-thick strips.
3 Heat the pitta breads in the oven for 3 minutes until warmed through, then
cut each one in half crossways. Push the sides together to form a hollow centre
and spoon 1 tbsp of the onion into the bread, followed by 2 slices of the lamb.
Add 1/2 tsp of the yogurt and season with salt and pepper. Top with 1 sprig of
watercress. Serve immediately.

294 Asparagus, Ham & Stilton Pastries

MAKES: 36   **PREPARATION TIME:** 20 minutes   **COOKING TIME:** 17 minutes
EQUIPMENT: 3 x 12-hole mini-muffin tins

36 asparagus tips
plain flour, for rolling the pastry
500g/1lb 2oz ready-to-roll puff pastry

60g/2¼oz thinly sliced ham,
  cut into thin strips
60g/2¼oz Stilton cheese, thinly sliced
1 egg yolk, beaten with 1 tbsp milk

1   Preheat the oven to 180°C/350°F/Gas 4. Bring a pan of water to the boil. Add the asparagus tips and boil for 1–2 minutes, then drain and set aside.
2   On a lightly floured surface, roll the pastry into a 30cm/12in square and, using a sharp knife, cut out 36 x 5cm/2in squares. Gently press the pastry squares into the holes of the mini-muffin tins so that the four corners of each square stick up a little.
3   Put a few strips of the ham in each pastry case, followed by 1 slice of Stilton, 1 asparagus spear and then another slice of Stilton. Brush with the egg yolk mixture and bake for 15 minutes until golden and puffed on the edges, then serve.

295 Ham Bonnes Bouches

MAKES: 18   **PREPARATION TIME:** 20 minutes   **COOKING TIME:** 35 minutes
EQUIPMENT: 6cm/2½in plain round pastry cutter

30g/1oz butter
4½ tsp plain flour, plus extra
  for rolling the pastry
500ml/17fl oz/2 cups milk

100g/3½oz cooked gammon
250g/9oz ready-to-roll puff pastry
1 egg yolk, beaten with 1 tbsp milk
salt and freshly ground black pepper

1   Preheat the oven to 180°C/350°F/Gas 4. Melt the butter in a saucepan over a medium-low heat. Stir in the flour. Slowly stir in the milk, 4 tbsp at a time. Continue cooking, stirring continuously, for 1–2 minutes until smooth. Reduce the heat to low and simmer for 15 minutes, stirring occasionally, until pale in colour and satiny in texture. Add the gammon, season with salt and pepper, and leave to cool.
2   On a lightly floured surface, roll the pastry into a 36 x 20cm/14½ x 8in rectangle and cut out 18 circles, using the pastry cutter. Put 1 tbsp of the sauce on each circle, then fold over to form a semi-circle. Press the edges together to seal and transfer to a baking sheet. Brush with the egg yolk mixture and bake for 12–15 minutes until puffed and golden, then serve.

296 Scotch Quail Eggs

MAKES: 18   **PREPARATION TIME:** 25 minutes   **COOKING TIME:** 25 minutes

18 quail eggs, at room temperature
½ tsp white wine vinegar
750g/1lb 10oz pork mince
150g/5½oz/scant 1¼ cups plain flour
3 eggs, beaten

300g/10½oz/3 cups breadcrumbs
4 tbsp olive oil
salt and freshly ground black pepper
250ml/9fl oz/1 cup tomato ketchup,
  to serve

1   Bring a saucepan of water to the boil. Add the eggs and vinegar and boil for 4 minutes, then drain and leave to stand until cool enough to handle, then peel.
2   Put the mince in a bowl and season with salt and pepper. Roll the quail eggs in the flour, then using your hands, firmly press 2 tbsp of the mince around each egg to cover. Dip into the beaten eggs and roll in the breadcrumbs to coat.
3   Heat half of the oil in a frying pan over a medium heat and fry half of the eggs for 10–12 minutes, turning occasionally, until they are golden brown all over and the pork is cooked through. Transfer to a plate and repeat with the remaining oil and eggs. Serve with the ketchup.

PREPARING AHEAD: The eggs can be boiled and peeled up to 1 day in advance and stored, covered, in cold water in the fridge. Do not cut the eggs until ready to use or they will discolour.

297 Honey-Glazed Spare Ribs

MAKES: 18 **PREPARATION TIME:** 15 minutes, plus overnight marinating
COOKING TIME: 35 minutes

3 tbsp soft brown sugar
3 tbsp clear honey
125ml/4fl oz/½ cup soy sauce
2 garlic cloves, finely chopped

1–2 small red chillies, halved
  and deseeded (optional)
600g/1lb 5oz pork ribs, about 9 ribs,
  cut into 18 x 5cm/2in lengths

1 To make the glaze, put the sugar, honey, soy sauce, garlic and chilli, if using, in a small saucepan. Cook over a medium heat, stirring, for 5 minutes until the sugar has dissolved.
2 Put the ribs in a baking dish and pour the glaze over the top. Mix well to coat. Leave to cool, then cover and chill in the fridge overnight or for up to 24 hours.
3 Preheat the oven to 180°C/350°F/Gas 4. Bake the ribs, uncovered, for 20 minutes, then turn them over and bake for a further 10 minutes until brown and glazed. Leave to cool for 5 minutes, as the glaze will be very hot, then serve.

298 Piglets in Blankets

MAKES: 24 **PREPARATION TIME:** 25 minutes **COOKING TIME:** 18 minutes

15g/½oz butter
1 leek, finely sliced
250g/9oz pork mince
½ tsp salt
plain flour, for rolling the pastry

250g/9oz ready-to-roll puff pastry
1 egg yolk, beaten with 1 tbsp milk
2 tbsp sesame seeds
2 tbsp poppy seeds

1 Preheat the oven to 180°C/350°F/Gas 4. Melt the butter in a saucepan over a medium heat. Add the leek and fry, stirring occasionally, for 5 minutes until soft. Put the mince in a bowl, add the leeks and salt and mix well.
2 On a lightly floured surface, roll the pastry into a 22 x 38cm/8½ x 15in rectangle. Cut the pastry in half lengthways and then crossways to create 4 pieces. Spread the pork mixture along the widest side of each rectangle and roll the pastry fairly tightly around it. Brush the egg yolk mixture along the edge of each roll and press to seal.
3 Cut each roll into 6 pieces of equal size and put them on a baking sheet.
4 Brush with the remaining egg yolk mixture and sprinkle with the sesame and poppy seeds. Bake for 12 minutes until golden brown. Serve hot.

PREPARING AHEAD: These can be made to the end of step 3 up to 4 hours in advance, covered with cling film and stored in the fridge before being brushed with the egg and baked.

299 Artichoke Hearts, Parma Ham & Sun-Dried Tomato Parcels

MAKES: 24   **PREPARATION TIME:** 15 minutes

12 bottled artichoke hearts,
   drained and halved

12 slices of Parma ham,
   halved lengthways
6 sun-dried tomatoes, quartered

1   Put 1 artichoke heart half on each piece of Parma ham. Top with 1 piece
    of sun-dried tomato and roll tightly.
2   Secure with cocktail sticks and serve.

300 Water Chestnuts Wrapped in Bacon

MAKES: 24   PREPARATION TIME: 15 minutes   COOKING TIME: 30 minutes

12 rindless, unsmoked streaky bacon
 rashers, halved widthways

24 tinned water chestnuts, about
 220g/7¾oz, drained and rinsed

1   Preheat the oven to 180°C/350°F/Gas 4. Wrap each strip of bacon tightly around
    each water chestnut and put them on a baking sheet.
2   Bake for 25–30 minutes until the bacon has begun to crisp. Serve immediately.

PREPARING AHEAD: These can be made to the end of step 1 up to 1 day in advance, covered
and stored in the fridge until ready to bake.

301 Pancetta, Fontina & Mushroom Piadini

MAKES: 18   PREPARATION TIME: 30 minutes   COOKING TIME: 30 minutes

300g/10½oz/scant 2½ cups
 plain flour
1½ tsp salt
30g/1oz butter, cubed
plain flour, for rolling the dough
3 tbsp olive oil

300g/10½oz button mushrooms,
 finely chopped
9 slices of pancetta, cut into quarters
100g/3½oz fontina cheese, cut into
 36 x thin slices
freshly ground black pepper

1   Put the flour, salt and butter in a large mixing bowl. Add 185ml/6fl oz/¾ cup
    lukewarm water and mix together until the mixture forms a dough. Turn the
    dough out onto a lightly floured surface and knead for 10 minutes until elastic.
2   On a lightly floured surface, roll the piadini dough into a log about 2.5cm/1in
    in diameter, then cut it into 18 x 2cm/1in-thick pieces and, on a lightly floured
    surface, roll each one into a 12cm/4¾in circle.
3   Heat a heavy frying pan over a medium-high heat for 3–4 minutes until hot. Put
    1–2 dough circles in the dry pan and cook for 1 minute until the surface bubbles
    slightly and dark brown spots appear on the underside, then turn over and cook
    for a further 1 minute. Transfer to a baking sheet and repeat with the remaining
    dough circles.
4   Heat the oil in a frying pan over a medium-high heat. Add the mushrooms and
    cook for 5 minutes until soft and beginning to brown. Remove from the heat and
    season with salt.
5   Preheat the grill to high. Divide the mushrooms evenly over the piadini bases, top
    each one with 2 pieces of the pancetta and 2 slices of the fontina. Grill for 4–5
    minutes until the pancetta is cooked and the fontina has melted. Season with
    pepper and serve immediately.

PREPARING AHEAD: The piadini dough can be made up to 2 hours in advance, wrapped in cling
film and stored in the fridge. The cooked piadini bases can also be made up to 2 hours in advance
and stored in an airtight container until needed.

02 Mint Chocolate-Chip Ice Cream

SERVES: 12 **PREPARATION TIME:** 5 minutes, plus churning and freezing the ice cream
COOKING TIME: 10 minutes **EQUIPMENT:** ice-cream machine, small ice-cream scoop

250ml/9fl oz/1 cup milk
150g/5oz/heaped ²/₃ cup caster sugar
5 egg yolks
250ml/9fl oz/1 cup double cream

1¹/₂ tsp peppermint extract
100g/3¹/₂oz dark chocolate,
   coarsely chopped
12 flat-bottom wafer cones, to serve

1 Put the milk in a saucepan, bring to the boil, then remove from the heat and set aside. Put the sugar and egg yolks in a heatproof bowl and, using a whisk or hand-held electric mixer, beat for 1 minute until pale and thick.
2 Pour the hot milk over the mixture and mix well, then pour the mixture back into the saucepan and cook over a very low heat for 8–10 minutes until thick and the mixture coats the back of a spoon. Remove from the heat and stir in the cream and peppermint extract, then leave to cool completely.
3 Churn the mixture in an ice-cream machine according to the manufacturer's instructions. Add the chocolate 5 minutes before churning finishes. Transfer the ice cream to a freezerproof container and freeze for 1 hour.
4 Working quickly, put 1 scoop of ice cream in each wafer cone, using the ice-cream scoop or a teaspoon, and serve immediately.

PREPARING AHEAD: The ice cream can be made up to 1 week in advance and stored in a freezerproof container in the freezer.

303 Iced Fairy Cakes

MAKES: 24 **PREPARATION TIME:** 15 minutes **COOKING TIME:** 10 minutes
EQUIPMENT: 2 x 12-hole mini-muffin tins

90g/3¹/₄oz/heaped ¹/₃ cup
   caster sugar
90g/3¹/₄oz unsalted butter, softened
2 eggs
90g/3¹/₄oz/¾ cup plain flour
1 tsp baking powder
2 tsp vanilla extract

1 egg white
300g/10¹/₂oz/heaped 2¹/₃ cups icing
   sugar, sifted, plus extra as needed
a few drops food colouring (optional)
1 tbsp colourful sugar balls, sprinkles
   or 24 glacé cherries, to decorate

1 Preheat the oven to 180°C/350°F/Gas 4 and line the mini-muffin tins with cupcake cases. Put the caster sugar, butter and eggs in a mixing bowl and beat, using a whisk or electric hand-held mixer, for 2–3 minutes until smooth. The mixture may appear to curdle, but simply keep beating and it will turn smooth. Sift in the flour and baking powder and mix gently until thick. Stir in the vanilla extract. Alternatively, put all the above ingredients in a food processor and process for 1–2 minutes until thick.
2 Fill each of the cupcake cases halfway with the batter and bake for 10 minutes until risen and golden brown. Remove from the oven and leave to cool completely.
3 To make the icing, put the egg white and icing sugar in a bowl and whisk until the mixture forms a thick paste. Add a little more icing sugar or a few drops of water if necessary to achieve a spreading consistency. Stir in the food colouring, if using.
4 Spread the icing over the cakes. Carefully drop the sugar balls, sprinkles or cherries, if using, over the wet icing to decorate. Leave the icing to set for a few minutes, then serve.

304 Pecan Tartlets

MAKES: 24   PREPARATION TIME: 15 minutes, plus making the tartlet cases
COOKING TIME: 12 minutes

125g/4½oz unsalted butter
125g/4½oz/⅔ cup soft brown sugar
100g/3½oz/1 cup pecan nut halves,
   plus 24 extra to decorate

1 egg
½ recipe quantity sweet Tartlet Cases,
   blind-baked (see page 14)

1   Preheat the oven to 180°C/350°F/Gas 4. Put the butter, sugar, pecan nuts and egg in a food processor and process for 2 minutes until thick.
2   Spoon the mixture into the tartlet cases and top each one with 1 pecan half. Put them on a baking sheet and bake for 10–12 minutes until brown. Remove from the oven and leave to cool for 10 minutes. Serve warm or at room temperature.

PREPARING AHEAD: These can be made up to 8 hours in advance, covered and stored at room temperature.

305 Lemon Meringue Tartlets

MAKES: 24   PREPARATION TIME: 20 minutes, plus 1 hour chilling and making the tartlet cases
COOKING TIME: 6 minutes

2 egg whites, at room temperature
juice of ½ lemon
90g/3¼oz/½ cup caster sugar
½ recipe quantity sweet Tartlet Cases,
   baked (see page 14)

LEMON CURD
2 eggs, beaten
150g/5oz/heaped ⅔ cup caster sugar
juice and grated zest of 2 lemons
55g/2oz unsalted butter, diced

1   To make the lemon curd, put the eggs and sugar in a heatproof mixing bowl and beat, using a whisk or hand-held electric mixer, for 3 minutes until pale and fluffy. Stir in the lemon juice and zest and put the bowl over a saucepan of barely simmering water, making sure the bottom of the bowl does not touch the water. Add the butter and cook, stirring continuously, for 5 minutes until the butter has melted and the mixture is glossy. Leave to cool and then chill, covered, for 1 hour.
2   When ready to serve, make the meringue. Beat the egg whites in a large mixing bowl, using a whisk or hand-held electric mixer, for 3 minutes until stiff peaks form. Stir in the lemon juice and 2 tbsp of the sugar, then, using a metal spoon, fold in the remaining sugar.
3   Preheat the grill to high. Spoon the lemon curd into the tartlet cases and top with 1 tbsp of the meringue. Put the tartlets on a baking sheet and grill for 30 seconds until the meringue has begun to brown. Serve immediately.

PREPARING AHEAD: The lemon curd in step 1 can be made up to 1 day in advance and stored in an airtight container in the fridge.

306 Lemonade Ice Lollies

MAKES: 12   **PREPARATION TIME:** 10 minutes, plus 4 hours freezing
COOKING TIME: 3 minutes   **EQUIPMENT:** 12 x 80ml/3fl oz lollipop moulds with sticks

5 lemons, cut into 8 wedges each
250g/9oz/heaped 1 cup caster sugar

1   Put the lemons and sugar in a large heatproof bowl and cover with 1l/35fl oz/
    4 cups boiled water. Stir until the sugar has dissolved. Leave to stand for 2 hours.
2   Using your hands, squeeze the lemons into the mixture to release as much juice
    as possible, then discard the rinds. Strain the lemon mixture into the lollipop
    moulds, insert the sticks and freeze for 4 hours until frozen solid.
3   Just before serving, dip the moulds in a basin of hot water for 30 seconds to loosen
    the lollies, then serve immediately.

PREPARING AHEAD: These can be made up to 1 week in advance and stored in a freezerproof
container in the freezer.

307 Profiteroles

MAKES: 36   PREPARATION TIME: 25 minutes, plus making the crème patissiere
COOKING TIME: 30 minutes   EQUIPMENT: 3 x 12-hole muffin tins or 3 baking sheets

45g/1½oz unsalted butter, plus
   extra for greasing
1 tbsp caster sugar
70g/2½oz/heaped ½ cup plain flour
2 eggs, beaten

150g/5½oz plain chocolate, chopped
150ml/5fl oz/scant ⅔ cup double
   cream, lightly whipped
½ recipe quantity Crème Patissiere
   (see page 15)

1   Preheat the oven to 200°C/400°F/Gas 6 and grease the muffin tins or baking sheets.
Put the butter in a medium saucepan and heat over a low heat until melted. Add
the sugar and 125ml/4fl oz/½ cup water and bring to the boil. Sift the flour into
the saucepan and stir until the mixture forms a ball that comes away from the sides
of the pan. Remove from the heat and leave to cool for 5 minutes.

2   Add the eggs, a little at a time, mixing in thoroughly before adding more. Spoon
the choux mixture into the muffin tins, filling them no more than ¾ of the way.
Alternatively, spoon 36 balls of the mixture directly onto the baking sheets.

3   Bake for 20 minutes until puffed and golden. Remove from the oven. Using a sharp
knife, make a cut in the top of each pastry, half-pulling off the top to release the
steam so the profiteroles don't get soggy. Transfer to a wire rack and leave to cool.

4   When ready to assemble, put the chocolate in a heatproof bowl and rest it over
a pan of gently simmering water, making sure the bottom of the bowl does not
touch the water. Heat for 4–5 minutes, stirring, until the chocolate has melted. Put
the cream and crème patisserie in a bowl and mix well. Spoon the cream mixture
into the centre of the pastries, then arrange on a serving plate. Carefully pour the
melted chocolate over the top, leave to set for a few minutes and then serve.

PREPARING AHEAD: The pastries should be made to the end of step 3 up to 6 hours in advance
and stored in an airtight container at room temperature.

308 Lemongrass, Mango & Chilli Sorbet

SERVES: 18   **PREPARATION TIME:** 10 minutes, plus churning the sorbet
COOKING TIME: 10 minutes   **EQUIPMENT:** ice-cream machine, small ice-cream scoop

380g/13½oz/1½ cups caster sugar
2 lemongrass stalks,
  coarsely chopped
1 large red chilli, coarsely chopped

4 tbsp liquid glucose (optional)
2 mangoes, peeled, halved,
  stoned and chopped
18 flat-bottom wafer cones, to serve

1   Put the sugar, lemongrass, chilli, glucose, if using, and 250ml/9fl oz/1 cup water
  in a saucepan and heat over a medium-low heat for 5 minutes, stirring occasionally,
  until the sugar has dissolved. Increase the heat to high and bring to the boil.
  Boil for 5 minutes until syrupy. Remove from the heat and leave to cool.
2   Put the mango in a blender and blend for 1–2 minutes until smooth. Strain the
  sugar syrup into the mango and mix well. Transfer the mixture to an ice-cream
  machine and churn according to the manufacturer's instructions until frozen.
3   Working quickly, put 1 scoop of sorbet on each wafer cone, using the ice-cream
  scoop or a teaspoon, and serve immediately.

PREPARING AHEAD: The sorbet can be made up to 1 week in advance and stored in a freezerproof
container in the freezer.

309 Hazelnut Ice Cream

SERVES: 12   **COOKING TIME:** 15 minutes   **PREPARATION TIME:** 15 minutes, plus churning and
freezing the ice cream   **EQUIPMENT:** ice-cream machine, small ice-cream scoop

500ml/17fl oz/2 cups milk
205g/7¼oz/scant 1 cup caster sugar
5 egg yolks

100g/3½oz/scant ¾ cup hazelnuts,
  toasted
12 flat-bottom wafer cones, to serve

1   Put the milk in a saucepan and bring to the boil, then remove from the heat
  and set aside. Put the egg yolks and 150g/5oz/heaped ⅔ cup of the sugar
  in a heatproof bowl and, using a whisk or hand-held electric mixer, beat for
  2–3 minutes until thick and pale yellow. Pour the hot milk over the mixture and
  mix well.
2   Set the bowl over a saucepan of simmering water, making sure the bottom
  of the bowl does not touch the water, and cook, stirring continuously to keep
  the eggs from scrambling, for 10 minutes until the mixture thickens into a custard.
  Remove from the heat and leave to cool completely, stirring occasionally to avoid
  a skin forming on the top.
3   Line a baking sheet with greaseproof paper. Put the sugar and 2 tbsp water
  in a saucepan and heat over a low heat, stirring occasionally, until the sugar has
  dissolved. Bring the mixture to the boil and boil for 5 minutes until bubbling and
  beginning to turn golden brown. Remove from the heat and quickly stir in the nuts
  to coat. Return to the heat and cook, stirring, for a further 30 seconds so the
  caramel remains liquid.
4   Turn the nuts out onto the greaseproof paper and spread the mixture into
  a single layer. Leave to cool and set for 5 minutes, then cover with another piece
  of greaseproof paper and crush with a rolling pin to form rough crumbs.
5   Put the custard in an ice-cream machine and churn, setting the timer for 5 minutes
  less than the manufacturer's instructions. Add the crushed hazelnuts in the final
  5 minutes and churn.
6   Working quickly, put 1 scoop of ice cream on each wafer cone, using the ice-cream
  scoop or a teaspoon, and serve immediately.

PREPARING AHEAD: The ice cream can be made up to 1 week in advance and stored
in a freezerproof container in the freezer.

310 Baklava

MAKES: 36 **PREPARATION TIME:** 15 minutes, plus 24 hours resting
COOKING TIME: 30 minutes

150g/5oz/1 cup pistachio nuts
100g/3½oz/scant 1 cup flaked
    almonds
100g/3½oz/scant ¾ cup blanched
    hazelnuts
2 tsp ground ginger
2 tsp ground cinnamon

2 tsp ground nutmeg
8 filo pastry sheets
30g/1oz unsalted butter, melted
380g/13½oz/heaped 1⅔ cups
    caster sugar
juice of 4 lemons

1 Preheat the oven to 180°C/350°F/Gas 4. Put the nuts in a food processor and pulse until coarsely chopped. Add the ginger, cinnamon and nutmeg and mix well.

2 Put 1 sheet of filo pastry in a roasting tin or cake tin that is the same size as the filo sheet. Brush with a little of the melted butter and top with another sheet of pastry. Evenly spread one third of the nut mixture over the top, then cover with another 2 sheets of pastry, brushing each with melted butter. Continue layering the nuts and pastry, ending with a top layer of filo. Then, using a sharp knife, carefully cut several evenly spaced diagonal lines through the pastry in one direction and then in the other to form 36 diamonds. Bake for 30 minutes until golden.

3 Meanwhile, prepare the sugar syrup. Put the sugar, lemon juice and 4 tbsp water in a saucepan. Cook over a low heat, stirring occasionally, for 5 minutes until the sugar has dissolved. Increase the heat slightly and bring to the boil. Boil for 5 minutes until syrupy.

4 Remove the baklava from the oven and leave to cool for 5 minutes, then evenly pour the syrup over the top. Leave to stand, covered, in a cool place for 24 hours, then serve with napkins, as it is very sticky!

PREPARING AHEAD: This can be made up to 3 days in advance, covered with cling film and stored at room temperature.

311 Gingerbread Loaf

SERVES: 18 **PREPARATION TIME:** 10 minutes **COOKING TIME:** 45 minutes
EQUIPMENT: 900g/2lb loaf tin

100g/3½oz unsalted butter, plus
    extra for greasing and to serve
90g/3¼oz/heaped ⅓ cup
    caster sugar
100g/3½oz/¼ cup plus 1 tbsp
    golden syrup
100g/3½oz/¼ cup plus 1 tbsp
    treacle or molasses
2 tbsp orange marmalade

125ml/4fl oz/½ cup milk
2 eggs, beaten
200g/7oz/heaped 1½ cups plain flour
2 tsp baking powder
1 tsp ground ginger
½ tsp ground cinnamon
½ tsp ground nutmeg
60g/2¼oz crystallized ginger,
    finely chopped

1 Preheat the oven to 170°C/325°F/Gas 3 and lightly grease and line the loaf tin. Put the butter, sugar, golden syrup, treacle and marmalade in a saucepan and heat over a medium heat, stirring occasionally, until the butter has melted. Add the milk and mix well.

2 Remove from the heat and stir in the eggs. Sift in the flour, baking powder, ginger, cinnamon and nutmeg. Add the crystalized ginger and mix well. Pour the mixture into the loaf tin.

3 Bake for 40 minutes until firm to the touch and cooked through. Leave to cool in the tin for 10 minutes, then turn out of the tin, transfer to a cooling rack and leave to cool completely.

4 Serve warm or at room temperature, spread with butter.

PREPARING AHEAD: This can be made up to 12 hours in advance, left to cool completely and then stored in an airtight container at room temperature.

12 Raspberry Meringues

MAKES: 36   **PREPARATION TIME:** 30 minutes   **COOKING TIME:** 1 hour 15 minutes

3 egg whites
85g/3oz/heaped ⅓ cup caster sugar
85g/3oz/⅔ cup icing sugar, sifted,
  plus extra for dusting

175g/6oz/¾ cup crème fraîche
36 raspberries

1   Preheat the oven to 130°C/250°F/Gas 1. Put the egg whites in a large mixing
    bowl and beat, using a whisk or hand-held electric mixer with a whisk attachment,
    for 2–3 minutes until soft peaks form. Slowly add the caster sugar and beat for
    a further 3–5 minutes until shiny and stiff. Gently but thoroughly fold in one third
    of the icing sugar, using a metal spoon, then fold in the remaining icing sugar.
2   Line a baking sheet with baking parchment and spoon the meringue mixture into
    36 x 3cm/1¼in circles, spacing them 2cm/¾in apart. Bake for 45 minutes, then turn
    the oven down to 70°C/150°F/Gas ¼ and bake for a further 30 minutes until hard.
    Remove from the oven and leave to cool completely.
3   When ready to serve, top each meringue with 1 tsp of the crème fraîche and
    1 raspberry. Dust with icing sugar and serve.

PREPARING AHEAD: The meringues can be made up to 1 month in advance and stored
in an airtight container.

CHAPTER 6

WEDDINGS

A wedding reception is the party of all parties – a celebration on a day when romance and happiness seem completely limitless. It's an occasion to indulge in sophisticated, grown-up flavours, and the stunning selection of world tapas recipes in this chapter will help you stamp your personality on the event of a lifetime.

Use this chapter to inspire a caterer or, if you're determined to do it yourself, make sure you have lots of help and make sure to organize a series of taste tests in the months leading up to the day. Designed for 24–36 guests, the recipes here can easily be adapted no matter how many guests you're inviting. Choose a few dishes that can be prepared ahead of time, such as Quail Eggs with Fiery Salt and Florentines, and some that are super quick to make, like Salmon Sashimi and Chicory Leaves with Blue Cheese & Mango Chutney. Spoil yourself and your guests with elegant dishes such as Lobster Tartlets, Figs & Mozzarella Wrapped in Honey-Drizzled Parma Ham and Oysters with Shallot Dressing. Top off the celebration with delicacies like Chocolate-Dipped Strawberries and Hazelnut Meringue Nests for a true taste of happy-ever-after.

CHOCOLATE-DIPPED STRAWBERRIES (SEE PAGE 207)

313　Asparagus California Rolls

MAKES: 24　**PREPARATION TIME:** 20 minutes, plus 20 minutes resting
COOKING TIME: 20 minutes　**EQUIPMENT:** sushi mat

210g/7¹/₂oz/1 cup sushi rice
1 tsp caster sugar
1 tbsp rice vinegar
2 tsp mirin
2 tsp sake
¹/₄ tsp salt
2 tbsp wasabi paste

4 nori sheets
125ml/4fl oz/¹/₂ cup rice wine
　　vinegar, mixed with 125ml/4fl oz/
　　¹/₂ cup water
16 asparagus spears
15g/¹/₂oz pickled ginger, to serve
125ml/4fl oz/¹/₂ cup soy sauce,
　　to serve

1　Cook the sushi rice according to the packet instructions. Set aside to rest for 20 minutes.
2　Put the sugar, rice vinegar, mirin, sake and salt in a bowl and mix well. Stir this mixture into the rice.
3　Put the wasabi paste and 2 tbsp water in a small bowl and mix well.
4　Put the sushi mat in a landscape position in front of you and put a sheet of nori on top, shiny-side down. Dip your hands into the vinegar and water mixture and spread a thin layer of the rice over the nori, leaving a 2.5cm/1in gap along the top.
5　Spread a thin line of the wasabi paste across the bottom third of the rice, then put 4 asparagus spears on top. Starting at the bottom edge and working upwards, roll the mat tightly around the filling, then slowly peel back the mat and seal the edge of the nori with a dab of water. Repeat with the remaining nori and fillings.
6　When ready to serve, slice each sushi roll into 6 pieces of equal size, using a very sharp knife. Serve with the ginger and soy sauce.

PREPARING AHEAD: The sushi rolls can be made up to 4 hours in advance, wrapped, uncut, in cling film and stored in the fridge. Slice and serve at room temperature.

314　Feta & Mint Filo Parcels

MAKES: 24　**PREPARATION TIME:** 25 minutes, plus making the dip　**COOKING TIME:** 30 minutes

125g/4¹/₂oz feta cheese, crumbled
1 egg yolk
1 handful mint leaves, finely chopped
8 sheets of filo pastry
55g/2oz butter, melted

375ml/13fl oz/1¹/₂ cups sunflower oil,
　　plus extra as needed
1 recipe quantity Mint & Yogurt Dip
　　(see page 11)

1　Put the feta, egg yolk and mint in a large bowl and mix well.
2　Put 1 sheet of filo pastry on a work surface and keep the rest covered with a clean damp tea towel while you work. Brush the pastry with a little of the melted butter, then cover with a second filo sheet and butter again. Cut the filo lengthways into 6 long strips.
3　Position 1 pastry strip vertically in front of you. Put scant 1 tbsp of the filling at the bottom end of the pastry, leaving a little space between the edges of the pastry and the filling. Fold the bottom-right corner of the pastry diagonally up over the filling to form a triangle, then fold the lower left-hand corner up the left edge, keeping the triangular shape. Continue folding until you reach the end of the pastry and the filling is enclosed. Repeat with the remaining pastry and filling.
4　Heat the oil in a deep saucepan or wok until a small piece of pastry sizzles when dropped in. Fry the parcels for 1–2 minutes on each side until golden brown, working in batches to avoid overcrowding the pan. Remove from the pan, using a slotted spoon, and drain on kitchen paper. Repeat with the remaining parcels, adding more oil to the pan, if necessary. Serve hot, warm or cool with the dip.

PREPARING AHEAD: These can be made to the end of step 3 up to 1 day in advance, covered with cling film and stored in the fridge.

15 Quail Eggs with Fiery Salt

MAKES: 24   **PREPARATION TIME:** 15 minutes   **COOKING TIME:** 5 minutes

24 quail eggs, at room temperature
3 tbsp salt

1 tsp ground coriander
$1/2$–1 tsp cayenne pepper

1   Bring a large saucepan of water to the boil. Carefully add the quail eggs and cook for 4 minutes. Drain, rinse under cold water and peel.
2   Put the salt, coriander and cayenne pepper in a shallow bowl and mix well. Serve the eggs at room temperature with the spice mixture for dipping.

PREPARING AHEAD: The eggs can be boiled and peeled up to 1 day in advance and stored, covered, in cold water in the fridge. Do not cut the eggs until ready to use or they will discolour.

16 Potato Latke with Crème Fraîche

MAKES: 24   **PREPARATION TIME:** 25 minutes   **COOKING TIME:** 40 minutes

5 potatoes, peeled and
   coarsely grated
2 tbsp sunflower oil, plus extra
   as needed
1 tbsp finely chopped onion
2 eggs, beaten

1 handful parsley,
   finely chopped
75g/2$1/2$oz/$1/3$ cup crème fraîche
salt and freshly ground black pepper

1   Put the potatoes in a clean dry tea towel and squeeze out as much of the excess liquid as possible, then transfer to a large bowl.
2   Heat 1 tbsp of the oil in a frying pan over a medium heat. Add the onion and cook, stirring occasionally, for 5 minutes until soft and translucent. Remove from the heat and add to the potatoes. Stir in the eggs and season with salt and pepper.
3   Shape the mixture into 24 small balls of equal size, using your hands, then gently flatten them.
4   Heat the remaining oil in a frying pan over a medium heat. Working in batches, fry the latke for 4 minutes on each side until golden brown, adding more oil to the pan as needed.
5   Put the parsley and crème fraîche in a bowl and mix well. Top each latke with 1 tsp of the crème fraîche, season with pepper and serve.

17 Chicory Leaves with Blue Cheese & Mango Chutney

MAKES: 24   **PREPARATION TIME:** 10 minutes

125g/4$1/2$oz blue cheese, crumbled
24 chicory leaves, about 2 heads
125g/4$1/2$oz/$1/2$ cup mango chutney

1   Put 1 tsp of the cheese on each chicory leaf.
2   Top with 1 tsp of the chutney and serve.

318 Honeyed Crostini with Grapes & Camembert

MAKES: 24   PREPARATION TIME: 10 minutes   COOKING TIME: 15 minutes

1/2 x 50cm/20in baguette, cut into
    24 thin slices
2 tbsp olive oil, for brushing
4 tbsp clear honey

250g/9oz Camembert cheese,
    cut into 24 slices
12 white seedless grapes,
    quartered lengthways

1   Preheat the oven to 200°C/400°F/Gas 6. Put the bread slices on a baking sheet,
    brush with the oil and bake for 8 minutes until lightly toasted. Drizzle the honey
    over the crostini and bake for a further 7 minutes until golden.
2   Put 1 slice of the cheese on each of the crostini, top with 2 grape quarters
    and serve.

319 Paneer Tikka Skewers

MAKES: 9 double or 18 single skewers   PREPARATION TIME: 10 minutes, plus 1–8 hours
marinating   COOKING TIME: 10 minutes   EQUIPMENT: 9 or 18 x 10cm/4in skewers

2 tsp olive oil
1 tbsp garam masala
1 tbsp finely grated root ginger
1 red chilli, chopped
1 tsp black mustard seeds

juice of 1/2 lemon
4 tbsp natural yogurt
250g/9oz paneer cheese,
    cut into 18 x 3cm/11/4in cubes
salt

1   Heat the oil in a frying pan over a medium heat. Add the garam masala, ginger,
    chilli and mustard seeds and cook, stirring, for 2 minutes until well mixed and
    aromatic. Remove from the heat and leave to cool.
2   Put the spice mixture, lemon juice and yogurt in a coffee grinder or small food
    processor and process for 1 minute, or until well combined. Season with salt.
3   Put the paneer and yogurt marinade in a non-metallic bowl and mix gently until
    the cheese is well coated. Cover and leave to marinate in the fridge for at least
    1 hour and up to 8 hours.
4   If using wooden skewers, soak them in cold water for at least 30 minutes before
    grilling. Heat the grill to high and line a baking tray with foil. Put 1 or 2 paneer
    cubes on each skewer and place on the baking sheet. Grill for 6 minutes, turning
    halfway through, until starting to brown. Serve immediately.

320 Halloumi & Tomato Puff-Pastry Croûtes

MAKES: 18   PREPARATION TIME: 15 minutes   COOKING TIME: 8 minutes
EQUIPMENT: 6cm/21/2in plain round pastry cutter

plain flour, for rolling the pastry
250g/9oz ready-to-roll puff pastry
125g/41/2oz halloumi cheese,
    chopped

125g/41/2oz cherry tomatoes,
    finely diced
1 tsp olive oil
leaves from 1–2 oregano sprigs
salt and freshly ground black pepper

1   Preheat the oven to 200°C/400°F/Gas 6. On a lightly floured surface, roll out the
    pastry into a 24 x 30cm/91/2 x 12in rectangle. Cut out 18 circles, using the pastry
    cutter. Put the circles on a baking sheet and cover with a sheet of baking
    parchment. Top with another baking sheet to weigh the pastry down, then
    bake for 8 minutes until golden. Remove the top baking sheet and baking
    parchment and set the croûtes aside until ready to assemble.
2   Top each croûte with a little of the halloumi, followed by a few pieces of the
    tomato. Drizzle with the oil, sprinkle with the oregano leaves and season with
    salt and pepper, then serve.

21 Red Pepper & Pesto Tartlets

MAKES: 24 **PREPARATION TIME:** 10 minutes, plus making the tartlet cases and pesto
COOKING TIME: 20 minutes

4 red peppers, halved lengthways,
  deseeded and deveined
1 garlic clove, peeled and chopped
125ml/4fl oz/½ cup olive oil
½ recipe quantity savoury Tartlet
  Cases, baked (see page 14)

½ recipe quantity Pesto (see page 11)
12 pitted black olives, quartered
24 very small basil leaves, to serve
salt and freshly ground black pepper

1   Preheat the oven to 200°C/400°F/Gas 6. Put the peppers, skin-side up, in a roasting
    tin. Bake for 20 minutes, or until the skin is wrinkled and slightly charred. Leave to
    cool, then peel the skin from the peppers, using a sharp knife

2   Put the peppers, garlic and oil in a food processor and process for 1 minute until
    smooth. Season with salt and pepper.

3   Divide the red pepper mixture into the tartlet cases. Top with ½ tsp of the pesto,
    1 piece of black olive and 1 basil leaf. Serve immediately.

PREPARING AHEAD: The red pepper mixture can be made to the end of step 2 up to 1 day
in advance and stored in an airtight container in the fridge.

322 Gazpacho Shot Glasses with Chive Straws

MAKES: 30   **PREPARATION TIME:** 20 minutes, plus 1–2 hours chilling   **EQUIPMENT:** 30 shot glasses

1kg/2lb 4oz tomatoes
3 garlic cloves, finely chopped
1 green pepper, deseeded and
  finely diced
½ cucumber, halved lengthways,
  deseeded and finely diced

2 slices of day-old white bread,
  finely diced
leaves from 2 mint sprigs
125ml/4fl oz/½ cup red wine vinegar
125ml/4fl oz/½ cup olive oil
30 chives, trimmed, to serve

1 Cut a small cross in the bottom of each tomato and put them in a large
heatproof bowl. Cover with boiled water, leave to stand for 8 minutes, then drain.
Peel the tomatoes, using a sharp knife, then coarsely chop them and transfer to
a mixing bowl. Stir in the garlic, pepper and cucumber.

2 Add the bread, mint, vinegar and oil and mix well. Cover and chill for 1–2 hours.

3 Divide the gazpacho into the shot glasses, put 1 chive 'straw' in each glass and serve.

PREPARING AHEAD: The gazpacho can be made up to 1 day in advance and stored in an airtight
container in the fridge.

23 Smoked Salmon, Cream Cheese & Cucumber Crostini

MAKES: 24   PREPARATION TIME: 20 minutes, plus making the crostini

360g/12³/₄oz smoked salmon,
  cut into thin strips
1 cucumber, halved lengthways,
  deseeded and finely diced
1 tbsp olive oil

150g/5¹/₂oz/²/₃ cup cream cheese
¹/₂ recipe quantity Crostini
  (see page 15)
freshly ground black pepper

1 Put the salmon, cucumber and oil in a bowl and mix gently.
2 Spread 1 heaped tsp of the cream cheese onto each of the crostini and top with 1 tbsp of the salmon mixture. Season with pepper and serve.

24 Spicy Squid

SERVES: 24   PREPARATION TIME: 20 minutes   COOKING TIME: 10 minutes

2 large bunches coriander leaves,
  finely chopped
2 large red chillies,
  finely chopped
2 lemongrass stalks,
  finely chopped

600g/1lb 5oz small squid with
  tentacles, washed and dried
2 tbsp olive oil
2 tbsp sunflower oil
salt

1 Put the coriander, chillies and lemongrass in a bowl and mix well.
2 Put the squid and olive oil in another bowl. Season with salt and mix well.
3 Heat the sunflower oil in a frying pan over a medium-high heat. Working in batches, fry the squid for 1 minute until starting to brown. Remove the squid from the pan, using a slotted spoon, and add it to the coriander mixture. Toss to coat, then transfer to a shallow serving bowl and serve.

325 Gem Lettuce Boats with Prawn & Lime Mayonnaise

MAKES: 24   PREPARATION TIME: 20 minutes, plus making the mayonnaise

grated zest of 1 lime
1 recipe quantity Mayonnaise
  (see page 12), replacing the lemon
  juice with lime juice

24 peeled, cooked prawns
24 Little Gem lettuce leaves,
  about 2 heads
freshly ground black pepper

1 Stir the lime zest into the mayonnaise.
2 Put 1 prawn on each lettuce leaf and top with 1 tsp of the mayonnaise. Season with pepper and serve.

326 Smoked Eel & Horseradish on Rye

MAKES: 24　**PREPARATION TIME:** 20 minutes, plus 30 minutes resting

125ml/4fl oz/½ cup
　double cream
2 tbsp grated horseradish
juice of ½ lemon
85g/3oz skinless smoked eel

3 slices of rye bread, each cut
　into 8 small squares
2 large gherkins, finely chopped
salt and freshly ground black pepper

1　Put the cream in a mixing bowl and beat, using a whisk or electric hand-held mixer, for 1–2 minutes until soft peaks form. Add the horseradish and lemon juice and mix well, then season with salt and leave to stand for 30 minutes.

2　Cut the eel into small slices similar in size to the bread squares. Spread 1 tsp of the horseradish mixture onto each bread square, then cover with 1 slice of eel and a few pieces of the gherkin. Season with pepper and serve.

327 Smoked Haddock & Quail Egg Tartlets

MAKES: 24　**PREPARATION TIME:** 25 minutes, plus making the tartlet cases and mayonnaise
COOKING TIME: 10 minutes

250g/9oz undyed smoked haddock
1 recipe quantity Mayonnaise
　(see page 12)
12 quail eggs, at room temperature

½ recipe quantity savoury Tartlet
　Cases, baked (see page 14)
5 chives, finely chopped
freshly ground black pepper

1　Put the haddock in a large frying pan and cover with water. Bring to the boil over a high heat, then reduce the heat to medium-low and simmer gently for 5 minutes until white but still firm. Drain and leave to cool for a few minutes.

2　Flake the fish into a bowl, carefully removing and discarding any bones and skin. Gently stir in the mayonnaise.

3　Bring a large saucepan of water to the boil. Carefully add the quail eggs and cook for 4 minutes. Drain, rinse under cold water and peel. Cut in half lengthways.

4　To assemble, put 1 tbsp of the haddock mayonnaise in each tartlet case. Top with ½ quail egg, sprinkle with the chives and season with pepper. Serve immediately.

PREPARING AHEAD: The haddock mayonnaise can be made to the end of step 2 up to 1 day in advance and stored in an airtight container in the fridge until ready to use. The eggs can be boiled and peeled up to 1 day in advance and stored, covered, in cold water in the fridge. Do not cut the eggs until ready to use or they will discolour.

328 Oysters with Shallot Dressing

MAKES: 24   **PREPARATION TIME:** 25 minutes   **EQUIPMENT:** oyster knife and protective glove

1 shallot, finely chopped
80ml/2½fl oz/⅓ cup red wine vinegar

24 oysters
3 tsp Tabasco sauce

1   Put the shallot and red wine vinegar in a small non-metallic bowl and mix well.
2   To shuck the oysters, wear a protective glove or use a folded tea towel as a barrier between the hand holding the oyster and the oyster. Hold the oyster, flat-side up, and push the tip of the oyster knife as far as you can into the shell at the narrow end and prize it open. Remove the top shell and the muscle attaching the oyster to its shell. If not serving immediately, pack the shucked oysters, in their bottom shells, in crushed ice and keep in the fridge for up to 2 hours.
3   Put ½ tsp of the dressing on each oyster and add 1–2 drops of the Tabasco sauce, if using, and serve immediately.

PREPARING AHEAD: The shallot dressing in step 1 can be made up to 1 day in advance, covered and stored in the fridge until ready to use.

329 Salmon Sashimi

MAKES: 24   **PREPARATION TIME:** 10 minutes

250g/9oz skinned very fresh
   salmon fillet, cut into 24 x 1cm/
   ½in-thick slices

4 tbsp soy sauce, to serve
30g/1oz pickled ginger, to serve
4 tbsp wasabi paste, to serve

1   Arrange the salmon on a serving plate.
2   Serve with the soy sauce, ginger and wasabi.

330 Smoked Mackerel & Horseradish Cream Tartlets

MAKES: 24   **PREPARATION TIME:** 20 minutes, plus 30 minutes chilling and making the tartlet cases
COOKING TIME: 15 minutes

250ml/9fl oz/1 cup double cream
2 tsp grated horseradish
juice of ¼ lemon
1 egg
90g/3oz skinless smoked mackerel

½ recipe quantity savoury Tartlet
   Cases, blind-baked (see page 14)
24 parsley leaves
salt and freshly ground black pepper

1   Put half of the cream in a mixing bowl and whisk for 1 minute until just stiff. Stir in the horseradish and lemon juice and chill, covered, for 30 minutes.
2   Preheat the oven to 180°C/350°F/Gas 4. Put the egg and the remaining cream in a mixing bowl and beat well, using a fork. Flake the mackerel into little pieces and stir it into the mixture. Season well with salt and pepper.
3   Put 1 tsp of the mixture in each tartlet case, then put them on a baking sheet and bake for 15 minutes until golden. Leave to cool completely, then top each one with 1 tsp of the horseradish cream and 1 parsley leaf. Season again with pepper and serve.

PREPARING AHEAD: The horseradish cream in step 1 can be made up to 4 hours in advance, covered and stored in the fridge until ready to use.

331　Ceviche in Little Gem Lettuce Leaves

MAKES: 24　**PREPARATION TIME:** 20 minutes, plus 45 minutes resting

250g/9oz salmon or any firm white
  fish, cut into 5mm/¼in-thick strips
juice and grated zest of 2 limes
juice of 3 lemons
2 small red chillies, deseeded and
  finely chopped

2 small handfuls coriander leaves
1 avocado, peeled, stoned and
  finely diced
12 cherry tomatoes, cut into eighths
24 Little Gem lettuce leaves, about
  2 heads

1　Put all the ingredients, except the lettuce leaves, in a bowl and mix well.
　　Leave to stand for 45 minutes.
2　Divide the mixture onto the lettuce leaves and serve.

32 Chicory Leaves with Smoked Salmon & Dill

MAKES: 24 **PREPARATION TIME:** 20 minutes

100g/3½oz/½ cup crème fraîche
24 chicory leaves, about 2 heads
100g/3½oz smoked salmon,
    cut into thin strips

a few dill sprigs
freshly ground black pepper

1 Put 1 tsp of the crème fraîche on each chicory leaf.
2 Divide the smoked salmon onto the crème fraîche and top with a few fronds of dill.
   Season with pepper and serve.

33 Gravadlax on Rye

MAKES: 36 **PREPARATION TIME:** 10 minutes, plus 2–3 days resting

150g/5½oz/1 cup flaked salt
190g/6¾oz/heaped ¾ cup
    caster sugar
1 large handful dill, stems discarded
    and fronds finely chopped

2 very fresh salmon or sea trout fillets,
    about 400g/14oz each
9 slices of rye bread, each cut into
    4 squares

1 Put the salt, sugar and dill in a bowl and mix well. Line a board with foil and put
   1 of the fish fillets on it, skin-side down. Cover the fillet with the salt and sugar
   mixture and position the other fillet neatly on top, skin-side up. Wrap the fillets
   tightly in the foil and then again with another piece of foil.
2 Put the fish on a flat board that will fit in the fridge and weigh it down with another
   suitably sized board or plate. Chill for 2–3 days to cure.
3 When ready to serve, remove the gravadlax from the foil and cut into 36 thin slices.
   Serve on the rye bread squares.

34 Salmon Caviar & Dill Blinis with Crème Fraîche

MAKES: 36 **PREPARATION TIME:** 20 minutes, plus 1 hour resting
COOKING TIME: 30 minutes

150g/5½oz/scant 1¼ cups plain flour
1 tsp dried active yeast
1 egg, separated
250ml/9fl oz/1 cup milk
1 tsp salt, plus extra for seasoning
1 small handful dill, finely chopped

1 tbsp sunflower oil, plus extra
    as needed
120g/4¼oz smoked salmon,
    cut into 36 pieces
250g/9oz/1 cup crème fraîche
50g/1¾oz lumpfish caviar
freshly ground black pepper

1 Put the flour, yeast and egg yolk in a mixing bowl and mix well. Heat the milk
   in a saucepan over a low heat until lukewarm, then stir it into the flour mixture
   to form a batter. Stir in the salt, season with pepper and leave to rest at room
   temperature for 1 hour.
2 Put the egg white in a clean mixing bowl and beat, using a whisk or electric
   hand-held mixer, for 2–3 minutes until stiff peaks form. Fold the egg white and dill
   into the batter, using a metal spoon.
3 Heat 1 tbsp of the oil in a frying pan over a medium heat. Working in batches,
   drop a few teaspoonfuls of the batter into the pan, spacing well apart. Cook for
   2–3 minutes until bubbles appear on the surface, then turn the blini over and cook
   for a further 2–3 minutes until lightly golden. Add more oil to the pan as needed.
4 Put 1 piece of the smoked salmon on each blini, followed by 1 tsp of the crème
   fraîche. Top with ¼ tsp of the caviar and serve immediately.

335 King Prawns with Coconut-Yogurt Dip

MAKES: 24   PREPARATION TIME: 15 minutes   EQUIPMENT: 24 x 10cm/4in skewers

24 large peeled, cooked king prawns,
  deveined
6 green chillies, finely chopped
juice and grated zest of 4 limes
1 handful coriander leaves,
  coarsely chopped

COCONUT-YOGURT DIP
200g/7oz/scant 1 cup coconut cream
250ml/9fl oz/1 cup natural yogurt
2 tbsp olive oil
salt and freshly ground black pepper

1   Put the prawns, chillies, lime juice and zest in a bowl and mix well to coat.
2   To make the dip, put the coconut cream, yogurt and oil in a bowl and mix well.
    Season with salt and pepper.
3   Put 1 prawn on each skewer. Sprinkle with the coriander leaves and serve with
    the dip.

PREPARING AHEAD: The prawns can be made to the end of step 1 up to 12 hours in advance and
stored in an airtight container in the fridge. The dip can be made up to 1 day in advance and stored
in an airtight container in the fridge. Stir well before serving.

336 Crab & Apple Croustades

MAKES: 24   PREPARATION TIME: 30 minutes, plus making the croustades and mayonnaise

100g/3½oz crab meat, about
  1 dressed crab
½ recipe quantity Mayonnaise
  (see page 12)
1 small apple, peeled, cored and cut
  into thin strips

juice of ½ lemon
1 recipe quantity Croustades
  (see page 14)
salt and freshly ground black pepper

1   Put the crab meat and mayonnaise in a bowl, season with salt and pepper
    and mix well.
2   Put the apple in a bowl, sprinkle with the lemon juice and toss to coat.
3   Put 1½ tsp of the crab mayonnaise in each croustade. Top with 2 pieces of the
    apple and serve.

337 Lobster Tartlets

MAKES: 36   PREPARATION TIME: 35 minutes, plus making the mayonnaise
COOKING TIME: 15 minutes   EQUIPMENT: 4 x 12-hole mini muffin tins, 5cm/2in plain
round pastry cutter

500g/1lb 2oz ready-to-roll puff pastry
plain flour, for rolling the pastry
1 tomato, quartered, deseeded and
  finely diced
1 tbsp soy sauce

1 recipe quantity Mayonnaise
  (see page 12)
meat from 1 cooked, dressed lobster
6 chives, finely chopped
freshly ground black pepper

1   Preheat the oven to 180°C/350°F/Gas 4. Cut the pastry block in half and, on a lightly
    floured surface, roll one half into a 25 x 20cm/10 x 8in rectangle. Cut out 18 circles,
    using the pastry cutter, and gently press them into 18 bases of the mini muffin tins.
    Repeat with the remaining half of the pastry.
2   Line each tartlet with a small square of foil and stack the tins on top of one another,
    ending with the empty one. Bake for 12–15 minutes until lightly golden. Remove
    from the oven, unstack the tins, remove the foil and leave to cool.
3   Put the tomato and soy sauce in a small bowl and mix well.
4   To assemble, put heaped ½ tsp of mayonnaise into each tartlet case and top with
    1½ tsp of the lobster meat. Top with ¼ tsp of the tomato, draining off most of the
    liquid. Sprinkle with the chives, season with black pepper and serve immediately.

38 Chilli-Salted King Prawns

MAKES: 24 **PREPARATION TIME:** 25 minutes **EQUIPMENT:** 24 x 10cm/4in skewers

24 large peeled, cooked king prawns
   with tails, deveined
2 small red chillies, deseeded and
   finely chopped

juice and grated zest of 2 lemons
24 sweet Thai basil leaves

1   Put the prawns, chillies, lemon juice and zest in a bowl and mix well.
2   Put each prawn on a skewer, followed by 1 basil leaf. Arrange the skewers
    on a plate and pour the remaining juice mixture over, then serve.

339 Mussels with Lemongrass & Chilli

MAKES: 24 **PREPARATION TIME:** 15 minutes, plus 20 minutes soaking
COOKING TIME: 12 minutes

680g/1lb 8oz mussels
1 tbsp olive oil
1 onion, very finely chopped
1 lemongrass stalk, finely chopped

1 red chilli, finely chopped
250ml/9fl oz/1 cup coconut milk
24 coriander leaves

1   Discard any mussels with broken shells or that do not close when tapped. Pull out the beards and put the mussels in a basin of cold water. Soak for 10 minutes, then change the water. Soak for a further 10 minutes, then drain and rinse.
2   Put 250ml/9fl oz/1 cup water in a large saucepan and bring to the boil. Add the mussels and cook for 2 minutes, covered, or until all the mussels are open. Discard any that have not opened. Transfer the mussels to a colander and leave to cool for 5 minutes, or until cool enough to handle, then remove the empty top shells and discard.
3   Heat the oil in a frying pan over a medium heat. Add the onion, lemongrass and chilli and fry, stirring occasionally, for 5 minutes, until soft. Add the coconut milk and cook for a further 5 minutes until the liquid has almost all evaporated.
4   Put 1/2 tsp of the lemongrass mixture on each mussel. Top with 1 coriander leaf and serve.

PREPARING AHEAD: The mussels can be made to the end of step 2 up to 8 hours in advance and stored in an airtight container in the fridge.

40 Sesame & Coriander Chicken

MAKES: 18 **PREPARATION TIME:** 5 minutes **COOKING TIME:** 7 minutes

1 tbsp olive oil
2 boneless, skinless chicken breasts,
about 185g/6¹/₂oz each, cut into
18 chunks of equal size

juice of 1 lemon
2 tsp clear honey
2 tsp sesame seeds
18 coriander leaves, torn

1 Heat the oil in a frying pan over a medium-high heat. Add the chicken and cook, stirring occasionally, for 5 minutes until brown and cooked through. Stir in the lemon juice and honey and cook for 1 minute until the honey colours slightly.
2 Add the sesame seeds and stir to coat the chicken evenly, then remove from the heat and transfer to a serving platter. Sprinkle with the coriander leaves and serve.

41 Green Tandoori Chicken with Minty Mango Dip

MAKES: 24 **PREPARATION TIME:** 20 minutes, plus 1–2 hours marinating
COOKING TIME: 20 minutes **EQUIPMENT:** 24 x 10cm/4in skewers

250ml/9fl oz/1 cup natural yogurt
1 small garlic clove, flattened
1 handful mint leaves
1 handful coriander leaves
juice of ¹/₂ lemon
¹/₄ tsp ground cumin seeds

¹/₄ tsp salt
2 boneless, skinless chicken breasts,
about 125g/4¹/₂oz each
2 mangoes, peeled, stoned
and chopped

1 Put the yogurt, garlic, mint, coriander, lemon juice, cumin and salt in a food processor and process for 1–2 minutes until smooth. Transfer half of the mixture to a shallow dish, add the chicken and turn well to coat. Cover with cling film and leave to marinate in the fridge for 1-2 hours.
2 To make the dip, add the mango flesh to the remaining yogurt mixture in the food processor and process for 2–3 minutes until smooth.
3 If using wooden skewers, soak them in cold water for at least 30 minutes before baking. Preheat the oven to 180°C/350°F/Gas 4. Remove the chicken from the marinade and cut it into 24 thin slices. Thread 1 piece of chicken onto each skewer and put them on a baking sheet. Bake for 10–15 minutes until cooked through. Alternatively, grill under a hot grill for 10 minutes on each side. Serve hot with the dip.

42 Oriental Chicken Satays

MAKES: 24 **PREPARATION TIME:** 30 minutes, plus 1 hour marinating
COOKING TIME: 12 minutes **EQUIPMENT:** 24 x 10cm/4in skewers

1 small red chilli, finely chopped
2 tbsp soft brown sugar
1 tsp soy sauce
170ml/5¹/₂fl oz/²/₃ cup sweet sherry

6 boneless, skinless chicken thighs,
quartered
1 handful coriander leaves, chopped

1 Put the chilli, sugar, soy sauce and half of the sherry in a bowl and mix well. Add the chicken, mix to coat and leave to stand for 1 hour. If using wooden skewers, soak them in cold water for at least 30 minutes before grilling.
2 Preheat the grill to high. Put 1 piece of the chicken on each skewer, reserving the marinade. Stretch the chicken out so that it lies as flat as possible to allow for even cooking. Put the skewers on a baking sheet. Transfer the marinade to a saucepan and bring to the boil. Boil, stirring, for 5 minutes until syrupy. Be careful not to overcook it or the sugar will turn to toffee. Brush the skewers with the sauce, then grill for 3–4 minutes on each side until cooked through and brown. Sprinkle with the coriander and serve.

343 Hoisin Duck Pancakes

MAKES: 24   **PREPARATION TIME:** 40 minutes, plus making the duck
COOKING TIME: 20 minutes   **EQUIPMENT:** 10cm/4in plain round pastry cutter

125g/4½oz/1 cup plain flour,
  plus extra for rolling the dough
1 tbsp olive oil, plus extra for
  brushing and frying

250ml/9fl oz/1 cup Hoisin sauce
1 cucumber, cut into matchsticks
½ recipe quantity Crispy Duck, about
  250g/9oz, (see page 13), chopped

1   Sift the flour into a bowl, add 1 tbsp of the oil and 125ml/4fl oz/½ cup boiling
    water and mix to form a smooth dough. Roll into a 20cm/8in-long log and cut into
    8 x 2.5cm/1in pieces. On a floured surface, roll each piece into a 12cm/4½in circle.
    Brush 4 of the circles with olive oil and sandwich with the remaining 4 circles.
    Roll each one into a 20cm/8in circle. Cut out 3 circles from each large circle, using
    the pastry cutter, and keep covered with a clean damp tea towel.
2   Brush a frying pan with oil and heat over a medium heat. Working in batches,
    cook the pancakes for 1 minute on each side until bubbles appear. Do not let the
    pancakes turn colour or they will be dry and brittle. Separate each pancake into
    2 by carefully peeling them apart. Keep covered with a clean damp tea towel.
3   When ready to serve, spread 1 tsp of the Hoisin sauce over each pancake, then put
    2–3 cucumber pieces and 1 tbsp of the duck slightly off-centre along the bottom
    half. Roll into a log and serve.

344 Chicken, Mozzarella & Thyme Filo Parcels

MAKES: 24   **PREPARATION TIME:** 25 minutes, plus making the dip   **COOKING TIME:** 20 minutes

1 small boneless, skinless chicken
  breast, about 100g/3½oz,
  coarsely chopped
55g/2oz mozzarella cheese,
  coarsely chopped
leaves from 2 thyme sprigs

2 tbsp olive oil
8 filo pastry sheets
55g/2oz butter, melted
375ml/13fl oz/1½ cups sunflower oil
1 recipe quantity Mint & Yogurt Dip
  (see page 11)

1   Put the chicken, mozzarella, thyme and oil in a food processor and process for
    20 seconds until the mixture forms a paste. Put 1 sheet of filo pastry on a work
    surface and keep the rest covered with a clean damp tea towel while you work.
    Brush the pastry with a little of the melted butter, then cover with a second filo
    sheet and butter again. Cut the filo lengthways into 6 long strips.
2   Position 1 pastry strip vertically in front of you. Put scant 1 tbsp of the filling at the
    bottom end of the pastry, leaving a little space between the edges of the pastry
    and the filling. Fold the bottom-right corner of the pastry diagonally up over the
    filling to form a triangle, then fold the lower left-hand corner up the left edge,
    keeping the triangular shape. Continue folding until you reach the end of the
    pastry and the filling is enclosed. Repeat with the remaining pastry and filling.
3   Heat the oil in a deep saucepan or wok until a small piece of pastry sizzles when
    dropped in. Fry the parcels for 1–2 minutes on each side until golden brown,
    working in batches to avoid overcrowding the pan. Remove from the pan, using
    a slotted spoon, and drain on kitchen paper. Repeat with the remaining parcels,
    adding more oil to the pan if necessary. Serve warm with the dip.

45 Indonesian Chicken Satays

MAKES: 18   **PREPARATION TIME:** 15 minutes, plus 12 hours chilling
COOKING TIME: 4 minutes   **EQUIPMENT:** 18 x 10cm/4in skewers

1 boneless, skinless chicken breast,
   about 185g/6½oz
½ tsp coriander seeds
½ tsp cumin seeds
1 handful coriander leaves

PEANUT DIP
2 tbsp crunchy peanut butter
2 tsp clear honey
½ tsp chilli powder
2 tsp dark soy
juice of ½ a lime

1 Put all the ingredients for the dip in a bowl and mix well. Cover and leave to stand for 1 hour.
2 Butterfly the chicken breast by making a deep cut lengthways along the centre of the breast. Open the breast out and put it, cut-side down, on a work surface. Cover with a piece of cling film and flatten, using a rolling pin, to 5mm/¼in-thick.
3 Crush the coriander and cumin seeds using a pestle and mortar. Mix them in a bowl with the coriander leaves and then press the chicken into them to coat. Put on a plate, cover with cling film and refrigerate for 12 hours.
4 If using wooden skewers, soak them in cold water for at least 30 minutes before grilling. Preheat the grill to high. Cut the chicken into 18 strips of equal size. Fold each strip into thirds and thread it onto a skewer so that it forms an 's' shape. Put the skewers on a baking sheet.
5 Grill for 2 minutes on each side until cooked through. Serve with the peanut dip.

PREPARING AHEAD: The dip in step 1 can be made up to 2 days in advance and stored in an airtight container in the fridge. The satays can be made to the end of step 4 up to 1 day in advance and stored in an airtight container in the fridge.

346 Duck Breast, Camembert & Membrillo Croustades

MAKES: 24 **PREPARATION TIME:** 15 minutes, plus making the croustades
COOKING TIME: 8 minutes

235g/8¹/₂oz duck breast
1 tsp salt
1 tsp olive oil
¹/₂ recipe quantity Croustades
(see page 14)

50g/1³/₄oz membrillo (quince
cheese), cut into 24 slices
50g/1³/₄oz Camembert cheese,
cut into 24 slices

1 Put the duck in a colander, skin-side up, and pour boiling water over it. Pat dry
with a clean tea towel and rub the skin with the salt. Heat the oil in a frying pan
over a medium-high heat. Cook the duck, skin-side down, for 5 minutes until
brown, then turn and cook for 2–3 minutes until brown but still pink in the middle.
Remove from the heat and leave to rest for a few minutes.
2 Slice the duck into small, thin pieces and divide into the croustades. Add 1 slice
each of the membrillo and Camembert and serve.

347 Antipasti Skewers

MAKES: 24 **PREPARATION TIME:** 25 minutes, plus making the pesto
COOKING TIME: 30 minutes **EQUIPMENT:** 24 x 10cm/4in skewers

2 red peppers
1 tsp olive oil
12 pitted black olives
12 slices of salami
3 slices of mortadella

60g/2oz pecorino cheese,
cut into 12 thin slices
1 recipe quantity Pesto (see page 11),
to serve

1 Preheat the oven to 200°C/400°F/Gas 6. Put the whole peppers in a baking dish
and bake for 25–30 minutes until the skin is charred and wrinkled. Leave to cool
for a few minutes until cool enough to handle, then peel the peppers, remove the
stems and deseed. Slice into thin strips and toss in a bowl with the oil.
2 Wrap each olive in 1 slice of the salami.
3 Fold 1 pepper strip into thirds and thread it onto a skewer to form an 's' shape,
then add 1 salami-wrapped olive. Repeat with 11 more skewers.
4 Cut each slice of mortadella into 4 strips. Fold the strips into thirds and thread each
one onto a skewer to form an 's' shape, then add 1 slice of the pecorino. Repeat
with the remaining 11 skewers. Serve with the pesto to dip.

348 Roasted Red Pepper & Parma Ham Crostini

MAKES: 48 **PREPARATION TIME:** 25 minutes, plus making the crostini and pesto
COOKING TIME: 20 minutes

3 red peppers, halved lengthways
and deseeded
1 tbsp olive oil
300g/10¹/₂oz/1¹/₂ cups cream cheese

1 recipe quantity Crostini
(see page 15)
125g/4¹/₂oz Parma ham, cut into
48 thin strips about 4cm/1¹/₂in long
1 recipe quantity Pesto (see page 11)

1 Preheat the oven to 200°C/400°F/Gas 6. Put the peppers, skin-side up, on a baking
sheet and bake for 20 minutes or until the skin is charred and slightly wrinkled.
Leave to cool for a few minutes until cool enough to handle, then peel the peppers
and cut into 48 strips. Toss in a bowl with the oil.
2 When ready to serve, spread 1 tsp of the cream cheese over each of the crostini.
Cover with 1 strip of Parma ham, followed by 1 piece of the roasted pepper. Top
with 1 tsp of the pesto and serve.

PREPARING AHEAD: The red peppers can be made to the end of step 1 up to 1 day in advance
and stored in an airtight container in the fridge.

49 Beef Carpaccio & Horseradish Cream

MAKES: 18   **PREPARATION TIME:** 15 minutes   **COOKING TIME:** 20 minutes
EQUIPMENT: 5cm/2in plain round pastry cutter

125ml/4fl oz/$\frac{1}{2}$ cup double cream
2 tsp grated horseradish or bottled
   'hot' horseradish (not creamed
   horseradish)
juice of $\frac{1}{2}$ lemon

110g/3$\frac{3}{4}$oz beef fillet
9 slices of white bread,
   crusts removed
3 chives, finely chopped
salt and freshly ground black pepper

1   Preheat the oven to 200°C/400°F/Gas 6. Put the cream in a mixing bowl and
    whip, using a whisk or hand-held electric mixer, for 1–2 minutes until soft peaks
    form. Stir in the horseradish and lemon juice and season with salt and pepper.
2   Put the beef in a roasting tin and bake for 10 minutes until brown on the
    outside and pink in the middle. Remove from the oven and leave to rest for
    10 minutes.
3   Cut 2 circles out of each slice of bread, using the pastry cutter. Put the bread
    circles on a baking sheet and bake for 10 minutes until lightly toasted.
4   Slice the beef as thinly as possible and layer 1 piece on each toast circle. Top with
    $\frac{1}{4}$ tsp of the horseradish cream and sprinkle with the chives. Season with salt and
    pepper and serve.

50 Beef Teriyaki Skewers

MAKES: 24   **PREPARATION TIME:** 10 minutes   **COOKING TIME:** 25 minutes
EQUIPMENT: 24 x 10cm/4in skewers

250ml/9fl oz/1 cup white
   wine vinegar
250ml/9fl oz/1 cup soy sauce

125g/4$\frac{1}{2}$oz/heaped $\frac{1}{2}$ cup
   caster sugar
500g/1lb 2oz beef fillet, chilled for
   at least 30 minutes

1   Put the vinegar, soy sauce and sugar in a small saucepan and slowly bring to the
    boil over a medium heat, stirring until the sugar has dissolved. Reduce the heat to
    medium-low and simmer for 15 minutes until thick and syrupy. Leave to cool.
2   Slice the beef as thinly as possible and add to the sauce. Leave to marinate at room
    temperature for 10 minutes. If using wooden skewers, soak them in cold water for
    at least 30 minutes before grilling.
3   Thread 1 slice of beef onto each skewer and straighten them out as flat as possible
    along the skewer.
4   Heat a griddle pan over a high heat until smoking hot, then cook the skewers for
    1–2 minutes on each side. Serve hot or cold.

PREPARING AHEAD: These can be made to the end of step 3 up to 8 hours in advance and stored
in an airtight container in the fridge.

351 Asparagus Wrapped in Parma Ham

MAKES: 18   **PREPARATION TIME:** 20 minutes   **COOKING TIME:** 3 minutes

18 asparagus tips, about
   6cm/2$\frac{1}{2}$in long
6 slices, Parma ham, cut into thirds

2 tsp olive oil
2 tbsp grated Parmesan cheese
salt

1   Bring a saucepan of water to the boil. Add the asparagus tips and boil for 1 minute,
    then drain immediately. Roll 1 asparagus tip in each piece of Parma ham.
2   Drizzle the oil over and sprinkle with the Parmesan. Season with salt and serve.

PREPARING AHEAD: These can be made to the end of step 1 up to 4 hours in advance and stored
in an airtight container in the fridge.

352 Figs & Mozzarella Wrapped in Honey-Drizzled Parma Ham

MAKES: 24   **PREPARATION TIME:** 15 minutes

200g/7oz buffalo mozzarella
6 figs, quartered lengthways

12 slices of Parma ham,
    halved lengthways
80ml/2¹/₂oz/¹/₃ cup clear honey

1   Drain the mozzarella, halve lengthways and cut into 24 thin slices, about 5mm/¹/₄in thick.
2   Put 1 piece of fig and 1 slice of mozzarella on the end of each slice of Parma ham and roll tightly, then arrange on a serving plate.
3   Drizzle the honey over and serve.

PREPARING AHEAD: These can be made to the end of step 2 up to 4 hours in advance, covered and stored in the fridge.

53 Chocolate Whisky Truffles

MAKES: 18 **PREPARATION TIME:** 20 minutes, plus 2 hours chilling
COOKING TIME: 6 minutes **EQUIPMENT:** 18 paper petit four cases

100g/3¹/₂oz dark chocolate,
   coarsely chopped
30g/1oz unsalted butter

1 tbsp whisky
2 tbsp double cream
1 tbsp cocoa powder, for coating

1 Put the chocolate, butter and whisky in a heatproof bowl and rest it over a pan of gently simmering water, making sure the bottom of the bowl does not touch the water. Heat for 4–5 minutes, stirring, until the chocolate has melted, then remove from the heat.
2 Put the cream in a saucepan and bring to the boil, then stir it into the chocolate and mix well. Leave to cool to room temperature, then chill, covered, in the fridge for 1 hour, or until hard but still pliable.
3 Shape the chocolate mixture into 18 small balls of equal size, using two teaspoons or a melon baller. Roll each ball in the cocoa powder and transfer to a petit four case. Chill for 1 hour, then serve.

PREPARING AHEAD: These can be made up to 1 week in advance and stored in an airtight container in the fridge.

354 Chocolate-Dipped Strawberries

MAKES: 24 **PREPARATION TIME:** 20 minutes, plus 1 hour chilling **COOKING TIME:** 5 minutes

100g/3¹/₂ dark chocolate,
   coarsely chopped
24 strawberries, about 400g/14oz

1 Line a baking sheet with greaseproof paper and set aside. Put the chocolate in a heatproof bowl and rest it over a pan of gently simmering water, making sure the bottom of the bowl does not touch the water. Heat for 4–5 minutes, stirring, until the chocolate has melted.
2 Dip each strawberry three-quarters of the way into the chocolate and put on the greaseproof paper. Repeat with the remaining strawberries. Chill for 1 hour until set, then serve.

PREPARING AHEAD: These can be made up to 1 day in advance and stored in an airtight container in the fridge.

355 Strawberry Tartlets

MAKES: 24 **PREPARATION TIME:** 15 minutes, plus making the tartlet cases and crème pâtissière

125ml/4fl oz/¹/₂ cup double cream
¹/₂ recipe quantity Crème Patisserie
   (see page 15)
¹/₂ recipe quantity sweet Tartlet Cases,
   baked (see page 14)

24 strawberries, about 400g/14oz,
   hulled
icing sugar, for dusting

1 Put the cream in a mixing bowl and whip, using a whisk or hand-held electric mixer with a whisk attachment, for 1 minute, or until soft peaks form. Fold in the crème pâtissière and divide the mixture into the tartlet cases.
2 Top each tartlet with 1 strawberry, top-end up. Dust generously with icing sugar and serve.

PREPARING AHEAD: The crème pâtissière can be made to the end of step 2 up to 1 day in advance and stored in an airtight container in the fridge.

356 Florentines

MAKES: 24   **PREPARATION TIME:** 30 minutes   **COOKING TIME:** 15 minutes

55g/2oz unsalted butter, plus extra
  for greasing
55g/2oz caster sugar
55g/2oz/¹/₄ cup glacé cherries,
  chopped

55g/2oz/¹/₄ cup flaked almonds
55g/2oz/¹/₄ cup mixed candied peel,
  chopped
120g/4¹/₄oz dark chocolate,
  coarsely chopped

1   Preheat the oven to 170°C/325°F/Gas 3 and lightly grease a baking sheet. Melt the butter in a saucepan over a medium-low heat, then stir in the sugar. Increase the heat to medium and slowly bring to the boil. Add the cherries, almonds and mixed peel and mix well.

2   Spoon the florentine mixture into 24 circles on the baking sheet, spacing well apart. Bake for 7 minutes until the mixture has thinly spread and is brown. Remove from the oven and, while still hot, tidy up the edges, using the edge of a spoon or a rubber spatula. Leave to set for 4–5 minutes, then carefully transfer to a cooling rack and leave to cool completely.

3   Put the chocolate in a heatproof bowl and rest it over a pan of gently simmering water, making sure the bottom of the bowl does not touch the water. Heat for 4–5 minutes, stirring, until the chocolate has melted. Carefully spread a layer of the chocolate onto the underside of each Florentine and return, chocolate-side up, to the cooling rack. Leave to set at room temperature or put the cooling rack in the fridge to set, then serve.

PREPARING AHEAD: These can be made up to 2 weeks in advance and stored on sheets of greaseproof paper in an airtight container in the fridge.

357 Passionfruit Meringues

MAKES: 36   **PREPARATION TIME:** 25 minutes   **COOKING TIME:** 1 hour 15 minutes

3 egg whites
85g/3oz/heaped ¹/₃ cup caster sugar
85g/3oz/²/₃ cup icing sugar, sifted

5 passionfruit
250g/9oz/1 cup mascarpone cheese

1   Preheat the oven to 130°C/250°F/Gas 1. Put the egg whites in a clean mixing bowl and beat, using a whisk or hand-held electric mixer, for 2–3 minutes until soft peaks form. Slowly add the caster sugar and beat for a further 3–5 minutes until shiny and stiff. Gently but thoroughly fold in one third of the icing sugar, using a metal spoon, then fold in the remaining icing sugar.

2   Line a baking sheet with baking parchment and spoon the meringue mixture into 36 x 3cm/1¹/₄in circles, spacing them 2cm/³/₄in apart. Bake for 45 minutes, then turn the oven down to 70°C/150°F/Gas ¹/₄ and bake for a further 30 minutes until hard. Remove from the oven and leave to cool completely.

3   Cut the passionfruit in half and, using a spoon, scrape the seeds and juice into a bowl and mix well. Spread the top of each meringue with some of the mascarpone, top with 1 tsp of the passionfruit and serve immediately.

PREPARING AHEAD: The meringues can be made up to 1 month in advance and stored in an airtight container.

58 Macaroons with Mascarpone & Raspberries

MAKES: 24   **PREPARATION TIME:** 25 minutes   **COOKING TIME:** 10 minutes

butter, for greasing (optional)
100g/3½oz/⅔ cup whole
   blanched almonds
125g/4½oz/heaped ½ cup
   caster sugar

1 egg white
200g/7oz/1 cup mascarpone cheese
24 raspberries
icing sugar, for dusting

1   Preheat the oven to 190°C/375°F/Gas 5 and lightly grease two baking sheets,
    or line them with baking parchment. Set aside 24 of the almonds and put the rest
    in a food processor. Add the sugar and process for 1–2 minutes until the mixture
    resembles fine breadcrumbs. Transfer to a mixing bowl.
2   Put the egg whites in a clean mixing bowl and beat, using a whisk or hand-held
    electric mixer, for 3 minutes until stiff. Gently fold the egg white into the almond
    mixture, using a metal spoon, and mix well until the mixture comes away from the
    sides of the bowl.
3   Spoon the macaroon mixture into 24 circles on the baking sheets, spacing well
    apart as the macaroons will spread to double in size during baking. Bake for
    10 minutes until golden. Leave to cool completely on the baking sheets.
4   When ready to serve, top each macaroon with scant 1 tbsp of the mascarpone.
    Add 1 raspberry and 1 of the reserved almonds, dust with icing sugar and serve.

PREPARING AHEAD: The macaroons can be made to the end of step 3 up to 1 day in advance
and stored in an airtight container at room temperature.

359 Mango Sorbet with Heart-Shaped Biscuits

SERVES: 24 **PREPARATION TIME:** 15 minutes, plus making the pastry and churning and freezing the ice cream **COOKING TIME:** 35 minutes **EQUIPMENT:** 4cm/1½in heart-shaped pastry cutter, ice-cream machine, small ice-cream scoop

380g/13½oz/1½ cups caster sugar
4 mangoes, peeled, stoned
   and chopped
juice of 2 lemons

plain flour, for rolling the pastry
1 recipe quantity Sweet Shortcrust
   Pastry (see page 13)
24 flat-bottomed wafer cups

1 Put the sugar and 500ml/17fl oz/2 cups water in a saucepan and slowly bring to the boil over a medium heat, stirring continuously, until the sugar has dissolved. Increase the heat and boil rapidly for 10 minutes until the mixture becomes syrupy. Remove from the heat and leave to cool completely.

2 Put the mango flesh, lemon juice and sugar syrup in a blender and blend for 2–3 minutes until smooth. Transfer the mixture to an ice-cream machine and churn according to the manufacturer's instructions, then put the sorbet in a freezerproof container and freeze in the freezer for 1 hour.

3 Meanwhile, preheat the oven to 180°C/350°F/Gas 4. On a lightly floured surface, roll the pastry out so that it is 3mm/⅛in thick and cut out 24 hearts, using the pastry cutter. Put the hearts on a baking sheet and bake for 8–10 minutes until golden. Transfer to a cooling rack and leave to cool completely.

4 Working quickly, put 1 scoop of sorbet in each wafer cup, using the ice-cream scoop or a teaspoon, and serve immediately with the heart-shaped biscuits.

PREPARING AHEAD: The sorbet can be made up to 1 week in advance and stored in a freezerproof container in the freezer.

60 Lemon Tartlets

MAKES: 24 **PREPARATION TIME:** 15 minutes, plus making the tartlet cases
COOKING TIME: 25 minutes

150g/5½oz/heaped ⅔ cup
    caster sugar
3 eggs
125ml/4fl oz/½ cup double cream

juice and grated zest of 2 lemons
½ recipe quantity sweet Tartlet Cases,
    blind-baked (see page 14)
icing sugar, for dusting

1   Preheat the oven to 160°C/315°F/Gas 2–3. Put the sugar and eggs in a mixing bowl and beat, using a whisk or hand-held electric mixer, for 1–2 minutes until thick and pale yellow. Add the cream, lemon juice and zest and beat for a further 1 minute until well mixed. Transfer the mixture to a jug.
2   Put the tartlet cases in their muffin tins on a baking sheet and carefully fill them with the lemon mixture. Bake for 20–25 minutes until just starting to set and turn brown. Remove from the oven and leave to cool completely. Dust with icing sugar and serve at room temperature.

61 Mini Scones with Mixed Jam & Clotted Cream

MAKES: 48 **PREPARATION TIME:** 20 minutes **COOKING TIME:** 12 minutes
EQUIPMENT: 3cm/1¼in fluted round pastry cutter

250g/9oz/2 cups plain flour, plus
    extra for rolling the dough
1 tbsp baking powder
85g/3oz unsalted butter
a pinch salt
1 egg

1–3 tbsp buttermilk
1 egg yolk, beaten with 1 tbsp milk
a selection of jams, such as apricot,
    strawberry and fig
200g/7oz/1 cup clotted cream
    or whipped cream

1   Preheat the oven to 200°C/400°F/Gas 6. Put the flour, baking powder, butter and salt in a food processor and process for 1–2 minutes until the mixture resembles fine breadcrumbs. Add the egg and the buttermilk, 1 tbsp at a time, and pulse until the mixture forms a rough dough, adding the remaining buttermilk as needed if the dough seems too dry. Alternatively, rub the butter into the flour and salt, using your fingertips, then add the egg and enough of the buttermilk to form a dough.
2   On a lightly floured surface, very gently roll the dough out to 1.5cm/¾in thick and cut out 24 circles, using the pastry cutter, then put them on a baking sheet. Brush the circles with the egg yolk mixture and bake for 10–12 minutes until golden.
3   Slice each scone in half horizontally and top each half with 1 tsp of the clotted cream and ½ tsp of the jam, alternating among the three different jams, then serve.

362 Hazelnut Meringue Nests

MAKES: 36 **PREPARATION TIME:** 25 minutes **COOKING TIME:** 1 hour 15 minutes

3 egg whites
85g/3oz/heaped 1/3 cup caster sugar
150g/51/2oz/scant 11/4 cups icing
  sugar, sifted

250ml/9fl oz/1 cup double cream
65g/21/4oz/scant 1/2 cup hazelnuts,
  lightly toasted and chopped
30g/1oz dark chocolate

1   Preheat the oven to 130°C/250°F/Gas 1. Put the egg whites in a clean mixing bowl
    and whisk, using a whisk or hand-held electric mixer, for 2–3 minutes until soft
    peaks form. Slowly add the caster sugar and whisk for a further 3–5 minutes until
    shiny and stiff. Gently but thoroughly fold in 30g/1oz/1/4 cup of the icing sugar,
    using a metal spoon, then fold in a further 55g/2oz/scant 1/2 cup of the icing sugar.
2   Line a baking sheet with baking parchment and spoon the meringue mixture into
    36 x 3cm/11/4in circles, spacing them 2cm/3/4in apart. Bake for 45 minutes, then turn
    the oven down to 70°C/150°F/Gas 1/4 and bake for a further 30 minutes until hard.
    Remove from the oven and leave to cool completely.
3   Put the cream in a bowl and whip, using a clean whisk or hand-held electric mixer
    with a whisk attachment, for 1–2 minutes until soft peaks form. Stir in half of the
    hazelnuts and the remaining 65g/21/4oz/heaped 1/2 cup icing sugar and mix well.
4   Top each meringue with 1 tbsp of the cream mixture, then sprinkle with the
    remaining hazelnuts. Grate the chocolate over the meringues and serve.

PREPARING AHEAD: The meringues can be made up to 1 month in advance and stored in an
airtight container.

363 Raspberry Cream Sorbet with White Chocolate Sauce

SERVES: 18 **PREPARATION TIME:** 15 minutes, plus churning and freezing the sorbet
COOKING TIME: 15 minutes **EQUIPMENT:** ice-cream machine, small ice-cream scoop

190g/63/4oz/heaped 3/4 cup
  caster sugar
450g/1lb raspberries
juice of 1 lemon

125ml/4fl oz/1/2 cup double cream
250g/9oz white chocolate,
  coarsely chopped
18 waffle cones

1   Put the sugar and 4 tbsp water in a saucepan and slowly bring to the boil over
    a medium heat, stirring continuously, until the sugar has dissolved. Increase the
    heat to high and bring to the boil. Boil for 5 minutes until the mixture becomes
    syrupy. Remove from the heat and leave to cool completely.
2   Put the sugar syrup, raspberries and lemon juice in a blender and blend for
    30 seconds until smooth. Add the cream and pulse briefly to combine. Transfer
    the mixture to an ice-cream machine and churn according to the manufacturer's
    instructions, then put the sorbet in a freezerproof container and freeze for 3 hours,
    or until hard.
3   Shortly before serving, put the chocolate in a heatproof bowl and rest it over a pan
    of gently simmering water, making sure the bottom of the bowl does not touch
    the water. Heat for 4–5 minutes, stirring, until the chocolate has melted. Remove
    from the heat and leave to cool for 10 minutes.
4   Working quickly, put 1 scoop of ice cream in each waffle cone, using the ice-cream
    scoop or a teaspoon. Top with 1 tbsp of the melted chocolate and serve
    immediately.

PREPARING AHEAD: The sorbet can be made up to 1 week in advance and stored in a freezerproof
container in the freezer.

364 Rich Dark Chocolate Cake

SERVES: 18   **PREPARATION TIME:** 30 minutes   **COOKING TIME:** 45 minutes
EQUIPMENT: 23cm/9in square cake tin

175g/6oz unsalted butter, plus extra
   for greasing
250g/9oz dark chocolate,
   coarsely chopped
6 eggs, separated
170g/6oz/³/₄ cup caster sugar
4 tbsp plain flour

CHOCOLATE ICING
125g/4¹/₂oz dark chocolate,
   coarsely chopped
125g/4¹/₂oz unsalted butter

1   Preheat the oven to 180°C/350°F/Gas 4. Lightly grease a 23cm/9in square cake tin
    and line the base and sides with baking parchment. Put the butter and chocolate
    in a heatproof bowl and rest it over a pan of gently simmering water, making sure
    the bottom of the bowl does not touch the water. Heat for 4–5 minutes, stirring,
    until smooth.
2   Put the egg yolks and caster sugar in a large bowl and beat, using a whisk or hand-
    held electric mixer, for 2–3 minutes until pale yellow. Stir in the melted butter and
    chocolate and mix well, then sift in the flour and fold together.
3   Put the egg whites in a clean mixing bowl and whisk, using a whisk or hand-held
    electric mixer, for 3–4 minutes until stiff. Fold the egg whites into the chocolate
    mixture a little at a time, using a metal spoon and mixing well after each addition.
4   Pour the cake mixture into the prepared tin and bake for 25–35 minutes until a thin
    crust forms on the top and the cake wobbles only a little bit. Remove from the
    oven and leave to cool completely in the tin. The centre of the cake will continue
    to cook and then set once out of the oven, but it should be somewhat gooey in
    the middle. Turn the cake out onto a cooling rack and peel off the baking paper.
5   To make the icing, melt the chocolate and butter together as in step 1. Pour the
    icing over the cake, using a palette knife to coat the sides. Leave to cool completely
    and set, then cut into 18 squares and serve.

PREPARING AHEAD: The cake can be made up to 2 days in advance and stored in an airtight
container. Its flavour will improve with time.

365 Caramelized Physalis

MAKES: 36   **PREPARATION TIME:** 15 minutes   **COOKING TIME:** 15 minutes

36 physalis, about 200g/7oz
200g/7oz/scant 1 cup caster sugar

1   Line a baking sheet with greaseproof paper. Pull back the thin papery skins
    on the physalis to expose the orange fruit.
2   Put the sugar and 80ml/2¹/₂fl oz/¹/₃ cup water in a saucepan over a low heat
    and slowly bring to the boil, stirring continuously, until the sugar has dissolved.
    Increase the heat to medium-low and cook for a further 10–12 minutes, or until
    the mixture thickens and turns dark brown. Remove from the heat.
3   Using the papery skin as a handle, dip each physalis into the caramel. Transfer
    to the baking sheet, leave to set, then serve.

PREPARING AHEAD: These can be made up to 3 hours in advance and stored in an airtight
container at room temperature. Do not chill or the caramel will become soggy.

INDEX